Communications
in Computer and Information Science 2132

Editorial Board Members

Joaquim Filipe , *Polytechnic Institute of Setúbal, Setúbal, Portugal*
Ashish Ghosh , *Indian Statistical Institute, Kolkata, India*
Lizhu Zhou, *Tsinghua University, Beijing, China*

Rationale
The CCIS series is devoted to the publication of proceedings of computer science conferences. Its aim is to efficiently disseminate original research results in informatics in printed and electronic form. While the focus is on publication of peer-reviewed full papers presenting mature work, inclusion of reviewed short papers reporting on work in progress is welcome, too. Besides globally relevant meetings with internationally representative program committees guaranteeing a strict peer-reviewing and paper selection process, conferences run by societies or of high regional or national relevance are also considered for publication.

Topics
The topical scope of CCIS spans the entire spectrum of informatics ranging from foundational topics in the theory of computing to information and communications science and technology and a broad variety of interdisciplinary application fields.

Information for Volume Editors and Authors
Publication in CCIS is free of charge. No royalties are paid, however, we offer registered conference participants temporary free access to the online version of the conference proceedings on SpringerLink http://link.springer.com by means of an http referrer from the conference website and/or a number of complimentary printed copies, as specified in the official acceptance email of the event.

CCIS proceedings can be published in time for distribution at conferences or as post-proceedings, and delivered in the form of printed books and/or electronically as USBs and/or e-content licenses for accessing proceedings at SpringerLink. Furthermore, CCIS proceedings are included in the CCIS electronic book series hosted in the Springer-Link digital library at http://link.springer.com/bookseries/7899 Conferences publishing in CCIS are allowed to use Online Conference Service (OCS) for managing the whole proceedings lifecycle (from submission and reviewing to preparing for publication) free of charge.

Publication process
The language of publication is exclusively English. Authors publishing in CCIS have to sign the Springer CCIS copyright transfer form, however, they are free to use their material published in CCIS for substantially changed, more elaborate subsequent publications elsewhere. For the preparation of the camera-ready papers/files, authors have to strictly adhere to the Springer CCIS Authors' Instructions and are strongly encouraged to use the CCIS LaTeX style files or templates.

Abstracting/Indexing
CCIS is abstracted/indexed in DBLP, Google Scholar, EI-Compendex, Mathematical Reviews, SCImago, Scopus. CCIS volumes are also submitted for the inclusion in ISI Proceedings.

How to start
To start the evaluation of your proposal for inclusion in the CCIS series, please send an e-mail to ccis@springer.com.

Marten Van Sinderen · Slimane Hammoudi ·
Fons Wijnhoven
Editors

Smart Business Technologies

20th International Conference, ICSBT 2023
Rome, Italy, July 11–13, 2023
Revised Selected Papers

Editors
Marten Van Sinderen
University of Twente
Enschede, The Netherlands

Slimane Hammoudi
ESEO
Angers, France

Fons Wijnhoven
University of Twente
Enschede, The Netherlands

ISSN 1865-0929 ISSN 1865-0937 (electronic)
Communications in Computer and Information Science
ISBN 978-3-031-67903-2 ISBN 978-3-031-67904-9 (eBook)
https://doi.org/10.1007/978-3-031-67904-9

© The Editor(s) (if applicable) and The Author(s), under exclusive license
to Springer Nature Switzerland AG 2024

This work is subject to copyright. All rights are solely and exclusively licensed by the Publisher, whether the whole or part of the material is concerned, specifically the rights of translation, reprinting, reuse of illustrations, recitation, broadcasting, reproduction on microfilms or in any other physical way, and transmission or information storage and retrieval, electronic adaptation, computer software, or by similar or dissimilar methodology now known or hereafter developed.
The use of general descriptive names, registered names, trademarks, service marks, etc. in this publication does not imply, even in the absence of a specific statement, that such names are exempt from the relevant protective laws and regulations and therefore free for general use.
The publisher, the authors and the editors are safe to assume that the advice and information in this book are believed to be true and accurate at the date of publication. Neither the publisher nor the authors or the editors give a warranty, expressed or implied, with respect to the material contained herein or for any errors or omissions that may have been made. The publisher remains neutral with regard to jurisdictional claims in published maps and institutional affiliations.

This Springer imprint is published by the registered company Springer Nature Switzerland AG
The registered company address is: Gewerbestrasse 11, 6330 Cham, Switzerland

If disposing of this product, please recycle the paper.

Preface

The present book includes extended and revised versions of a set of selected papers from the 20th International Conference on Smart Business Technologies (ICSBT 2023), held in Rome, Italy, from 11–13 July, 2023.

ICSBT 2023 received 30 paper submissions from 18 countries, of which 9 (30%) were included in this book.

The papers were selected by the event chairs and their selection was based on a number of criteria that included the classifications and comments provided by the program committee members, the session chairs' assessment, and the program chairs' global view of all papers presented at ICSBT 2023. The authors of selected papers were then invited to submit revised and extended versions of their papers having at least 30% innovative material.

The International Conference on Smart Business Technologies (formerly known as ICE-B - International Conference on e-Business), aims to bring together researchers and practitioners who are interested in e-Business technology and its current applications. The scope of the conference covers technology-related topics, such as technology platforms, internet of things and web services, but also business-relevant topics, such as business processes, business intelligence, value setting and business strategy. Furthermore, it covers different approaches to address these issues and different possible applications with their own specific business needs and requirements on technology. These are all areas of theoretical and practical importance within the broad scope of e-Business, whose growing importance can be seen from the increasing interest of the IT research community.

The papers selected to be included in this book contribute to the understanding of relevant trends of current research on Smart Business Technologies, including: Business Analytics, Business Processes, Collaborative Systems, Sustainability, Data Collection, Cloud Technology, Business-IT Alignment, Data-Driven Value Creation, Integration/Interoperability and Knowledge Sharing.

We would like to thank all the authors for their contributions and also extend our gratitude to the reviewers who helped to ensure the quality of this publication.

July 2023

Marten Van Sinderen
Slimane Hammoudi
Fons Wijnhoven

Organization

Conference Chair

Marten van Sinderen — University of Twente, Netherlands

Program Co-chairs

Slimane Hammoudi — ESEO, ERIS, France
Fons Wijnhoven — University of Twente, Netherlands

Program Committee

Andreas Ahrens	Hochschule Wismar, University of Technology, Business and Design, Germany
Abdullah Al Ghamdi	King Abdul Aziz University, Saudi Arabia
Saadat Alhashmi	University of Sharjah, UAE
Karim Baina	ENSIAS, Morocco
Fernando Paulo Belfo	Polytechnic Institute of Coimbra, Portugal
Zorica Bogdanovic	University of Belgrade, Serbia
Ana Bologa	Academy of Economic Studies, Romania
Alexandros Bousdekis	National Technical University of Athens, Greece
Chun-Liang Chen	National Taiwan University of Arts, Taiwan, Republic of China
Amita Goyal Chin	Virginia Commonwealth University, USA
Dorian Cojocaru	University of Craiova, Romania
Cristina Costa	CISUC/IPC, Portugal
Sergio de Cesare	University of Westminster, UK
Valerio Frascolla	Intel, Germany
Andreas Gadatsch	Hochschule Bonn-Rhein-Sieg, Germany
Giulio Di Gravio	Sapienza University of Rome, Italy
Ahasanul Haque	International Islamic University Malaysia, Malaysia
Keith Harman	Oklahoma Baptist University, USA
Junichi Iijima	Tokyo Institute of Technology, Japan
Amin Jalali	Stockholm University, Sweden
Jae-Yoon Jung	Kyung Hee University, Korea, Republic of

Slim Kallel	University of Sfax, Tunisia
Gamal Kassem	German University in Cairo, Egypt
Dimitrios Katehakis	FORTH, Greece
Zaheer Khan	University of the West of England, UK
Vinay Kulkarni	Tata Consultancy Services, India
Lam-Son Lê	Vietnamese-German University, Vietnam
Ulrike Lechner	University of the Bundeswehr Munich, Germany
Peter Loos	German Research Center for Artificial Intelligence, Germany
Wenhong Luo	Villanova University, USA
Ali Montazemi	McMaster University, Canada
Hans Moonen	University of Twente, Netherlands
Mihaela Muntean	West University of Timisoara, Romania
Valentina Ndou	University of Salento, Italy
Daniel O'Leary	University of Southern California, USA
Umberto Panniello	Polytechnic University of Bari, Italy
Wilma Penzo	University of Bologna, Italy
Charmaine Plessis	University of South Africa, South Africa
Ela Pustulka-Hunt	FHNW Olten, Switzerland
Alexander Rossmann	Reutlingen University, Germany
Jarogniew Rykowski	Poznan University of Economics, Poland
Friedhelm Schwenker	University of Ulm, Germany
Rong-An Shang	Soochow University, Taiwan, Republic of China
Gheorghe Silaghi	Independent Researcher, Romania
Agostinho Sousa Pinto	CEOS.PP, ISCAP, Polytechnic of Porto, Portugal
Vesna Spasojevic Brkic	University of Belgrade, Serbia
Alessandro Stefanini	University of Pisa, Italy
Emmanouil Stiakakis	University of Macedonia, Greece
Christine Strauss	University of Vienna, Austria
Jianwen Su	University of California, Santa Barbara, USA
Yinshan Tang	Henley Business School, University of Reading, UK
Ben van Lier	Rotterdam University of Applied Sciences, Netherlands/Steinbeis University Berlin, Germany

Additional Reviewer

Shahrzad Khayatbashi	Linköping University, Sweden

Invited Speakers

Ali Emrouznejad	University of Surrey, UK
Paolo Bellavista	Alma Mater Studiorum, Università di Bologna, Italy
Agnes Koschmider	University of Bayreuth, Germany

Contents

A Conceptual Approach for an AI-Based Recommendation System
for Handling Returns in Fashion E-Commerce 1
   Soeren Gry, Marie Niederlaender, Aena Nuzhat Lodi, Marcel Mutz,
   and Dirk Werth

Business Models Innovation in the Realm of Grand Challenges:
Empowering It Through Emerging Technologies 24
   Davide Moiana, Jacopo Manotti, Antonio Ghezzi, and Andrea Rangone

Digital Transformation Roadmap for Danish SME Smart Factories:
Benefits and Future Research 41
   Richard Addo-Tenkorang, Charles Møller, and Kuan-Lin Chen

Roadmap Proposal for the Implementation of Business Intelligence
Systems in Higher Education Institutions 61
   Nuno Sequeira, Arsénio Reis, Frederico Branco, and Paulo Alves

A Study Partner Recommender System Using a Community Detection
Algorithm 76
   Chukwuka Victor Obionwu, Devi Prasad Ilapavuluri, David Broneske,
   and Gunter Saake

Exploring the Impact of Innovation and Competition on Profitability
in Internet-Based SMEs: A Survey Analysis 99
   Nabil Mohammad Abu Bakar and Mahady Hasan

Evolution and Comparative Analysis of Enterprise Architecture Tools 113
   Federico Heras

Real-Time Context Monitoring and Analysis for Detecting Process
Adaptation Needs 132
   Jamila Oukharijane, Mohamed Amine Chaâbane, Imen Ben Said,
   Eric Andonoff, and Rafik Bouaziz

Indoor and Outdoor Navigation for Personalised Shopping: Assisted Path
to Desired Products 160
   Mehmed Cihan Sakman, Oliver Cvetkovski, Panagiotis Gkikopoulos,
   Francesco Martella, Massimo Villari, and Josef Spillner

Author Index 187

A Conceptual Approach for an AI-Based Recommendation System for Handling Returns in Fashion E-Commerce

Soeren Gry[✉][iD], Marie Niederlaender[iD], Aena Nuzhat Lodi[iD], Marcel Mutz[iD], and Dirk Werth[iD]

August-Wilhelm Scheer Institut, Saarbrücken, Germany
{soeren.gry,marie.niederlaender,aenanuzhat.lodi,
marcel.mutz,dirk.werth}@aws-institut.de
https://www.aws-institut.de/research/

Abstract. The benefits of fashion E-commerce for customers are undisputed. Ordering clothes is easy, fast and usually free of delivery and return charges. Fashion E-commerce is moving the changing room from the brick-and-mortar store to the consumer's living room. These efforts, and the associated ever-increasing E-commerce sales, are accompanied by a consumer return behaviour that has high environmental and economic costs. Most studies in this area focus on the prevention of returns. However, many returns cannot be avoided, e.g. those based on selection orders or quality problems. This is the starting point for this study, which investigates how AI can be used to improve reverse logistics from an environmental and economic perspective, based on return forecasts. To this end, a literature review of existing approaches is conducted, followed by a detailed concept of an AI-based recommendation system for the best possible further processing of returns, with the aim of routing the returned product to a suitable sales channel as quickly as possible.

Keywords: Returns forecasting · Returns prediction · Recommendation system · ERP system · Sustainable return management · Logistics · Sustainable supply chain · E-commerce · Fashion · Apparel · Artificial intelligence · Machine learning

1 Introduction

The corona pandemic provided a catalyst for the global growth of E-commerce, which has grown from 15% of all retail sales in 2019 to 21% in 2021 [31]. E-commerce is expected to continue to grow strongly after the pandemic. In this context, the E-commerce market is expected to grow from $6.3 trillion in 2023 to $8.1 trillion in 2026, representing 24% of all retail sales [14]. This means that logistics and returns will increase accordingly. While E-commerce has many advantages over brick-and-mortar stores from the customer's point of view, it also has some disadvantages when it comes to seeing, feeling and trying products before buying. Among other things, this discrepancy between the virtual and the real world leads to inevitable returns [4]. In terms of the number of returns, Germany is the leader in Europe. Overall, 24% of parcels were returned in Germany in 2021, which corresponds to 530 million parcels with 1.3 billion items in absolute figures. Of these, 91% came from the apparel and shoe segment. This consumer behaviour can be observed not only in Germany with regard to returns, where up to 60% of apparel and shoes are returned, but also at the European level, where an almost congruent consumer behaviour can be noted. From an economic and ecological perspective, this represents an immense burden for companies and the environment. For retailers, the high volume of returns makes it difficult to achieve positive margins and at the same time the impact on the environment is immense. In Germany alone, around 795,000 tonnes of CO_2 are already emitted solely due to returns, which is equivalent to 5.3 billion kilometres driven by car [15]. The fashion and apparel industry is a major contributor to climate change, accounting for 5% of global emissions, more than cruise shipping and international air travel combined. This makes the fashion and apparel industry one of the top three greenhouse gas emitters, which explains the strong political efforts to make the industry more sustainable [55]. There are both preventative and reactive approaches to tackling the problem of high volumes of returns [11]. This study, like the previous study by Gry et al. [18] on which it is partly based, looks at reactive approaches to mitigating the environmental and economic impacts of returns. Following on from the previous study, this paper looks at how returns forecasting can be used by manufacturers and retailers to best manage returns in the fashion and apparel sector in terms of Second Life planning and avoid the destruction of goods [18]. The emphasis lies in Artificial Intelligence (AI) and in particular Machine Learning (ML) as part of AI research to identify regularities and patterns in large data sets [27, 41].

The underlying work is based on a paper presented at the International Conference on Smart Business Technologies in Rome in July 2023 and published as part of the Conference Proceedings [18]. Following this publication, this study will first provide an overview of current scientific approaches that deal with 1) the forecasting of returns and 2) the best possible processing of these returns. The focus is on scientific approaches based in the field of AI. Current research gaps are identified. Due to the large environmental impact of the industry, the focus is also on the fashion and apparel industry. The structure of the research paper is as follows. Similar to the underlying publication, the first step is to identify AI-based approaches for returns forecasting, return quantity and return reasons [18]. In a second step, AI-based approaches that deal with the further processing of returns in the context of the reverse logistics process are investigated in order to enable an economically and ecologically sensible decision. Table 2 in the appendix provides an overview of the findings in the two areas of returns forecasting and processing. Unlike Gry et al. [18], this study not only discusses at a high level the use of an AI-based recommendation system that can be part of reverse logistics planning, but also uses a returns process to illustrate in detail the possible structure and components of the recommendation system, the use and benefits of the system, and suggestions for integration into the system landscape of a fashion manufacturer or retailer. The final section summarises the results, particularly with regard to the AI-based recommendation system, and gives an outlook on future developments in the field.

2 Methodology

This study seeks to offer a review of contemporary practices and advancements within the domain of return management with a focus on Artificial Intelligence and Machine Learning. Thereby, particular attention has been paid to their application potential in the fashion and apparel industry. The studies examined fall under two subject areas (as illustrated in Fig. 1):

1. Returns Forecasting and Consumer Returns Behaviour
2. Reverse Logistics Network Design and Optimization (including Returns Management)

The literature review has been conducted with a specific focus on publications from 2018 to 2022. Older literature was incorporated if its relevance remained significant or when no recent studies were available. The online databases Google Scholar, Wiley Online Library, ScienceDirect, and Springer Link served as sources, and snowballing techniques were applied.

This work is meant to serve as a comprehensive overview of the most relevant advancements in the textile and fashion industry, providing a guide for future research. It does not constitute a systematic review of return management practices. Table 1 provides a detailed understanding of the keywords employed in the literature search for the contexts. Recently published or notably relevant works that have a connection to the fashion and apparel industry or have the potential for adaptation within those fields, were incorporated into this work.

Table 1. Search keywords for each of the research areas (Topic 1&2), including context keywords.

Topic	Keywords
Topic 1	Returns Forecasting, Product Return Prediction, Consumer Return Behaviour, Prediction of Consumer Returns
Topic 2	Reverse Logistics Network Design, Reverse Logistics Network Optimization, Reverse Logistics, Returns Management
Context	Sustainability, AI, Artificial Intelligence, Machine Learning, Fashion, Apparel, Online Retail, E-commerce

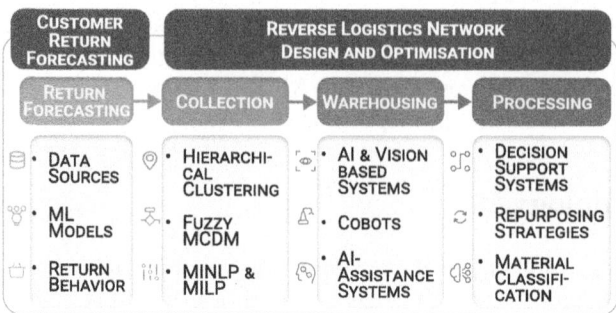

Fig. 1. Structure of topics along the supply chain with top-down increasing detail level, adapted from Gry et al. [18].

3 Literature Review

3.1 A Review of Return Behaviour and Forecasting

Behaviour of Consumers and Retailers Surrounding Product Returns. Consumers return products due to a variety of reasons. Advertisements and promotions often cause people to make spontaneous purchases, which they may later regret and end up returning. Some products may not meet each customer's expectations, while at other times, customers order multiple items with a premeditated intention to return some of them. This section explores the reasons for product returns that have been found in prior research, particularly of wearable garments.

Consumer Behaviour Leading to Returns. Information from a German online retailer selling clothing for women was used in a study by Asdecker et al. [5] to examine some common motivations behind the returning of consumer products. The dataset used by the authors for this study came from a German online retailer selling women's apparel, and contained data on customer behaviour such as the assortment of items that they bought together in each order, payment methods and promotions applicable on the purchased items. The study had some revealing findings about bracketing, including the observation that purchasing the same item in a variety of colours actually reduced the likelihood of their return. Bracketing is a practise in which customers buy numerous items in a single order, with a premeditated intention to return a subset of them [8]. Similar to the findings by Makkonen et al. [29], they found that paying by invoice was associated with a higher rate of return [5]. It was also inferred that the use of coupons may result in more impulse-buys by customers, as the rate of return was higher for orders that used a coupon, than the orders purchased without a coupon. Based on this dataset, the authors deduced that the most informative features in the dataset were those that described the return history of particular items and customers. These features were found to be the most predictive of future returns, and are thus crucial to the building of an ML model aiming to predict product returns.

Shipping Practises. Some types of products are difficult for customers to form opinions about before making a purchase, especially online. It has been found that when free shipping promotions apply to such products, customers are more likely to make a return [44]. This perhaps owes again to impulse buying, especially because this statistic excludes free shipping policies. Shehu et al. [44] carried out their study using a Type II Tobit model [54].

Similarly, Lepthien et al. [25] found that when customers avail free shipping policies as a result of their order total exceeding a certain threshold, then they are more likely to return products. This study used OLS and logistic regression to analyze data from a retailer of streetwear and sportswear.

Customer Reviews and Product Pricing. Another pair of informative features have been explored with respect to their impact on the predictability of online product returns by Sahoo et al. [37]: product reviews and pricing. When customers shop online, it is often the case that the expectations in their minds may not match up with the real product, and they may have no other way of learning about the product prior to their purchase, than by the reviews of the product made by previous customers. The authors of this study found that the higher the number of unbiased reviews on a product, the lower its return rate was. On the other hand, a higher number of biased reviews on a product was associated with a higher return rate of the product.

Concerning the pricing of products, it was found that expensive products are much less likely to be returned than cheaper products. This may likely be because the customer is compelled to spend more time and effort considering the purchase prior to making it, due to the high price tag.

To carry out the analysis in their study, the authors created an analytical model, and alongside it made use of two-stage Probit model [19].

Sharing Asymmetric Data. In the Business-to-Business (B2B) relations between companies, suppliers only have access to returns data from the distributors, but not from individual customers. In such cases, it has been found to be very beneficial if a retailer agrees to share returns data with the manufacturer of the products, even lessening the number of B2B returns [63]. Yan et al. [63] conducted a study in which information from a retailer was passed on to the manufacturer of the footwear, clothing and accessories. Some of their findings has shown, for example, that customers paying by credit card took on a 'buy-now-pay-later' mindset which led them to make unnecessary purchases which they later ended up returning. Conversely, customers who paid by cash considered their purchases more carefully, and returned items less often. It was also found that diverse assortments of items (such as clothing, footwear and accessories) bought together were in general less likely to be returned. This shows that there is a distinction between bracketing and simply buying many items at once. The importance of historical data on customers and their previous purchases was also reinforced, as the return rate was found to be inversely proportional to the number of items purchased by the customer in the past. Thus, B2C level information is very important for predicting returns.

Product Return Rates by Demographics and Payment Preferences. Prior work has explored the connections of customers' demographics with rates of returns of products bought online [29]. This study by Makkonen et al. [29] was a general survey of consumers situated in Finland, but not limited to any particular shop, category of items, or brand, so the findings are applicable to a wide range of items. The questionnaire distributed by the authors inquired the respondents regarding their age, education, gender, income, and the mode of payment that they preferred to use, such as by invoice or online payment, along with their behaviour surrounding returns. The authors then examined the responses in three stages: Firstly, they used cumulative odds ordinal logistic regression to calculate the correlations relating to frequency of product returns by the customer. Secondly, they organized the causes for returns stated by the respondents, using content analysis. Thirdly, they made use of binomial logistic regression to identify specific causes for returns.

The findings showed that more than 60% of the participants mentioned returning products due to a mismatch in the size or fitting of clothes or shoes. A majority of these responses were from women, a demographic also found to return products more often in general, according to the survey. Alongside them, younger shoppers and those who preferred making payments using invoice were also found to be more likely to return products. Products that were returned due to damage or faultiness were most often returned by men, although this may be more related to online purchases of electronics than garments. Those respondents who stated that they returned products due to the product not meeting their expectations were often from amongst those who returned products very frequently, as much as making monthly returns [29].

Some respondents also mentioned practising bracketing. This frequently occurs with clothing and shoes, and most of the respondents mentioning bracketing were between the ages of 20 and 29 inclusive [29].

Assessing Machine Learning Approaches to Predicting Product Returns. A vast collection of prior literature has covered a wide array of ML models for the purpose of predicting returns of products. Many of the features of the datasets used in such experiments are likely to be similar to one another simply by their inherent nature as sales information. The following selection of prior work covers ML predictions on datasets concerning garment returns as well as other products.

Simple vs. Complex Methods. Asdecker et al. [4] compared the performance of simple data mining methods with complex methods, to determine whether it is possible to make fairly accurate returns predictions with limited resources. This can be very beneficial in cases where retailers have limited knowledge of ML models, or limited time in which to implement such a model. Unlike many other similar studies, this study did not use historical customer information, instead relying only on shipments and returns information. The study demonstrated that even the very simplest methods such as binary logistic regression and linear discriminant analysis provided results competitive to more complex methods such as ensembles. The simple models provided valuable insights on product properties that were associated with higher return rates. The return rate was found to be directly proportional to the total value and number of items in an order, and the age of the account used to place an order. The return rate was found to be inversely proportional to the delivery time. Additionally, orders sent to women were most likely to be returned.

Feature Extraction for Returns Forecasting. The most important building block of any ML model is the dataset that it is trained upon, and feature engineering is an essential part of creating a high-quality dataset. Urbanke et al. [52] have presented Mahalanobis feature extraction, which is a method that aims to reduce dimensionality of datasets whilst retaining the most useful information from it. The study made use of a real-world dataset from a German fashion retailer having a return rate of 57.3%. The authors were able to reduce the memory requirement of the dataset by 99% using a sparse matrix format. The newly-proposed feature extraction method was compared with seven existing feature extraction methods, outperforming all of them for the given dataset. The authors also carried out a comparison of different models after using Mahalanobis feature extraction, in which adaptive boosting was shown to work well with the new technique. Their combination worked better than logistic regression and linear kernel support vector machine. This study shows the importance of engineering useful features for a model aiming to predict apparel returns.

Return Forecasting as a Time Series Problem. Shang et al. [43] made use in their 2020 study of a time-series model and lagged sales to explore the prediction of product returns. They found that using such models reduced the prediction error by up to 18%, given the optimal configurations. The dataset that they used was from an online jeweller retailer that accepted returns within 30 days of each purchase, and also did not reject late returns. Following a comparison between the time series-based model ARIMA [22] and a lagged sales regression model, it was found that the lagged sales regression model outperformed ARIMA on the majority of measured metrics.

A Preliminary Selection of Algorithms. A study by Tüylü and Eroglu [51] created a comparison of ML models falling into the following four categories: lazy, rule-based, decision tree, and functional. This comparison was carried out on a dataset containing information mainly on women's fashion and apparel products, particularly trousers. The highest accuracy achieved on this dataset was consistently owed to the M5P decision tree algorithm. This algorithm makes use of the concepts behind decision trees for data mining as well as multiple linear regression [35]. Rule-based algorithms M5Rules and Decision Table were likewise a good fit for the problem. M5Rules makes predictions for both nominal and numerical values by selecting the most informative rule created in each cycle of tree creation [20]. Linear regression and support vector regression were shown to be two effective functional algorithms for predicting returns as well, whilst multilayer perceptron fell behind in performance.

Based on our literature search, no approach was found that created a recommendation system to guide retailers on the optimal next-steps for returned items. The first step towards such a recommendation system is to implement a method to accurately predict product returns. Following this, the reverse logistics processes can be optimized to accommodate for the recommendations.

3.2 On Designing and Optimising Reverse Logistics Networks

Unlike forward logistics planning, reverse logistics planning is much more complicated due to the uncertainty of the timing, quantity and quality of the returned item [13]. Reverse logistics can be defined as "the process of moving goods from their typical final destination for the purpose of capturing value or ensuring proper disposal" [9]. In order to improve the reverse logistics process, it is essential that the time and volume of returns are more accurately pinpointed on the basis of AI-based predictions [18]. This enables the best possible performance to be achieved in terms of transportation, collection, remanufacturing and recycling [50]. Return forecasts are an important basis for improving the design of the reverse logistics network and ensuring the control and adequate planning of the re-marketing of apparel items [61]. Following Agrawal et al. [2], Wilson et al. [60] and Gry et al. [18], this research focuses on the four main activities within the reverse logistics process that are also explicitly relevant to the fashion and apparel industry: network design, collection, warehousing and processing. What follows is a summary of how AI can play, or is already playing, a role in these four main reverse logistics activities.

Designing Networks in Reverse Logistics. Due to the differences between forward and reverse logistics, it is not possible to simply transfer the forward logistics process to the reverse logistics process. When products are returned to the manufacturer or retailer, they arrive at the central warehouse from many, often initially unknown, points and in very different conditions [60]. The size of the retailer and the existing logistics locations determine the strategic considerations in the planning and design of reverse logistics, as well as the transport between logistics locations. To reduce uncertainty in the context of reverse logistics, AI-based and non-AI-based approaches can be used, which have already been outlined in previous sections of this research [18].

Digital Reverse Logistics Twin: To create a digital twin of reverse logistics in the sense of Reverse Logistics 4.0, computer-aided simulations and mathematical models can be used and supplemented with AI-based data predictions and real-time data [21]. In this context, AI and real-time data integration are seen as the basis for making operational, tactical and strategic decisions for sustainable and intelligent reverse logistics network designs [48]. The resulting digital twin can be used to make informed decisions about the design of the reverse logistics network, such as optimal route planning and scheduling [65]. Decision parameters for route planning can include greenhouse gas reduction, truck availability, driver utilisation and, last but not least, economic costs [48]. In order to develop an intelligent digital reverse logistics twin, comprehensive methodological integration and system integration are necessary. This integration involves analytical models, visualization tools, and smart robots and devices, all of which must be effectively and seamlessly connected [47].

Third-Party Reverse Logistics Provider Selection. When it comes to making decisions about the appropriate selection of third-party reverse logistics providers for outsourcing logistics tasks, current research tends to use mathematical models rather than AI [18]. In the course of the continuous growth of E-commerce, an increased demand for third-party reverse logistics providers (3PRLP) has also emerged, the best possible selection of which Wang et al. [56] would like to support through their research. For this purpose, they use a hybrid multicriteria decision making (MCDM) approach that combines FAHP with FTOPSIS, which supports 3PRLP evaluation and selection. One of the central issues in reverse logistics is the selection of an appropriate initial collection centre (ICC), where customer returns are temporarily stored until they are sent to the final storage facility. Das et al. [10] address this issue in their empirical case study of a fashion retailer and investigate which logistics locations are best suited as ICCs. In order to minimise the costs of the reverse logistics network from an environmental and economic point of view, they used Mixed Linear Programming (MILP) as an approach in their study.

Using AI Methods for Collection Approaches. The Optimisation of vehicle routing forms an essential part of reverse logistics, especially when the aim is to make the network as sustainable and efficient as possible. Destinations for returned goods include repair workshops, primary or secondary sales channels, reusing, remanufacturing or recycling destinations [3]. Due to the variety of destinations, the choice of collection locations is an important factor and intelligent methods become necessary, which makes the application of mathematical models and Machine Learning an important tool. In recent years, Artificial Intelligence models have been investigated for these purposes with the aim to make collection processes more resource efficient [60].

Fuzzy Logic. The utilisation of fuzzy logic as well as probabilistic models are popular approaches when it comes to decision making in uncertain contexts. The collection of goods, especially those that reached the end of their life cycle (End-of-Life, EoL), poses such a context where the time required, quantity and the number of involved parties remains unpredictable until the process has already started. The combination of approaches such as multi criteria decision making (MCDM) or mixed-integer linear and non-linear programming with fuzzy set theory (FST) and fuzzy logic is extensively applied for improving the product disposition process, as it increases the robustness of said methods.

MCDM is a frequently used method for the selection of collection centre locations as multiple complex criteria can be considered, even when they pose contradictions [36]. Common MCDM methods are, but are not limited to Best-

Worst, analytic network or analytic hierarchy process (ANP, AHP), TOPSIS, VIKOR and DEMATEL [33,36,45,49].

The incorporation of fuzzy logic for the solution of the collection problem is also used in combination with multi-objective non-linear programming (MONLP) models. In this context, Soleimani et al. [46] investigate the collection EoL products utilising fuzzy theory, while employing MONLP for green vehicle routing. Efficiency improvements in facility location-allocation have been reached by a possibilistic mixed non-linear programming model in closed loop supply chain network design [53]. The Problem of location-allocation is also addressed by Yang and Chen [64], using multi-objective mixed integer linear programming (MOMILP). The decision-making process is thereby supported by fuzzy ANP.

Hierarchical Clustering. Hierachical Clustering, the exploration of cluster patterns of data, is a unsupervised Machine Learning method, which is suitable for solving location-allocation problems such as for determining locations of collection facilities, taking into account both transportation and routing, but also costs [28]. Supervised Machine Learning methods such as k-means clustering have also been employed for the purpose of facility location allocation in different contexts [57,67]. Lin et al. [28] provide a framework for logistics process optimisation utilising hierarchical clustering. Facility nodes in the logistics network are selected from a set of options, which include warehouses, terminal stations, and distribution centres. The location is optimized using practical constraints from real-world scenarios such as the limited capacity of nodes as well as adding new nodes to an already existing network. The 'greedy trap' is avoided by a looking-forward mechanism, leveraging global information at each step [28]. A case study shows that the framework outperforms models like gradient based genetic algorithms (GGA) and variable neighborhood search (VNS) [28]. Nanayakkara et al. [32] introduce a three-step approach, where either the locations of collection facilities are optimised, or, if preexisting facilities are already present, geographical areas are sought out to be assigned to them. This study was performed based on summary data for 2,484 cities in Brazil. In the first step, ward-like hierarchical clustering is applied, utilising geographical constraints. Second, depending on the preconditions, either the best location for initial collection centres (ICCs) or the selection of the most suitable preexisting ICC is determined for each cluster. Thereby, a centre of gravity calculation serves as a selection method. The third step constitutes the network design, which is then optimised in terms of economical and ecological sustainability. The results of 4 clusters as the optimum were further validated by k-means clustering.

The techniques employed for smart collection are not limited to the methods mentioned above. Industry 4.0 technologies such as IoT, big data, cloud, virtual reality and robot technology give rise to a variety of other collection approaches [48].

Using AI Methods for Warehousing Approaches. The warehousing process is the next step in reverse logistics after the returned items have been collected. Associated with this are process steps such as sorting, consolidation, inspection and inventory management [60]. Inspection is an essential and labour-intensive step in the warehousing process, as returned items can vary widely in condition, which is also unknown at the outset [6]. Not only is the condition of the returned items unknown. The quantity and time of arrival are also unknown. This is where the returns forecasting approaches described earlier come in, providing valuable time and quantity information to help plan the warehousing process [18]. On this basis, capacities (personnel, storage capacity) can be planned and inventory management activities can be coordinated at an early stage [60].

AI- and Vision-Based Approaches. When returned items arrive at the warehouse and have been inspected, the next step is to sort the items according to their condition. Based on this assessment, it is decided whether the garments should be repaired, reused, recycled or refurbished and sorted accordingly. Storing items in consolidated form requires steps such as counting, sorting and tracking, all of which can be categorised as reverse logistics warehousing, with the aim of getting the returned garment back into use as quickly as possible [18,60]. AI and vision-based systems can be used to support recycling, helping to identify and sort different materials for recycling [58,66].

Collaborative Robots and AI-Based Assistance Systems. So-called collaborative robots ('cobots') are increasingly being used to sort goods in warehouses. Their role is usually to complete a task started by a human worker. As well as increasing efficiency, this automated sorting is intended to ensure that the human worker does not come into contact with toxic materials [39]. Even though toxic materials play a minor role in the fashion and apparel industry in the warehousing process step, attention should be paid to how decisions on reprocessing, reuse or recycling can be supported and accelerated. This will provide the basis for the most economical and environmentally sound decision [18]. According to Gry et al. [18] and the research conducted in the context of this work, there are no approaches yet in the fashion and apparel sector that address the warehousing process with an AI-based assistance system.

Using AI Methods for Processing Approaches. The most crucial step, especially when aiming at creating a closed-loop supply chain and avoiding waste and destruction of garments, is finding the final destination for the returned items. Thereby significant effort must be invested in the further processing of the returned goods. The processing is highly dependent on the condition of the goods, but final disposal should be the last resort. Following inspection and sorting, individual processing options include reuse, reparation, remanufacturing, recycling or disposal [60]. Especially in remanufacturing, IoT technologies like RFID have been investigated in recent years. Testing the effects of RFID in reverse logistics has been conducted by Kumar et al. [24], employing an Chaos-based Interactive Artificial Bee Colony (CI-ABC) algorithm, showing that the implementation of RFID causes substantial increase in overall costs caused by investments in equipment. Nevertheless, the increase in operational time performance is more substantial.

Recycling techniques in the fashion industry are still limited or not widely adapted, due to limited technology in the field of material separation and the fragmentation of supply chains, that reduces traceability of material compositions and pretreatments, which makes maintenance of fibre quality a challenging endeavor in the recycling process [38]. For that reason, fabric and apparel recycling methods have been sought out in recent years [62]. Lewis et al. [26] investigate repurposing strategies for second-hand clothing, following zero-waste principles. Open- and closed-loop recycling strategies for textiles and fashion have been explored by Payne [34]. Innovative materials create potential for simplified or standardised recycling processes in the future. Further, improved collection practices and strengthened cooperation between stakeholders are necessary to work towards a circular economy [38]. Durham et al. [12] explore aspects to focus on in the design process in order to achieve increased recyclability for apparel at the end of its life cycle, in the future. Wool is known to be a material with a comparably good recyclability, however, due the variety of wool materials and colours, a sorting process is required. Furferi and Governi [16] performed colour classification of wool clothing, incorporating differences in recycling processes to find optimal similarity in colour and material when several wool materials are combined to be recycled. For this purpose, a matrix approach with a self-organising feature map (SOFM) and a feed-forward backpropagation artificial neural network (FFBP ANN)-based has been employed.

Decision Support Systems. The most essential part of the processing of garments and other returned goods is the decision which strategy is chosen. In order to make comprehensible, strategic and far-sighted decisions, keeping the aim of a circular economy in mind, recommendation systems and decision support systems can be of great benefit, as they offer the possibility of including many complex parameters in the decision-making process. In this context, Abdessalem et al. [1] introduce a decision modeling approach aimed at identifying the optimal reprocessing strategy for End-of-Life (EoL) returns. This methodology has been applied in two distinct industrial cases. Disassembly, a crucial step of the reverse logistics process, represents a promising area for the application of AI techniques, but remains relatively unexplored, particularly within the apparel sector [60]. Recent developments include the application of social media analysis to support consumer-centric decision-making in reverse logistics management, as demonstrated by Shahidzadeh and Shokouhyar [42]. This method utilizes Convolutional Neural Networks (CNNs) and Long short-term memory (LSTM) to interpret consumer sentiments in the digital space. For instance, it examines happiness levels expressed in social media posts to gauge consumer contentment with specific product features. This information aids in decisions regarding refurbishment, repair, or recycling. Additionally, benchmarks tailored for both developing and developed economies were derived from the results of the study [42].

In the majority of instances, where products, such as garments, retain their quality and condition, they can be reintroduced to the primary market or secondary markets. Determining the most suitable market for these items is a crucial task, often involving integration into the forward supply chain. While a multitude of recommendation systems exist to support consumers on the front end, in the scope of our literature review no instances of AI or non-AI-based recommendation systems for the optimised selection of a sales channel for returned items based on their inherent properties have been found [7,23,30]. As the need for such a recommendation system catering to the needs of supply chain managers and retailers for a more cost-effective and less wasteful processing of returned garments has been identified from this research, the next section outlines the structure and functionalities of such a system. All findings from the literature review above are summarised in Table 2 in the appendix.

4 Concept of an AI-Based Recommendation System in Return Process

In the following, the main components are conceptualized. Afterwards the basic idea of the AI-based recommendation system is presented and how the system is intended to provide professional users with an important basis for making ecologically and economically sensible decisions. This is followed by a discussion of the necessary data base for the system and the integration of the system into the existing system landscape. The section ends with the limitations and the presentation of further necessary development steps.

4.1 High-Level System Components

Based on workshops and discussions with stakeholders in the garment manufacturing and E-commerce sectors, which took place between October 2022 and October 2023, two main components, located at different stages of the return process, are identified. In Sect. 4.3 the for the below conceptualized functionalities necessary database and data structure is described.

Returns Forecasting and Prediction. In the first component, users will be able to get an automated prediction of return probabilities for currently open orders. Machine Learning functions will make use of several data sources and output a prediction of how likely a certain item or basket will be returned. Additionally, the reason for the return will be determined. Customer as well as product data are included in the model training. Existing return data and completed orders will be used to train the models. The results are shown on a user friendly dashboard. While time passes, predictions can be automatically evaluated with the ground truth, introducing a cyclical retraining to optimize the Machine Learning output. With this component, companies have a more detailed basis on which to make returns management decisions, can analyse the reasons for returns, and can even implement communication functions with the customer prior to the creation of a likely return offer, which could potentially be aimed at preventing returns.

Optimizing Return Management Towards a Sustainable Second Life Planning. Returned items enter a complex return process. The outcome is determined by the reason of return as well as information gathered within the return process. A with historical return data as well as sustainability metrics trained Machine Learning model will recommend decisions within the return process based on optimizing costs and sustainability. Also, an according second life planning will be issued by choosing the correct sales channel. By assisting the complete return process, the system component incorporates a new sustainability dimension to decision making and improves the quality of decisions made.

4.2 Starting Points for the Use of an AI-Based Recommendation System

In order to design a practical recommendation system that is actually used by professional users, it is essential that ecological and economic aspects go hand in hand. Only if the recommendations made by the system make sense to the retailer from an economic point of view, the system will have a chance of being used to its full potential, including its environmental potential. A return prediction should be made at the order stage, based on the customer's individual shopping basket. The system should determine the likely reason for return and the likelihood of return for each item. Possible reasons or patterns can result from the fact that the customer has, for example, placed a selection order in the form of bracketing. Another reason may be based on product history. For example, if a shirt in the colour yellow was returned 80% of the time, this can be used to predict the likelihood of returns for the current order. In addition to product history, customer history and individual customer behaviour also play a key role in returns and provide information about the likelihood of returns. Another common reason for returns is quality. Although this is to some extent part of the product history, it is also recorded separately by most retailers.

The retailer's main objective is to get the returned fashion product back on sale as quickly as possible. Further returns are to be avoided at all costs, from both an economic and an environmental perspective. In order to avoid returns in the future, it may make sense to select other distribution channels for the return in question. For example, if a product is frequently returned when sold via the online channel, it may make sense to select the brick-and-mortar or outlet stores as the next sales channel (Fig. 2). The role of the AI-based recommendation system in this context is to find a suitable sales channel for the return in question, where there is the lowest probability of a return at the next sale. This ensures that the garment is delivered as quickly as possible to the channel or location where the chances of a sale are high and the chances of a return are low. This avoids the destruction of garments at the end of the season after countless returns and unnecessary logistical movements.

In order to get the returned goods back to the sales channel as quickly as possible, the AI system will determine not only the likelihood of returns, but also the most appropriate logistics address for the returned item. This ensures that the item can be returned directly to a channel with a lower likelihood of

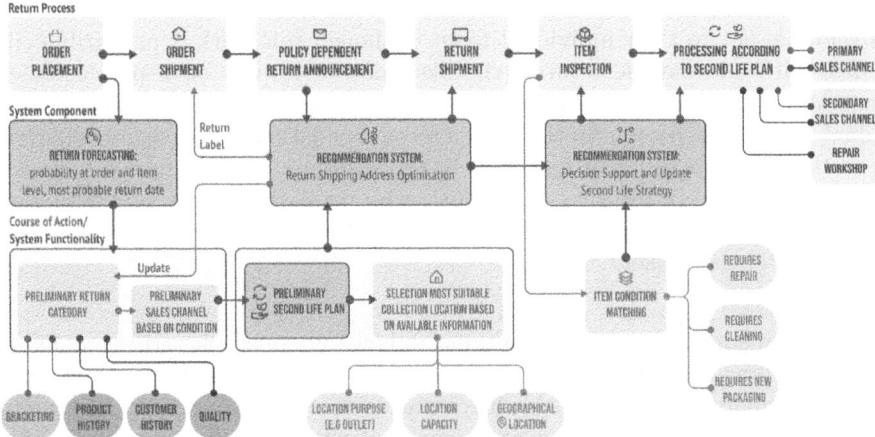

Fig. 2. Process of return and points of contact of a forecasting and recommendation system.

returns and good sales prospects. As the system is designed to determine the likelihood of the item being returned when the customer places the order, the return label sent to the customer with the order can already be matched to the most likely next sales channel for the return.

4.3 Necessary Database and Possible System Integration

A comprehensive database is required in order to make reliable return forecasts. The following information is particularly important for making the predictions described above.

Product History. Product history can be used as a basis for determining the likelihood of returns. At the level of an individual garment, historical return rates should be recorded in order to predict return probabilities at the product level for future orders more accurately. If a garment has an increased return rate for a particular fit, size or colour, this information can be used as an important basis for determining the likelihood of returns. If available, the product history can be enriched with return reasons given by customers when returning garments.

Customer History. Another important variable in determining the likelihood of returns is customer history. To do so, the order history of all known orders per client must be available. This makes it possible to identify patterns in order and return behaviour for each customer. It is conceivable, for example, that customers may return garments with a particular cut more often than the average. Also possible are correlations between colours or fabric compositions and the individual likelihood of returns in relation to individual customers. For instance, certain customers might regularly return garments that contain synthetic fibres as they are not to their individual taste. Although this work is primarily concerned with unavoidable returns, the likelihood of returns on a per-customer basis also allows an approach to avoiding returns. For example, based on individual customer behaviour in the past, a recommendation system could be developed that suggests different garments to the customer that are associated with a lower likelihood of returns. A customer who regularly returns synthetic garments could be recommended a 100% cotton garment the next time a synthetic garment is in the basket.

Quality. In addition to product-specific and customer-specific returns, quality-related returns should be considered as a separate factor. Although quality can be attributed to product-specific characteristics, it is considered separately because quality-related returns are associated with limited opportunities for reuse. Quality-related returns often require more intensive reprocessing or are sent directly to a secondary distribution channel, such as an outlet store. For instance, it might be the case that the item is not necessarily damaged but simply does not fulfill the quality expectations of the target group for the primary sales channel. In order to ensure that reprocessing or reuse in a secondary sales channel, such as an outlet, makes economic sense, it is important to consider this category of returns separately in the system to be developed.

System Integration. The ERP system provides information on current and past orders on a customer basis (Fig. 3). This information is used to make returns predictions based on the trained ML models and to keep the ML models up to date through continuous training.

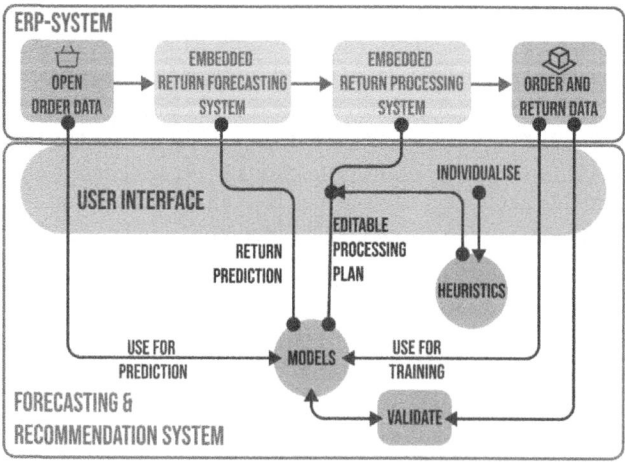

Fig. 3. Possible system integration of the forecast and recommendation system.

The ML models can be validated with actual returns data from the ERP system. The returns data can also be used to train the ML models. In this context, it is possible to compare the actual forecast accuracy based on the trained models and the order data. The user interface of the forecasting and recommendation system, which can be visualised as a pop-up in the ERP system, should allow the business user to view the expected returns quantities and to edit the displayed options for the use of the returns (online, brick-and-mortar store, outlet, repair). By involving the user in a human-in-the-loop approach, the system will be improved and business user acceptance will be increased.

5 Conclusion and Future Work

The fashion and apparel sector is responsible for a large proportion of global CO_2 emissions. Despite the industry's awareness of its environmental impact, many E-commerce retailers in affluent developed countries are taking the approach of moving the fitting room to the customer and making the ordering and returns process very convenient for the customer. There are already signs of a shift in the industry, with some retailers reintroducing return fees, but these initiatives are very cautious. Retailers do not want to lose customers by adding inconvenience to the ordering and returns process. At this point, customers should also be made to rethink their consumer behaviour. But even this will only reduce the number of returns to a limited extent due to the increasing sales volumes in E-commerce. For this reason, the study looked at ways of using AI to predict unavoidable returns at the point of ordering and to optimise the processing of returns in terms of environmental and economic variables. Only if the economic side is sufficiently taken into account, is it realistic that retailers will recognise the benefits of the recommendation system outlined in this study. Between October 2022 and October 2023, expert interviews were conducted with executives and general managers of medium to large fashion and apparel manufacturers or retailers to inform the design of the AI-based recommendation system presented in this study. To gain further practical insights into the development of the system, additional expert interviews should be conducted at the level of the end users who will use the system on a daily basis, e.g. as a system component of the ERP system. This would ensure that a system to be developed would be used in the everyday work of a user in the supply chain sector, for example. Furthermore, the literature review, which together with the expert interviews conducted, can be seen as the basis for the design of the AI system presented here, has shown that many questions remain unanswered, particularly with regard to the design of reverse logistics using AI in terms of economically and ecologically sensible further processing. Although the literature review does not claim to provide a systematic and complete overview, it is clear that there is currently a lack of research that addresses returns handling in an industry that is responsible for a greater environmental impact than other industries. For this reason, it would be useful for further research to address this issue in the future.

Acknowledgements. This research was funded in part by the German Federal Ministry of Education and Research (BMBF) under the project OptiRetouren (grant number 01IS22046B). It is a joint project of the August-Wilhelm Scheer Institut, INTEX, HAIX and h+p. August-Wilhelm Scheer Institut is mainly entrusted with conducting research in AI for forecasting returns volume and for recommendations based on AI.

Appendix

Table 2. Overview of research topics, adapted from Gry et al. [18].

Topic	Subcategory	Approaches	Sources
Consumer Returns Fore-casting	Comparison of Machine Learning Methods	Tree-based models, lazy, rule-based & functional algorithms	[51]
		Data mining methods	[4]
		Mahalanobis feature extraction	[52]
		Time-series based model	[43]
	Observations of Consumer Behaviour	Subject to demographics, payment method preference, bracketing	[5, 29]
		Effect of pricing, effect of accuracy and availability of product reviews	[37]
		Free shipping promotions, threshold-based free shipping policies	[25, 44]
		Effects of payment methods, assortment diversity, and past customer records	[63]
Reverse Logistics Network Design	Digital reverse logistics twin	Real-time data, smart robots and AI-based data predictions (e.g. for vehicle routing)	[21, 47, 48, 65]
	Mathematical Programming	Mixed linear programming (MILP) (e.g. facility location-allocation)	[10]
		Hybrid multicriteria decision-making (MCDM) (e.g. selection of 3PRLP)	[17, 56]
Collection	Machine Learning	Hierarchical Clustering for facility location allocation	[28, 32]
	Mathematical Programming	Fuzzy MCDM for collection optimization	[33, 36, 45, 49]
		Fuzzy MONLP green vehicle routing	[46]
		MINLP facility location-allocation	[53]
Ware-housing	AI- and vision-based systems	AI- and vision-based identification, inspection and sorting in combination with smart robots/Cobots	[39, 40, 58, 65]
Pro-cessing	Remanu-facturing	RFID, Chaos-based Interactive Artificial Bee Colony (CI-ABC)	[24]
	Textile Recycling	Artificial Neural Networks	[16]
		Zero-waste, second hand clothing	[26]
		Design for improved recycling	[12]
		Textile to textile: drivers & inhibiters	[38]
		Recycling and reuse of clothing in general	[59, 62]

References

1. Abdessalem, M., Hadj-Alouane, A.B., Riopel, D.: Decision modelling of reverse logistics systems: selection of recovery operations for end-of-life products. Int. J. Logist. Syst. Manage. **13**(2), 139–161 (2012). https://doi.org/10.1504/IJLSM.2012.048933
2. Agrawal, S., Singh, R.K., Murtaza, Q.: A literature review and perspectives in reverse logistics. Resour. Conserv. Recycl. **97**, 76–92 (2015). https://doi.org/10.1016/j.resconrec.2015.02.009
3. Alkahtani, M., Ziout, A., Salah, B., Alatefi, M., Abd Elgawad, A.E.E., Badwelan, A., Syarif, U.: An insight into reverse logistics with a focus on collection systems. Sustainability **13**(2), 548 (2021). https://doi.org/10.3390/su13020548
4. Asdecker, B., Karl, D.: Big data analytics in returns management-are complex techniques necessary to forecast consumer returns properly? In: 2nd International Conference on Advanced Research Methods and Analytics. Proceedings, pp. 39–46 (2018). https://doi.org/10.4995/CARMA2018.2018.8303
5. Asdecker, B., Karl, D., Sucky, E.: Examining drivers of consumer returns in e-tailing with real shop data. In: Hawaii International Conference on System Sciences, pp. 4192–4201 (2017). https://doi.org/10.24251/HICSS.2017.507
6. Bai, C., Sarkis, J.: Flexibility in reverse logistics: a framework and evaluation approach. J. Clean. Prod. **47**, 306–318 (2013). https://doi.org/10.1016/j.jclepro.2013.01.005
7. Bellini, P., Palesi, L.A.I., Nesi, P., Pantaleo, G.: Multi clustering recommendation system for fashion retail. Multimedia Tools and Applications, pp. 1–28 (2022). https://doi.org/10.1007/s11042-021-11837-5
8. Bimschleger, C., Patel, K., Leddy, M.: Bringing it back: retailers need a synchronized reverse logistics strategy. Tech. rep., Deloitte Development LLC (2019). https://www2.deloitte.com/content/dam/Deloitte/us/Documents/process-and-operations/us-bringing-it-back.pdf
9. Chileshe, N., Rameezdeen, R., Hosseini, M.R.: Drivers for adopting reverse logistics in the construction industry: a qualitative study. Eng. Constr. Archit. Manag. **23**(2), 134–157 (2016). https://doi.org/10.1108/ECAM-06-2014-0087
10. Das, D., Kumar, R., Rajak, M.: Designing a reverse logistics network for an e-commerce firm: a case study. Oper. Supply Chain Manage. Int. J. **13**(1), 48–63 (2020). https://doi.org/10.31387/oscm0400252
11. Deges, F.: Retourencontrolling im online-handel. Controlling - Zeitschrift für erfolgsorientierte Unternehmenssteuerung **2/2021**, 61–68 (2021). https://doi.org/10.15358/0935-0381-2021-2
12. Durham, E., Hewitt, A., Bell, R., Russell, S.: Technical design for recycling of clothing. In: Sustainable Apparel, pp. 187–198. Elsevier (2015). https://doi.org/10.1016/B978-1-78242-339-3.00007-8
13. Flapper, S.D.P.: One-way or reusable distribution items? TU Eindhoven Fac. TBDK, Vakgroep LBS: working paper series **9504** (1995). https://research.tue.nl/en/publications/65159e9c-19b5-4731-8b8b-3193b3c0b199
14. Forbes: 38 e-commerce statistics of 2023 (2023). https://www.forbes.com/advisor/business/ecommerce-statistics/. Accessed 18 Oct 2023
15. Forschungsgruppe Retourenmanagement: Ergebnisse des europäischen retourentachos veröffentlicht (2022), https://www.retourenforschung.de/info-ergebnisse-des-europaeischen-retourentachos-veroeffentlicht.html, online; accessed 2023-01-26

16. Furferi, R., Governi, L.: The recycling of wool clothes: an artificial neural network colour classification tool. Int. J. Adv. Manuf. Technol. **37**, 722–731 (2008). https://doi.org/10.1007/s00170-007-1011-2
17. Govindan, K., Kadziński, M., Ehling, R., Miebs, G.: Selection of a sustainable third-party reverse logistics provider based on the robustness analysis of an outranking graph kernel conducted with electre i and smaa. Omega **85**, 1–15 (2019). https://doi.org/10.1016/j.omega.2018.05.007
18. Gry., S., Niederlaender., M., Lodi., A., Mutz., M., Werth., D.: Advances in ai-based garment returns prediction and processing: A conceptual approach for an ai-based recommender system. In: Proceedings of the 20th International Conference on Smart Business Technologies - ICSBT, pp. 15–25. INSTICC. SciTePress (2023). https://doi.org/10.5220/0012010500003552
19. Heckman, J.J.: Sample selection bias as a specification error. Econometrica: J. Econometric Soc., 153–161 (1979). https://doi.org/10.2307/1912352
20. Holmes, G., Hall, M., Prank, E.: Generating rule sets from model trees. In: Australasian Joint Conference on Artificial Intelligence, pp. 1–12. Springer (1999). https://doi.org/10.1007/3-540-46695-9_1
21. Ivanov, D., Dolgui, A.: A digital supply chain twin for managing the disruption risks and resilience in the era of industry 4.0. Production Plann. Control **32**(9), 775–788 (2021). https://doi.org/10.1080/09537287.2020.1768450
22. Jenkins, G.M.: Time Series Analysis; Forecasting and Control [by] George EP Box and Gwilym M. Jenkins. San Francisco: Holden-Day (1970). https://doi.org/10.1111/jtsa.12194
23. Kottage, G.N., Jayathilake, D.K., Chankuma, K.C., Ganegoda, G.U., Sandanayake, T.: Preference based recommendation system for apparel e-commerce sites. In: 17th international Conference on Computer and Information Science, pp. 122–127. IEEE (2018). https://doi.org/10.1109/ICIS.2018.8466382
24. Kumar, V.V., Liou, F.W., Balakrishnan, S., Kumar, V.: Economical impact of rfid implementation in remanufacturing: a chaos-based interactive artificial bee colony approach. J. Intell. Manuf. **26**, 815–830 (2015). https://doi.org/10.1007/s10845-013-0836-9
25. Lepthien, A., Clement, M.: Shipping fee schedules and return behavior. Mark. Lett. **30**(2), 151–165 (2019). https://doi.org/10.1007/s11002-019-09486-8
26. Lewis, T.L., Park, H., Netravali, A.N., Trejo, H.X.: Closing the loop: a scalable zero-waste model for apparel reuse and recycling. Int. J. Fashion Des. Technol. Educ. **10**(3), 353–362 (2017). https://doi.org/10.1080/17543266.2016.1263364
27. Lickert, H., Wewer, A., Dittmann, S., Bilge, P., Dietrich, F.: Selection of suitable machine learning algorithms for classification tasks in reverse logistics. Procedia CIRP **96**, 272–277 (2021). https://doi.org/10.1016/j.procir.2021.01.086
28. Lin, T., Liu, Y., Liu, B., Wang, Y., Wu, S., Zhe, W.: Hierarchical clustering framework for facility location selection with practical constraints. IET Cyber-Phys. Syst. Theory Appl. **6**(4), 238–253 (2021). https://doi.org/10.1049/cps2.12021
29. Makkonen, M., Frank, L., Kemppainen, T.: The effects of consumer demographics and payment method preference on product return frequency and reasons in online shopping. In: Bled eConference, pp. 567–580. University of Maribor (2021). https://doi.org/10.18690/978-961-286-385-9.2
30. Mohammed Abdulla, G., Singh, S., Borar, S.: Shop your right size: a system for recommending sizes for fashion products. In: Companion Proceedings of the 2019 World Wide Web Conference, pp. 327–334 (2019). https://doi.org/10.1145/3308560.3316599

31. Morgan Stanley: Here's why e-commerce growth can stay stronger for longer (2022). https://www.morganstanley.com/ideas/global-ecommerce-growth-forecast-2022/. Accessed 26 Jan 2023
32. Nanayakkara, P.R., Jayalath, M.M., Thibbotuwawa, A., Perera, H.N.: A circular reverse logistics framework for handling e-commerce returns. Cleaner Logist. Supp. Chain **5**, 100080 (2022). https://doi.org/10.1016/j.clscn.2022.100080
33. Ocampo, L., Himang, C., Kumar, A., Brezocnik, M.: A novel multiple criteria decision-making approach based on fuzzy dematel, fuzzy anp and fuzzy ahp for mapping collection and distribution centers in reverse logistics. Adv. Prod. Eng. Manage. **14**(3), 297–322 (2019). https://doi.org/10.14743/apem2019.3.329
34. Payne, A.: Open-and closed-loop recycling of textile and apparel products. In: Handbook of Life Cycle Assessment (LCA) of Textiles and Clothing, pp. 103–123. Elsevier (2015). https://doi.org/10.1016/B978-0-08-100169-1.00006-X
35. Quinlan, J.R., et al.: Learning with continuous classes. In: 5th Australian Joint Conference on Artificial Intelligence, vol. 92, pp. 343–348. World Scientific (1992). https://api.semanticscholar.org/CorpusID:1056674
36. Sagnak, M., Berberoglu, Y., Memis, İ, Yazgan, O.: Sustainable collection center location selection in emerging economy for electronic waste with fuzzy best-worst and fuzzy topsis. Waste Manage. (Oxford) **127**, 37–47 (2021). https://doi.org/10.1016/j.wasman.2021.03.054
37. Sahoo, N., Dellarocas, C., Srinivasan, S.: The impact of online product reviews on product returns. Inf. Syst. Res. **29**(3), 723–738 (2018). https://doi.org/10.1287/isre.2017.0736
38. Sandvik, I.M., Stubbs, W.: Circular fashion supply chain through textile-to-textile recycling. J. Fashion Market. Manage. Int. J. **23**(3), 366–381 (2019). https://doi.org/10.1108/JFMM-04-2018-0058
39. Sarc, R., Curtis, A., Kandlbauer, L., Khodier, K., Lorber, K.E., Pomberger, R.: Digitalisation and intelligent robotics in value chain of circular economy oriented waste management-a review. Waste Manage. (Oxford) **95**, 476–492 (2019). https://doi.org/10.1016/j.wasman.2019.06.035
40. Schlüter, M., et al.: Ai-enhanced identification, inspection and sorting for reverse logistics in remanufacturing. Procedia CIRP **98**, 300–305 (2021). https://doi.org/10.1016/j.procir.2021.01.107
41. Schwaiger, R., Steinwendner, J.: Neuronale Netze programmieren mit Python. Rheinwerk Computing (2019)
42. Shahidzadeh, M.H., Shokouhyar, S.: Shedding light on the reverse logistics' decision-making: a social-media analytics study of the electronics industry in developing vs developed countries. Int. J. Sustain. Eng. **15**(1), 161–176 (2022). https://doi.org/10.1080/19397038.2022.2101706
43. Shang, G., McKie, E.C., Ferguson, M.E., Galbreth, M.R.: Using transactions data to improve consumer returns forecasting. J. Oper. Manag. **66**(3), 326–348 (2020). https://doi.org/10.1002/joom.1071
44. Shehu, E., Papies, D., Neslin, S.A.: Free shipping promotions and product returns. J. Mark. Res. **57**(4), 640–658 (2020). https://doi.org/10.1177/0022243720921812
45. Singh, R.K., Agrawal, S.: Analyzing disposition strategies in reverse supply chains: fuzzy topsis approach. Manage. Environ. Quality Int. J. (2018). https://doi.org/10.1108/MEQ-12-2017-0177
46. Soleimani, H., Govindan, K., Saghafi, H., Jafari, H.: Fuzzy multi-objective sustainable and green closed-loop supply chain network design. Comput. Ind. Eng. **109**, 191–203 (2017). https://doi.org/10.1016/j.cie.2017.04.038

47. Sun, X., Yu, H., Solvang, W.D.: System integration for smart reverse logistics management. In: 2022 IEEE/SICE International Symposium on System Integration (SII), pp. 821–826. IEEE (2022). https://doi.org/10.1109/SII52469.2022.9708743
48. Sun, X., Yu, H., Solvang, W.D.: Towards the smart and sustainable transformation of reverse logistics 4.0: a conceptualization and research agenda. Environmental Science and Pollution Research, pp. 1–19 (2022). https://doi.org/10.1007/s11356-022-22473-3
49. Tian, G., et al.: Selection of take-back pattern of vehicle reverse logistics in china via grey-dematel and fuzzy-vikor combined method. J. Clean. Prod. **220**, 1088–1100 (2019). https://doi.org/10.1016/j.jclepro.2019.01.086
50. Tibben-Lembke, R.S., Rogers, D.S.: Differences between forward and reverse logistics in a retail environment. Supply Chain Manage. Int. J. **7**(5) (2002). https://doi.org/10.1108/13598540210447719
51. Tüylü, A.N.A., Eroğlu, E.: Using machine learning algorithms for forecasting rate of return product in reverse logistics process. Alphanumeric J. **7**(1), 143–156 (2019). https://doi.org/10.17093/alphanumeric.541307
52. Urbanke, P., Kranz, J., Kolbe, L.M.: Predicting product returns in e-commerce: the contribution of mahalanobis feature extraction. In: International Conference on Interaction Sciences, pp. 1–19 (2015)
53. Vahdani, B., Razmi, J., Tavakkoli-Moghaddam, R.: Fuzzy possibilistic modeling for closed loop recycling collection networks. Environ. Modeling Assessment **17**, 623–637 (2012). https://doi.org/10.1007/s10666-012-9313-7
54. Van Heerde, H.J., Gijsbrechts, E., Pauwels, K.: Price war: what is it good for? store incidence and basket size response to the price war in dutch grocery retailing. Tilburg University, LE Tilburg, The Netherlands (2005)
55. Vogue/BCG: Consumers' adaption to sustainability in fashion. https://web-assets.bcg.com/27/f3/794284e7437d99a71d625caf589f/consumers-adaptation-to-sustainability-in-fashion.pdf (2021). Accessed 26 Jan 2023
56. Wang, C.N., Dang, T.T., Nguyen, N.A.T.: Outsourcing reverse logistics for e-commerce retailers: a two-stage fuzzy optimization approach. Axioms **10**(1), 34 (2021). https://doi.org/10.3390/axioms10010034
57. Wang, X., Shao, C., Xu, S., Zhang, S., Xu, W., Guan, Y.: Study on the location of private clinics based on k-means clustering method and an integrated evaluation model. IEEE Access **8**, 23069–23081 (2020). https://doi.org/10.1109/ACCESS.2020.2967797
58. Wang, Z., Li, H., Yang, X.: Vision-based robotic system for on-site construction and demolition waste sorting and recycling. J. Build. Eng. **32**, 101769 (2020). https://doi.org/10.1016/j.jobe.2020.101769
59. Wiedemann, S.G., Biggs, L., Clarke, S.J., Russell, S.J.: Reducing the environmental impacts of garments through industrially scalable closed-loop recycling: Life cycle assessment of a recycled wool blend sweater. Sustainability **14**(3), 1081 (2022). https://doi.org/10.3390/su14031081
60. Wilson, M., Paschen, J., Pitt, L.: The circular economy meets artificial intelligence (AI): understanding the opportunities of AI for reverse logistics. Manage. Environ. Quality Int. J. **33**(1), 9–25 (2021). https://doi.org/10.1108/MEQ-10-2020-0222
61. Xiaofeng, X., Tijun, F.: Forecast for the amount of returned products based on wave function. In: 2009 International Conference on Information Management, Innovation Management and Industrial Engineering, vol. 2, pp. 324–327. IEEE (2009). https://doi.org/10.1109/ICIII.2009.235

62. Xie, X., Hong, Y., Zeng, X., Dai, X., Wagner, M.: A systematic literature review for the recycling and reuse of wasted clothing. Sustainability **13**(24), 13732 (2021). https://doi.org/10.3390/su132413732
63. Yan, R., Cao, Z.: Product returns, asymmetric information, and firm performance. Int. J. Prod. Econ. **185**, 211–222 (2017). https://doi.org/10.1016/j.ijpe.2017.01.001
64. Yang, C., Chen, X.: A novel approach integrating fanp and momilp for the collection centre location problem in closed-loop supply chain. Int. J. Sustain. Eng. **13**(3), 171–183 (2020). https://doi.org/10.1080/19397038.2019.1644388
65. Zhang, Y., et al.: The 'internet of things' enabled real-time scheduling for remanufacturing of automobile engines. J. Clean. Prod. **185**, 562–575 (2018). https://doi.org/10.1016/j.jclepro.2018.02.061
66. Zhang, Z., Wang, H., Song, H., Zhang, S., Zhang, J.: Industrial robot sorting system for municipal solid waste. In: Yu, H., Liu, J., Liu, L., Ju, Z., Liu, Y., Zhou, D. (eds.) ICIRA 2019, Part II. LNCS, pp. 342–353. Springer, Cham (2019). https://doi.org/10.1007/978-3-030-27532-7_31
67. Zhou, Y., Xie, R., Zhang, T., Holguin-Veras, J.: Joint distribution center location problem for restaurant industry based on improved k-means algorithm with penalty. IEEE Access **8**, 37746–37755 (2020). https://doi.org/10.1109/ACCESS.2020.2975449

Business Models Innovation in the Realm of Grand Challenges: Empowering It Through Emerging Technologies

Davide Moiana(✉), Jacopo Manotti, Antonio Ghezzi, and Andrea Rangone

Department of Management Economics and Industrial Engineering, Politecnico Di Milano, Via Lambruschini 4B, 20156 Milan, Italy
{davide.moiana,jacopo.manotti,antonio01.ghezzi, andrea.rangone}@polimi.it

Abstract. Amidst a backdrop of pressing sustainability Grand Challenges (GCs), modern corporations face an imperative to actively engage in addressing these intricate and urgent societal and environmental issues. The United Nations' 2030 Agenda for Sustainable Development, encompassing 17 Sustainable Development Goals (SDGs), stands as a global call to action, urging companies to transition towards sustainable practices and undergo fundamental innovations in their business models. As management research underscores, emerging technologies emerge as powerful enablers for Business Model Innovation (BMI). In this context, blockchain technology has garnered attention for its potential to significantly reshape corporate structures and markets. This study, employing an inductive approach through a multi-case analysis of four startups in the Voluntary Carbon Market (VCM) sector, introduces a framework for BMI by leveraging blockchain within GC domains. This model elucidates three actionable characteristics (Asset enabler, Trust machine, Collaborative and coordinated action enhancer) through which blockchain technologies drive BMI, offering insights into how they facilitate the integration of managerial problems related to GCs into various components of novel business model designs.

Keywords: Business model innovation · Grand challenges · Emerging technology · Blockchain · Tokens · DAO

1 Introduction

In In the modern world, we grapple with pressing concerns such as resource limitations, the evolving climate, socioeconomic disparities, poverty, and unequal accessibility to quality education and healthcare. These fall under the category of "Grand challenges" (GCs), presenting intricate, multifaceted issues without clear-cut and unequivocal solutions [19, 24]. In this regard, in 2015 the United Nations ratified the so-called 2030 Agenda for Sustainable Development, which captures 17 Sustainable Development Goals (SDGs) with the aim of promoting social, environmental, and economic objectives.

In a globalized society, these threats are increasingly influencing public opinion; addressing them effectively requires a collaborative mobilization of governments, businesses and individuals [30, 33].

As economic players, firms cannot stand aside, without acting. The neoclassical vision of the company, a black box anthropomorphic entity with the aim of maximizing profit, is falling in favor of the idea of returns' generation for all stakeholders. An increasing number of organizations are seeking to achieve both profit and social and environmental impact, delivering shared value to the society [49]. Many firms are founded on unsustainable practices that cannot be changed quickly and cheaply. As a result, a transition is required to move towards new business models and adopt sustainable practices in all sectors [9].

However, it is difficult to fully integrate sustainable practices into a company's business model, defined as the system of activities, as well as the resources and capabilities to perform them, with whom the company create, deliver and capture value [58, 67]. For this purpose, technology can be a useful tool to conjugate the possibilities offered by new technologies with the needs of the sustainable challenges [21, 24]. The dazzling promises of blockchain technology have captured the attention of various practitioners and academics [18, 35], who consider blockchain to underlie the next generation of internet. Web3 is a term that has gained momentum to represent the idea of a new digitally-enabled environment that promise to be more open, transparent, and secure, as it is built upon a set of new digital affordances enabled by blockchain technology (e.g., [34, 47]).

Adopting a technological affordances perspective [4], we conduct an inductive multiple case study [16, 26, 66] in the field of the Voluntary Carbon Market (VCM) and present a novel conceptual model, anchored in the business model as activity-system view [67]. Our study proposes three blockchain actionable characteristics for sustainable BMI. We find that blockchain can serve as a lever for BMI by acting as asset enabler, trust machine and coordinated and collaborative action enhancer.

This research contributes to the extant call of researchers to investigate BMI as a mean to address GCs. Based on our empirical analysis, we introduce a framework of BMI, which denotes the design of new business model content, governance, and structure in a way that advance the progress towards advancing managerial problems associated to GCs [25], namely problem of knowing, valuating, coordination and trust, communication, access and reach and institutions. To this extent, we advance the consolidated work on technology diffusion [52, 60, 61], by "opening the black box" of an emerging technology, blockchain, in order to understand which affordances it offers for BMI in GC domains.

This research represents an extended version of the conference paper "Unveiling the Digital and Sustainability Convergence: Leveraging Blockchain for Grand Challenges Oriented Business Model Innovation" [44]. Significant enhancements have been introduced to elevate the overall quality and originality of the content. These improvements encompass four key areas. Firstly, the paper's literature review section has been expanded to provide a more comprehensive examination of the existing research landscape in the field. Second, an augmented emphasis on the inclusion of primary sources and data bolsters the empirical foundation of the research, fostering a more detailed and transparent portrayal of the research methodology and results. Third, the theoretical framework has undergone refinement, affording a clearer and more focused lens through which to explore the subject matter. Lastly, the discussion section has been sharpened, delving deeper into the unique contributions of the re-search, with particular emphasis on its relevance to Business Model Innovation (BMI).

2 Theoretical Background

2.1 The Role of Firms with in Grand Challenges

The most relevant definition of GCs has been done by George and colleagues [24], That describe them as "formulations of global problems that can be plausibly addressed through coordinated and collaborative effort" [24, 32]. Addressing these challenges requires innovative and sustainable solutions that balance economic growth with environmental protection, as well as the education and engagement of individuals, businesses, and governments to make positive changes. Failure to tackle these GCs could have catastrophic consequences for future generations and the planet's delicate ecosystem, making it imperative that we act decisively to protect the environment (e.g., [40]). Addressing GCs necessitates a collaborative and sustained endeavor involving diverse stakeholders across various organizational and societal tiers. It calls for reconfigurations in the approach to economic activities and demands progress in tools and technology [24, 29, 48]. In this context, for-profit businesses, whether independently or in partnership with governmental and non-profit entities, serve as key players, functioning as hubs of innovation and central agents in facilitating collaborative efforts for social impact [62, 63].

2.2 Emerging Technologies and Sustainable Business Model Innovation

The rise and diffusion of the Internet in the late 90s shed light on the limitation of traditional strategy models (e.g., Porter's value chain, network analysis) to capture the essence of the value creation mechanisms in the new e-business arena, thus opening the avenues for the conceptualization of a new holistic strategy construct: the business model [3, 67]. Defined as a system of interdependent activities performed by a focal firm and its key partners to create, deliver and capture value from a plethora of stakeholders [2, 58], the business model increasingly gained momentum as a suitable unit of analysis for strategy-making, given its boundary-spanning nature outside the domain of the focal firm, encompassing the distributed network of partners and new kinds of relationship typical of the new digital economy [7, 68]. The atms making the overall construct of the business model are "a different set of activities, as well as the resources and capabilities to perform them - either within the firm, or beyond it through cooperation with partners, suppliers or customers" [67]. Activities are defined as organized efforts that involve human, physical, and capital resources to achieve a specific objective. These can be performed by the focal firm, but also by other external actors, such as partners and suppliers, that forms an activity system. [67] Identify three main design elements, characterizing a business model: what are the activities present in the business model (content), how the various activities and actors are linked to each other (structure) and how they are managed (governance). These design elements can be combined together in an original manner to unlock four main sources of competitive advantage: differentiation, efficiency, complementarities and lock-in effects [2]. The business model construct has been recently welcomed by scholars studying the design of sustainable practices, following the Elkington' seminal concept of triple-bottom line in 1997 (e.g., [9, 17]). In their extensive review about business model literature, Foss and Saebi [21] highlight the potential of the business construct to advance research at the crossroads between strategy and sustainability, specifically because of the finer-grained perspective (i.e., activity-based) compared to other strategy models (e.g., business strategy formulation process). Moreover, one of the research areas still underdeveloped encompasses the antecedents and the enablers of business model design [3], very often approached in an aggregated manner without deep diving into their inherent characteristics. For instance, both as antecedents and enablers, emerging and digital technologies have been widely used in prior studies which focused on the process of business model design, but a link between their characteristics and strategic consequences at the business model level remains unexplored [11, 51]. Sustainable BMI is defined as the incorporation of heterogeneous logic within business, considering social and environmental aspects [9, 57]. According to [14], sustainable business models address the opportunity to solve market imperfections as the not-perfect efficiency of firms, the presence of negative externalities, pricing distortions, and the absence of perfect information. To this regard, George and colleagues [25] attempted to distill GCs into six managerial problems, that undermine firms' efforts to drive sustainable change: problems of knowing, valuating, communicating, coordination and trust, access and reach and institution. According to recent literature, the use of technologies may enable BMI potentially with a sustainable-oriented purpose [21]. Emerging technologies, as defined by [51], possess five attributes: radical novelty, fast growth, coherence, prominent impact, uncertainty and ambiguity. Emerging technology–enabled BMI simultaneously affects customers, suppliers, strategic partners, and others who participate in the ecosystem, creating new needs for stakeholders, so that novel resource configuration could arise [2, 25]. Intended as potential business-oriented characteristics derived from the technical architecture of the digital infrastructure, able to unlock the redesign of the value creation, delivery, and capture processes, the inclusion of "digital affordances" perspective in such debate may be enormously beneficial [4]. In terms of GCs indeed, George and colleagues [25] widely describe how some digital technologies – i.e., because of their specific digital affordances - can serve as enablers to overcome the traditional managerial problems associated to such wicked and complex problems to address from the firm-level.

Among emerging technologies, Blockchain in particular has stood out for its promise to represent a revolutionary foundational technology, capable of igniting a wide range of business-wide applications (e.g., [18, 35]). Blockchain can be classified as an emerging technology, as it fulfills the five parameters identified by Rotolo and colleagues [51]. However, these characteristics are not fundamental technological traits, but rather factors that explain the diffusion and impact of a technology, allowing it to be classified as "emergent" and advancing the consolidated work on technology diffusion [51, 60, 61]. It is instead left apart how affordances of the emerging technology may be used as levers for BMI [21]. Therefore, recognizing the emergent nature of blockchain and the possible consequent implications in terms of BMI within GCs, the research questions investigated in this study is "How blockchain act as a driver of BMI within GCs?".

3 Methodology

The theoretical background on which the research is based allows to identify the research question at the intersection between GCs, BMI and emerging technologies literatures. The unit of analysis aim of this research are the affordances of blockchain that enable new sources of innovation in the business model design elements proposed by Zott & Amit [67] in their activity-system view, and how they tackle the managerial problems formulated by George and colleagues [25].

Blockchain role for sustainable business models is a research field still unexplored, from which new theory can emerge [6, 15]. The research accomplishes the aim of generation of new theory for the emerging researched themes, from which subsequent studies may begin their investigation [15, 66]. As a result, it is advantageous to proceed with qualitative research [23]. More specifically, it was chosen to conduct an inductive multiple case study [15, 66]. This approach has been chosen because the literature recognizes it as more robust if compared to a single case study [66].

Multiple case studies enable comparisons between different manifestations of the phenomenon, elucidating whether emergent findings are simply idiosyncratic to a single case study or consistently replicated by several cases, resulting in greater generalizability of results [16, 43].

3.1 Empirical Setting

Climate change is currently considered one of the most critical challenges to face in the next years, representing a proper threat for human as species [50]. As a result, the UN established an appropriate SDG for it (SDG 13). The primary issue with climate change is the rising concentration of greenhouse gases in the atmosphere, which causes global warming. However, in most industries, there is no penalty for causing air pollution.

Carbon markets can be an effective tool for internalizing the negative externalities associated with greenhouse gas emissions. Voluntary Carbon Markets (VCM) are non-regulated markets, in which organizations participate based on self-imposed emissions reduction goals. Here, actors can offset their impact by buying carbon credits that are generated through the development of mitigation projects that follow precise international methodologies and that are verified and certified by external accreditation entities (i.e., standard entities such as Verra and Gold Standard). These projects usually allow the reduction, removal or avoidance of emission production in the atmosphere [36].

The Voluntary Carbon Market (VCM) comprises two primary facets: the supply side and the demand side. The supply side segment encompasses the foundational processes of carbon reduction projects. Its core objective is the substantiation of emissions reduction, avoidance, or removal. This validation process, known as MRV (Measurement, Reporting, and Verification), serves as the mechanism for gathering evidence that attests to the project's genuine emission mitigation efforts, according to methodologies that are developed by so-called standard's organizations. Subsequently, a third-party entity acts as an arbiter, ensuring the accuracy and validity of the gathered data. Upon successful validation, carbon credits are issued. The demand side revolves around the trade and utilization of certified carbon credits. Once certified, these credits transform into valuable assets. Businesses and organizations engage in the acquisition and the retirement of these credits to offset their carbon emissions [42].

According to the Taskforce on Scaling Voluntary Carbon Markets, the demand for carbon credits could increase by a factor of 15 or more by 2030 and by a factor of up to 100 by 2050. However, the market is characterized by some problems that prevent it to scale up: measurement technical issues, heterogeneity and illiquidity of carbon credits, greenwashing concerns, opaqueness and fragmentation, entry barriers and lack of regulation [42].

Practitioners are growing more confident in the use of blockchain technologies to better collaborate in the fight against climate change and for decarbonizing the global economy. The growing interest in the area is evidenced by the relevant number of new companies that are beginning to develop novel solutions adopting blockchain for carbon markets [45, 55].

3.2 Case Sampling

To carry out the case selection within the multiple case study, it was decided to look for instances where blockchain technologies were being used to create sustainable business models. The sampling approach was thus theoretical, high quality case study research needs to be based on cases chosen for appropriate theoretical reasons, for the likelihood that they will offer theoretical insight [14].

Table 1. Sample selection

Company	Value-chain position	Blockchain protocol	Headquarter Basis	Maturity stage
Company A	Integrated	Polygon	Singapore	Low $ 530.000
Company B	Integrated	Azure Distributed Ledger	Australia	Low $ 1.400.000
Company D	Demand side	Polygon	USA	High $ 14.410.000
Company C	Integrated	Cosmos	USA	High $ 10.500.000

The main source utilized to gather blockchain-based startups for the selection process was Pitchbook, a subscription-based website that delivers data and research covering private capital markets, including venture capital and private equity. Companies were searched including keywords such as "Blockchain" AND "Sustainability" or "Blockchain" AND "Environmental services". To produce a heterogeneous sample within the "region of homogeneity" subject of our analysis, we considered different cases considering value chain position in the market, adopted blockchain protocol, geographic location and maturity stage. Once the initial sample was sufficiently large, it was filtered to select the most notable cases to be examined to ensure the heterogeneity logic (according to Table 1). As a conclusion of the case selection phase, a final sample of 4 blockchain-based startups were extracted and investigated: Company A, Company B, Company C and Company D.

3.3 Data Collection and Analysis

Data were collected through multiple sources of information. A data triangulation approach was followed, mixing primary and secondary sources of information [66]. This approach was important for the creation of robust results for the qualitative research [10, 53].

The four cases were subjected to semi-structured interviews with founders and.

C-levels. Semi-structured interviews allow for a degree of flexibility in the interview process in balancing the necessity to drive the conversation towards the key issues identified from the research question while leaving the respondents the possibility to drive the conversation and to bring up important points that may not have been covered by the researchers. The researchers carried out eight semi-structured interviews over two distinct waves. For both the rounds, all sessions lasted between 31 and 76 min. The informant for each company remained the same during both rounds. The results of this phase of the research were recorded, for a total of 380 min of material, and transcribed, for a total of 107 pages. According Eisenhardt [15] and Yin [66], who argue that the use of multiple sources of information improves the overall rigor of a case study, the final outcome of primary data was "triangulated" with several secondary sources, coming from the companies' websites, whitepapers and from third party articles.

The protocol of the pilot interview was similar and consistent with the study's research question: the informants were asked to describe their business model; specifically, questions were created to understand the business models in terms of design elements and themes (with questions like: "Can you describe the main activities you perform as a company? Can you describe the main activities performed by your customer groups and partners? Can you describe how do you create value for each customer group?"). These questions were based on the business model conceptualization as an activity system [67]. A second set of questions sought to investigate the sustainability contribution through the lenses of GCs managerial problems [25], with a particular emphasis on the contribution of technology for the resolution of those problems (including questions such as: "How are you able to detect and measure information gaps about environmental issues you aim to address? How can you traduce the positive sustainable impact in measurable economic value? How can you foster and manage coordination and trust among activities and actors in the network? Are you able to reach customer groups previously unserved by the market?"). The second round of interviews led us to confirm the information acquired in the first interviews, investigate specific blockchain applications and in general to deep dive into some topics that both interviewers and interviewees unconsciously overlooked or ignored in the first phase [66].

Following the data collection phase, data analysis was carried out to support the research discussion. First, recordings were listened and transcribed. A within-case study data analysis was performed in accordance with Eisenhardt [15] and focused on bridging the dimensions of design themes and George's managerial concerns in order to determine which value creation sources of each company model were related to distinct GCs managerial problem. Ground theory methodology [27, 56] was adopted to study each case according to an open coding practice, allowing to investigate complex phenomena using labels, thus generating theory from interviews. Collected data allowed the generation of in-vivo codes dataset and the analysis following constant comparative method [26]. Subsequently, a comparison of codes from the different cases was carried out to obtain the formulation of first-order concepts. Following the identification of first-order concepts, second-order themes were created to achieve a higher level of abstraction by linking the previously identified concepts to more theoretical constructs. The second-order codes were then aggregated into two major overarching dimensions: (1) Business model design themes routed in Zott & Amit [67] seminal work; (2) Grand Challenges managerial problems, based on George and colleagues [25] work.

With reference to cross-case analysis, we looked for similarities and differences at different abstraction levels (first order concepts, second order themes and overarching dimensions) to compare the differences between the four cases, allowing for novel findings [15]. Finally, a further analysis crossed similarities within first order concept and second order themes of the two overarching dimensions. In this way, the correlation between GCs managerial problems and design themes was investigated. The final result was graphically represented using coding trees [26].

4 Results

The cross-case analysis, carried out triangulating primary data coming from interviews with secondary data, has been the foundation for the conceptual framework described in Fig. 1.

4.1 Overarching Dimension 1: GCs Managerial Problems

The GCs managerial problems described by George and colleagues [25], are routed in the business model design elements identified by Zott & Amit [66]. Namely, the first two problem - problem of knowing and problem of valuating – are associated to design content, being the knowledge and the valuation of natural and social capital, fundamental to act within sustainability domain. The third and fourth problem – problem of communicating and problem of coordination and trust – are tied to design structure, as they entail the reshaping of links between actors in the market and changes in the way they communicate. Finally, the last two problems – problem of access and reach and problem of institutions – concern design governance, as they deal with actors' access and the institutions' role in the activity system.

Our cases reveal that blockchain seems not to cover a role in addressing the technical difficulties in obtaining an accurate and reliable measurement of a project's impact (problem of knowing). Being blockchain a distributed ledger, it has significant implications for how data is managed and shared among actors, but not for how data is obtained (for which other technologies can be leveraged, i.e., oracles such as sensors or satellites).

According to the findings, blockchain can successfully contribute by addressing the heterogeneity and illiquidity issues of carbon markets (problem of valuating) – while allowing to tokenize and fractionalize carbon credits. As described by Company C CIO: "The liquidity has to do with creating baskets of tokens on chain where we take a certain quality of token. There will be a third party that will just determine which tokens would be allowed into the basket; in that way, you can have literally millions of carbon credits in the basket and a single tradable token can be traded on centralized or decentralized exchanges." Carbon credit baskets aggregate credits from comparable carbon offsetting initiatives, boosting the homogeneity of the supply of carbon credits. Increased liquidity results in correct price discovery for each credit class: "The current illiquid system can work for a company buying a bunch of credits. But, if you want to have traders in the market and people who are longing carbon credits, you need to have much larger liquidity" (CIO, Company C).

Concerning problem of communicating, blockchain could represent a mean to fight greenwashing. In the distributed ledger, all information about each carbon credit is shared and accessible: "when somebody buys one of our carbon credits, they are not only buying a net 0 carbon reduction. They're also buying ESG reporting data" (CEO, Company B).

All the startups evaluated addressed the VCM's opaqueness and fragmentation issues (problem of coordination and trust). Within blockchain protocols, all transactions are permanently recorded on the ledger. To retire a carbon credit, it's essential to deactivate the underlying smart contract. This process significantly restricts the ability to purchase a carbon credit, enjoy its benefits, and subsequently resell it through intermediaries, preventing the common issue of "double counting." The peer-to-peer nature of blockchain may lead to increased disintermediation within the carbon credit ecosystem, diminishing the significance of brokers, traders, and merchants, thus reducing transaction costs in credit exchanges. As described by Company A CEO: "we're disrupting the brokers, traders and exchanges; and shortening the value chain". Relying on blockchain's decentralization features, it is possible to establish new roles or coordination mechanisms - for example, new methodologies can be proposed with open innovation approaches and validated through decentralized governance mechanisms, as in Company C, or peer-to-peer lending mechanisms enabled, as in Company A.

As a result, blockchain can help by providing the tools for removing entry barriers (problem of access and reach). On the demand side, decreased transaction costs allow more end users to buy carbon credits; on the supply side, more projects can receive financing for their activities. Blockchain-based startups working on the supply side of the market are combining blockchain to other measuring technologies (i.e., Sensors and satellites) to develop new digital measurement, reporting and verification (MRV) methodologies. As a result, project developers' verification costs for doing the entire MRV process and getting their carbon offsetting approved are decreased, overcoming the slow and manual measuring methodologies typical of existing standard organizations. As described by Company C CEO: "The process of sequestering carbon is still going to be at the same speed. It works at the speed of biology. But the process to validate and verify and collect data will be quicker and more inexpensive than in other projects".

Finally, blockchain may fill institutional void or failures (problem of institutions); blockchain can serve as a global distributed platform infrastructure for transacting carbon credits, without heavy reliance on trust intermediaries. As highlighted by Company A CEO: "[stakeholders] They don't have to trust a close service report [standards' organizations services]; you can trust a much more distributed and decentralized validation of the proof of your carbon purchase or offsetting".

4.2 Overarching Dimension 2: Design Themes

The cross-case analysis points out that blockchain primarily fosters efficiency through the use of tokens. It is crucial to differentiate between governance tokens, which signify the governance and consensus mechanisms of a DAO, and utility tokens, which represent the revival of on-chain carbon credits. Governance tokens facilitate novel decentralized governance models, giving rise to new organizational structures such as DAOs, where token holders are actively involved in the decision-making process. Regarding carbon credits as digital assets, Company D whitepaper affirms: *"Tokens have multiple advantages over legacy offsets, including full transparency, programmability and fractionalization"*.

As a consequence, tokenization may enhance the liquidity of carbon markets, as the use of smart contracts to automate trustless transactions are also tied to efficiency. As the CIO of Company C, explained: "The liquidity has to do with creating baskets of tokens on chain where we group a certain quality of credits in an index". The improved openness and accountability of the decentralized ledger aid in the decrease of information asymmetry: "blockchain is creating a huge amount of transparency around the ownership of a specific assets. So obviously assets owned on chain are really trackable. You can see who owns them, who owned them before, how many times have they been traded, what did they trade for it so they could see what they paid for it". Finally, transaction costs are drastically reduced by the possibility of decreasing the of reliance on intermediaries on both the demand and supply side.

Concerning the value source of complementarity, two main discovers emerge. First, the application of blockchain is empowered with the usage of a combination of other emerging technologies to innovate the measurement phase: "There are complementarities from a technological point of view, with the convergence of IoT, Remote Sensing, Satellite's image and blockchain is possible to develop D-MRV methodologies" (CIO, Company C). Second, it has been founded that blockchain enabled activity systems exhibit composability, with open-source logics that encourage cooperation among numerous actors operating within a certain blockchain protocol (e.g., Polygon).

Finally, regarding the lock-in design theme, the use of governance tokens and the development of DAOs allow investors to become more closely associated with the businesses, allowing them to take part in decision-making and share in the profits. Company A CEO explained: "Think the governance token as a share in a company". Company C interviewed said: "Investment into the our token is one of those mechanisms where people have the opportunity to own the token and stake it and take earning rewards through the staking of that token while also taking a stake in the entire network".

5 Discussion and Conclusions

According to George and colleagues [24] "Grand Challenges are formulations of global problems that can be plausibly addressed through coordinated and collaborative effort". Therefore, in order to tackle them, changes in the way economic activities are planned and implemented (i.e., business models) are needed, as well as advancements in tools and technologies [29, 48]. This study contributes to the call by [8], who asked researchers to investigate BMI as a mean to address GCs. By drawing on the case of voluntary carbon market, we get to explore how blockchain can contribute to BMI in the domain of GCs. Building on the business model construct proposed by Zott & Amit [66] in their activity-system view, our framework illustrates three features that characterize blockchain as enabler of novel forms of design content, structure and governance guided by novel efficiency, complementarity and lock-in logics. Specifically, blockchain acts as asset enabler, as trust machine and as coordinated and collaborative action enhancer.

In particular, our contribution is twofold. First, we provide a theoretical contribution to the BMI and GCs literatures by studying BMI as a means of addressing managerial problems related to GCs. Secondly, we contribute by opening the "black box" of an emerging technology, the blockchain, by unpacking three emerging affordances for BMI.

In the following paragraphs, we will explore the relationship among the managerial problems related to the GCs, the actionable characteristics of blockchain technology, and

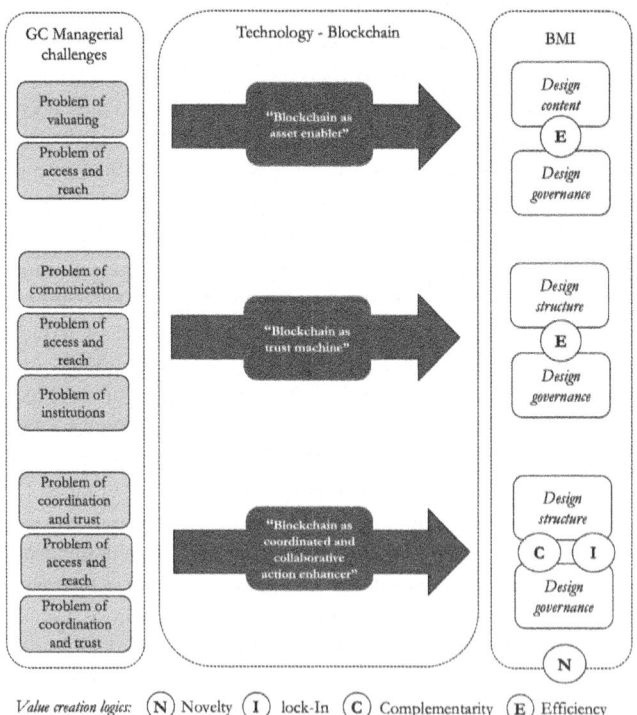

Fig. 1. Conceptual Framework (adapted from [44])

the value logics that drive BMI. This exploration will serve to elucidate our contribution, and illustrate the conceptual model presented in Fig. 1.

5.1 Feature 1: Blockchain as Asset Enabler

Blockchain acts as an *asset enabler* as it adds the fundamental attribute of "ownership" to the internet we use today [47], allowing new asset classes to emerge: (i) Governance tokens, which are built natively on-chain, govern the consensus mechanism of blockchain protocols and projects, as well as offering new kinds of stake, rights, and participation [28, 59]; (ii) Tokenized assets are digital twins of current real assets that are represented and transferrable on the distributed ledger [22, 25]. Tokens are a new source of design content, as they entail new activities related to the design of tokens, such as defining the conditions under which participants can earn new tokens for contributing resources to the network, or defining the rights associated with token ownership [12, 20, 28].

For sustainable development, tokens can be a source of efficiency as they contribute to the problem of valuation. In particular, our research empirically confirms what proposed by George-and-colleagues [25], observing that tokenization "contribute by transforming natural capital into precise, manageable, fungible or not fungible, tradeable units for which new markets can establish prices". Tokens may be a mean to change the manner of how we assess and value ecological and social assets. Accordingly, individual may gain access to asset classes and risks that may have been otherwise beyond their capacity, as it is possible to slice or group data into compact packets to create wider fractionalization and distribution of risk and ownership [52]. Thus, blockchain is employed to design content and governance driven by efficiency logics.

5.2 Feature 2: Blockchain as Trust Machine

Blockchain as *trust machine* property is linked to the nature of its distributed ledger and consensus mechanism. Smart contracts enable multiple parties who do not trust one another to engage in exchanges of value when certain conditions are met [20, 28, 46]. According to transaction costs economics (TCE), firm boundaries are determined by the need to internalize transactions that the market could not handle efficiently, because of the presence of transaction costs such as verification, searching and coordination costs [64, 65]. That is the reason why traditional and digital intermediaries emerge, enabling the possibility for large numbers of previously unconnected parties (e.g., buyers and sellers) to interact [5, 13, 39, 68].

Our study shows that blockchain technology enhance trust and transparency by reducing costs and time for validating trading partners. We find technological characteristic of blockchain technology shifts trust to the technology rather than to external entity, freeing actors to trade in a large-scale decentralized fashion, without the need for a trustworthy intermediary and allowing participation for actors who were previously excluded from existing activity systems.

Trust is important in many areas of sustainability, especially where there is an exchange of goods or services that have a social or ecological impact; these must be transparently communicated to the stakeholders and no mechanisms of opportunistic behaviours (moral hazard, adverse selection) due to information asymmetries should arise [25]. In these situations, pure commercial transactions can fail, while blockchain allows these transactions to happen despite the existing obstacles, such as by lowering costs or providing novel means of access [52]. Thus, blockchain is employed to design novel forms of structure and governance driven by efficiency logics.

5.3 Feature 3: Blockchain as Coordinated and Collaborative Action Enhancer

The name of this property stems from the definition of GCs provided by George and colleagues [24], according to whom solving GCs requires "coordinated and collaborative effort". As GCs lack centralized control over their participants, some researchers claim that current organizational structures are inappropriate [19, 33, 38]. Blockchain protocols pave the way to new distributed governance paradigms, incentives systems, and new open-source collaboration mechanisms. We show that governance tokens enable new forms of design governance and organizations, shifting towards forms of decentralized autonomous organizations (DAOs), where open innovation can be fostered with new roles and related reward mechanisms. Decentralized governance enabled by blockchain technology can serve as a mechanism for achieving structural alignment in addressing GCs. This is consistent with Adner [1], definition of "ecosystem-as-a-structure," which characterizes ecosystems as the structural alignment of multiple partners who must interact to realize a central value proposition. A social or environmental challenge may represent the focal value proposition the set of partners collectively tackle with their effort. Thus, blockchain is employed to design novel forms of structure and governance driven by complementarity and lock-in logics.

5.4 Blockchain Impact on Value Creation Logics

Our research provides an important contribution in in the understanding of blockchain as a BMI design enabler. Literature identifies some important properties that characterize good designs, most notably the occurrence of synergy across design themes [3]. We find not only that blockchain based business model exhibit all the value creation logics (novelty, efficiency, complementarity and lock-in), but also that there is strong inter-relationship among them. As can be seen, Novelty is a common logic that represents new ways of doing (content), structuring and governing activities. Thus, as showed in Fig. 1, Efficiency logics are promoted by "asset enabler" and "trust machine" properties Complementarity and lock-In are stimulated by "coordinated and collaborative action enhancer" property.

5.5 Blockchain and Technological Convergence

Second, we contribute from a technology-oriented perspective by "opening the black box" of an emerging technology. Blockchain fulfills the characteristics of an emerging technology described by Rotolo and colleagues' [51]: radical novelty, fast growth, coherence, uncertainty & ambiguity, prominent impact. However, these features are mainly related to the characteristics leading to the wider diffusion and adoption of the technology itself, advancing the consolidated work on technology diffusion [60, 61].

Despite the claims, it is instead very often left apart how the inner characteristics of an emerging and innovative technology may produce affordances (i.e., the three properties) that can be used as levers for BMI [21]. Our analysis also revealed that blockchain adoption is related to other technologies exploitation. We observe that the composability within different blockchain protocols (e.g., Ethereum, Polygon), as well as their integration with other consolidated and emerging technologies (i.e., third-party information sources, called oracles, including remote sensing and satellites) play a crucial role in unlocking the emerging technology's full potential. Through such advancements, the combination of blockchain with other emerging technologies unveils a realm of untapped digital affordances that can effectively address various managerial challenges. These developments align harmoniously with the concept of "digital convergence" put forth by Teece [58], which envisions the emergence of a fully digitized economy where the collective impact of technological convergence transcends the cumulative effect of individual technologies.

References

1. Adner, R.: Ecosystem as structure: an actionable construct for strategy. J. Manag. **43**, 39–58 (2017)
2. Amit, R., Han, X.: Value creation through novel resource configurations in a digitally enabled world: novel resource configurations in a digitally enabled world. Strateg. Entrep. J. **11**, 228–242 (2017)
3. Amit, R., Zott, C.: Value creation in E-business. Strateg. Manag. J. **22**, 493–520 (2001)
4. Autio, E., Nambisan, S., Thomas, L.D.W., Wright, M.: Digital affordances, spatial affordances, and the genesis of entrepreneurial ecosystems. Strateg. Entrep. J. **12**, 72–95 (2018)
5. Bailey, J.P., Bakos, Y.: An exploratory study of the emerging role of electronic intermediaries. Int. J. Electron. Commer. **1**, 7–20 (1997)
6. Bansal, P. (Tima), & Corley, K.: The Coming of Age for Qualitative Research: Embracing the Diversity of Qualitative Methods. Academy of Management Journal, 54, 233–237 (2011)
7. Bigelow, L.S., Barney, J.B.: What can Strategy Learn from the Business Model Approach? J. Manage. Stud. **58**, 528–539 (2021)
8. Bocken, N.M.P., Heidenreich S., Spieth P., Tucci L.C., Zott C.: SEJ Special Issue Call for Paper (2023)
9. Bocken, N.M.P., Short, S.W., Rana, P., Evans, S.: A literature and practice review to develop sustainable business model archetypes. J. Clean. Prod. **65**, 42–56 (2014)
10. Bonoma, T.V.: Case research in marketing: opportunities, problems, and a process. J. Mark. Res. **22**, 199 (1985)
11. Casadesus-Masanell, R., Ricart, J.E.: From strategy to business models and onto tactics. Long Range Plan. **43**, 195–215 (2010)
12. Catalini, C., Gans, J.S.: Some Simple Economics of the Blockchain (2020)
13. Clemons, E.K., Reddi, S.P., Row, M.C.: The impact of information technology on the organization of economic activity: the "move to the middle" hypothesis. J. Manag. Inf. Syst. **10**, 9–35 (1993)
14. Cohen, B., Winn, M.I.: Market imperfections, opportunity and sustainable entrepreneurship. J. Bus. Ventur. **22**, 29–49 (2007)
15. Eisenhardt, K.: Building theories from case study research. Acad. Manag. Rev. **14**, 532–550 (1989)

16. Eisenhardt, K.M., Graebner, M.E.: Theory building from cases: opportunities and challenges. Acad. Manag. J. **50**(1), 25–32 (2007). https://doi.org/10.5465/amj.2007.24160888
17. Elkington, J.: The triple bottom line. Environ. Manag.: Readings Cases **2**, 49–66 (1997)
18. Felin, T., Lakhani, K., Safari, an O.M.C.: What Problems Will You Solve with Blockchain? MIT Sloan Manag. Rev. (2018)
19. Ferraro, F., Etzion, D., Gehman, J.: Tackling grand challenges pragmatically: robust action revisited. Organ. Stud. **36**, 363–390 (2015)
20. Forman, C., et al.: The trust machine? The promise of blockchain-based algorithmic governance of Exchange. In: Academy of Management Proceedings, 2019, pp. 13603 (2019)
21. Foss, N.J., Saebi, T.: Fifteen years of research on business model innovation: how far have we come, and where should we go? J. Manag. **43**, 200–227 (2017)
22. Gan, J., Tsoukalas, G., Netessine, S.: Initial coin offerings, speculation, and asset tokenization. Manag. Sci. **67**(2), 914–931 (2021). https://doi.org/10.1287/mnsc.2020.3796
23. Gartner, W.B., Birley, S.: Introduction to the special issue on qualitative methods in entrepreneurship research. J. Bus. Ventur. **17**, 387–395 (2002)
24. George, G., Howard-Grenville, J., Joshi, A., Tihanyi, L.: Understanding and tackling societal grand challenges through management research. Acad. Manag. J. **59**, 1880–1895 (2016)
25. George, G., Merrill, R.K., Schillebeeckx, S.J.D.: Digital sustainability and entrepreneurship: how digital innovations are helping tackle climate change and sustainable development. Entrep. Theory Pract. **45**, 999–1027 (2021)
26. Gioia, D.A., Corley, K.G., Hamilton, A.L.: Seeking qualitative rigor in inductive research: notes on the gioia methodology. Organ. Res. Methods **16**, 15–31 (2013)
27. Glaser, B., Strauss, A.: The discovery of Grounded Theory. Aldine Transaction (1967)
28. Glaser, F.: Pervasive Decentralisation of Digital Infrastructures: A Framework for Blockchain enabled System and Use Case Analysis. Presented at Hawaii International Conference on System Sciences (2017)
29. Griggs, D., et al.: Sustainable development goals for people and planet. Nature, **495**, 305–307 (2013)
30. Grodal, S., O'Mahony, S.: How does a grand challenge become displaced? Explaining the duality of field mobilization. Acad. Manag. J. **60**, 1801–1827 (2017)
31. Holotiuk, F., Pisani, F., Moormann, J.: Radicalness of blockchain: an assessment based on its impact on the payments industry. Technol. Anal. Strateg. Manage. **31**, 915–928 (2019)
32. Howard-Grenville, J., Davis, G.F., Thomas Dyllick, C., Miller, C., Thau, S., Tsui, A.S.: Sustainable development for a better world: contributions of leadership, management, and organizations. Acade Manage. Discoveries **5**(4), 355–366 (2019). https://doi.org/10.5465/amd.2019.0275
33. Howard-Grenville, J., Spengler, J.: Surfing the grand challenges wave in management scholarship: how did we get here, where are we now, and what's next? In A. Aslan Gümüsay, E. Marti, H. Trittin-Ulbrich, C. Wickert (Eds.), Organizing for societal grand challenges, pp. 279–295. Emerald Publishing Limited (2022)
34. Hsieh, Y., Vergne, J.: The future of the web? the coordination and early-stage growth of decentralized platforms. Strateg. Manag. J. **44**, 829–857 (2023)
35. Iansiti, M., Lakhani, K. R.: The truth about blockchain. Harvard Business Review (2017)
36. Ieta.org, The anatomy of carbon market. https://www.ieta.org/resources/Resources/GHG_Report/2021/IETA-2021-GHG-Report.pdf (2021)
37. Klein, S.P., Spieth, P., Heidenreich, S.: Facilitating business model innovation: the influence of sustainability and the mediating role of strategic orientations. J. Prod. Innov. Manag. **38**, 271–288 (2021)
38. Luo, X.R., Zhang, J., Marquis, C.: Mobilization in the internet age: internet activism and corporate response. Acad. Manag. J. **59**, 2045–2068 (2016)

39. Malone, T.W., Yates, J., Benjamin, R.I.: Electronic markets and electronic hierarchies. Commun. ACM **30**, 484–497 (1987)
40. McCarthy, G.D., Haigh, I.D., Hirschi, J.J.-M., Grist, J.P., Smeed, D.A.: Ocean impact on decadal Atlantic climate variability revealed by sea-level observations. Nature **521**, 508–510 (2015)
41. McDonald, R.M., Eisenhardt, K.M.: Parallel play: startups, nascent markets, and effective business-model design. Adm. Sci. Q. **65**, 483–523 (2020)
42. McKinsey, Carbon credits: Scaling voluntary markets. Retrieved from https://www.mckinsey.com/capabilities/sustainability/our-insights/a-blueprint-for-scaling-voluntary-carbon-markets-to-meet-the-climate-challenge (2021)
43. Meredith, J.: Building operations management theory through case and field research. J. Oper. Manag. **16**, 441–454 (1998)
44. Moiana, D.; Manotti, J.; Ghezzi, A. and Rangone, A.: Unveiling the Digital and Sustainability Convergence: Leveraging Blockchain for Grand Challenges Oriented Business Model Innovation. In: Proceedings of the 20th International Conference on Smart Business Technologies, 136–143 (2023)
45. Morgan Stanley, Crypto & Carbon. Retrieved from https://www.morganstanley.com/im/publication/insights/articles/article_cryptoandcarbon_us.pdf (2022)
46. Murray, A., Kuban, S., Josefy, M., Anderson, J.: Contracting in the smart era: the implications of blockchain and decentralized autonomous organizations for contracting and corporate governance. Acad. Manag. Perspect. **35**, 622–641 (2021)
47. Murray, A., Kim, D., Combs, J.: The promise of a decentralized internet: what is web3 and how can firms prepare? Bus. Horiz. **66**, 191–202 (2023)
48. Muzio, D., Doh, J.: COVID-19 and the future of management studies. Insights from leading scholars. J. Manag. Stud. **58**(5), 1371–1377 (2021). https://doi.org/10.1111/joms.12689
49. Porter, M. E., Kramer, M. R.: Creating Shared Value. Harvard Business Review. (2011)
50. Pörtner, H.-O., Roberts, D. C.: Climate Change.: impacts, Adaptation and Vulnerability (n.d.) (2022)
51. Rotolo, D., Hicks, D., Martin, B.R.: What is an emerging technology? Res. Policy **44**, 1827–1843 (2015)
52. Santos, F., Pache, A.-C., Birkholz, C.: Making hybrids work: aligning business models and organizational design for social enterprises. Calif. Manage. Rev. **57**, 36–58 (2015)
53. Siggelkow, N.: Persuasion with case studies. Acade. Manag. J. (2007)
54. Snihur, Y., Zott, C., Amit, R.: Managing the value appropriation dilemma in business model innovation. Strategy Sci. **6**, 22–38 (2021)
55. Southpole, Blockchain and carbon: How to scale climate action while protecting investors and ensuring environmental integrity. Retrieved from https://www.southpole.com/fr/blog/blockchain-and-carbon
56. Strauss, A., Corbin, J.: Basics of qualitative research: Techniques and procedures for developing grounded theory (2nd ed.). Sage Publications (1998)
57. Stubbs, W.: Sustainable entrepreneurship and b corps. Bus. Strateg. Environ. **26**, 331–344 (2017)
58. Teece, D.J.: Profiting from innovation in the digital economy: enabling technologies, standards, and licensing models in the wireless world. Res. Policy **47**, 1367–1387 (2018)
59. Trabucchi, D., Moretto, A., Buganza, T., MacCormack, A.: Disrupting the disruptors or enhancing them? How blockchain reshapes two-sided platforms. J. Prod. Innov. Manag. **37**, 552–574 (2020)
60. Tushman, M.L., Anderson, P.: Technological discontinuities and organizational environments. Adm. Sci. Q. **31**, 439 (1986)
61. Utterback, J.M., Abernathy, W.J.: A dynamic model of process and product innovation. Omega **3**(6), 639–656 (1975)

62. Voegtlin, C., Scherer, A.G., Stahl, G.K., Hawn, O.: Grand societal challenges and responsible innovation. J. Manage. Stud. **59**, 1–28 (2022)
63. Wang, H., Tong, L., Takeuchi, R., George, G.: Corporate social responsibility: an overview and new research directions. Acad. Manag. J. **59**, 534–544 (2016)
64. Williamson, O.E.: Transaction-cost economics: the governance of contractual relations. J. Law Econ. **22**, 233–261 (1979)
65. Williamson, O.E.: Calculativeness, trust, and economic organization. J. Law Econ. **36**, 453–486 (1993)
66. Yin, R. K.: Case study research: Design and methods. Beverly Hills, Calif.: Sage Publications (1984)
67. Zott, C., Amit, R.: Business model design: an activity system perspective. Long Range Plan. **43**, 216–226 (2010)
68. Zott, C., Amit, R., Massa, L.: The business model: recent developments and future research. J. Manag. **37**, 1019–1042 (2011)

Digital Transformation Roadmap for Danish SME Smart Factories: Benefits and Future Research

Richard Addo-Tenkorang[1], Charles Møller[2,3(✉)], and Kuan-Lin Chen[2(✉)]

[1] University of Hertfordshire, SPECS, College Lane, Hatfield AL10 9AB, UK
r.addo-tenkorang@herts.ac.uk

[2] Department of Materials and Production, Centre for Production, Aalborg University, Fibigerstræde 16, 9220 Aalborg, Denmark
charles@mp.aau.dk, charles@mpe.au.dk, kuan_lin16@hotmail.com

[3] Department of Mechanical and Production Engineering, Aarhus University, Katrinebjergvej 89, 8200 Aarhus, Denmark

Abstract. Digitization has only penetrated certain supply chains. Some companies have made great strides in implementing Industry 4.0, where a digital twin connects virtual and real factories. SME interest in Industry 4.0, adopted by big OEMs in Germany, is low. The pressing challenge is crafting a practical transformation plan that resonates with SMEs, the backbone of any thriving economy. Danish SMEs' Smart Factories/Industry 4.0 model perspective is studied in this study. This study aims to provide a framework for companies to successfully transition to digitalization and adopt smart product and service development practices. SME-focused quantitative research methodologies like surveys, interviews, and literature reviews are used in this study. Large corporations started Industry 4.0, or the digital shift, according to a study. Comprehensive industrial growth, especially by SMEs, has not prioritised it. This research provides a well-defined and feasible path for industrial SMEs following the Danish Model's "digital change management process - Industry 4.0/Smart factory," industrial transformation process. This paper theoretically outlines an Industry 4.0 smart factory roadmap. This framework optimises and streamlines SME production. Danish Industry 4.0 views. The present study focuses on the development of a digital transformation roadmap specifically designed for Danish small and medium-sized enterprises (SMEs) operating in the smart factory sector. This research aims to explore the advantages of implementing such a roadmap and identify potential areas for future investigation.

Keywords: Digital transformation · Internet of Things (IoT) · Smart/Virtual factory · Supply Chain management (SCM) · Industry 4.0 · Small & Medium Enterprises (SMEs)

1 Introduction

The global community has witnessed three significant consecutive technological and industrial revolutions. The Industrial Revolution commenced in England during the late 18th century and extended into the mid-19th century. The advent of mechanised farming marked a significant departure from an agrarian economy towards a more structured system characterised by the implementation of mechanised and/or mechanical production techniques. During the late 1960s, a significant shift occurred in the industrial landscape, marking the onset of the second phase of radical industrial transformation. This time witnessed a transition from mechanised farming to the emergence of industrial production and manufacturing as dominant economic activities. Consequently, the advent of factories marked the initiation of a global shift towards the large-scale manufacturing of accessible consumer goods.

The revolution also facilitated the widespread adoption of electronics and information technology in industrial and manufacturing processes, leading to the emergence of an era characterised by enhanced efficiency and automated production. The global community is currently witnessing the culmination or onset of the much anticipated fourth industrial revolution. The current industrial revolution holds the potential to integrate and connect the realms of production and manufacturing through the utilisation of network interconnectivity, sometimes referred to as the "Internet of Things." Consequently, the current period commonly referred to as "Industry 4.0" has emerged ([1]; [2]; [3]). Industry 4.0, also known as the fourth industrial revolution, functions as a framework for the concept of "Smart production;" a concept that refers to the use of advanced technologies and intelligent systems in the manufacturing process. It involves the integration of artificial intelligence, machine learning, and data analytics to optimise production efficiency, reduce costs, and improve product quality. Smart production enables real-time monitoring.

A production or manufacturing process that operates as a fully integrated and automated system. The Smart production process or system facilitates and improves a production process by incorporating intelligent information and communication technology (ICT) machines, systems, technologies, and interconnected networks. This integration enables these components to autonomously exchange and respond to executed information, thereby automating the management of industrial production supply-chain processes and activities. Previous studies on Industry 4.0 have suggested that the emergence of the fourth industrial revolution was initially observed in Germany, thereby highlighting its distinctiveness in this context. Germany, as the domicile of prominent high-tech car original equipment manufacturers (OEMs), possesses a favourable position in relation to the substantial financial capital-intensive investment that is necessary. The integration of cyber-physical production systems (CPPS) is essential in the context of the fourth industrial revolution, which encompasses the use of intelligent equipment and gadgets. These advanced technologies provide superior interconnectivity through information and communication technology (ICT), resulting in a seamless integration and networked production environment.

The fourth revolution is characterised by the emergence of a decentralised intelligence platform that enables the autonomous processing and management of intelligent cyber-physical systems or objects. This platform also facilitates the integration of these systems or objects into both real and virtual environments, commonly referred to as the "Digital/Virtual Twin" ([3]). This introduces a critical novel element of the manufacturing and/or production paradigm shift. Hence, this represents a crucial transformation in the industrial landscape, transitioning from a centralised mode of production to a decentralised one. Hence, this presents the potential and capacity for transformative technological breakthroughs in the industrial sector. This paradigm change would facilitate the ability of industrial production machinery to not only enhance the value of materials and carry out various processes to create finished products but also enable the products themselves to possess physical configurations that allow them to interact with the machinery, providing precise instructions on how to operate.

The successful implementation of a comprehensive "Digital Change Management - (DCM)" strategy inside an industrial organisation necessitates the establishment of a strong awareness among top management and organisational employees who will play a crucial role in its achievement. Hence, this article aims to examine the potential for small and medium-sized enterprises (SMEs) to transition their traditional production processes into a "Smart Factory" or smart production. Therefore, our earlier research; [57], Addo-Tenkorang, R. et al., (2023) published in ICSBT 2023 on the unique title: "Industrial Transformation Roadmap for Digitalisation and Smart Factories: The Danish SMEs Model" has set the tone for this current further research which builds on the findings and observations of the previous. Thus, this current study endeavours to present a much more detailed and straightforward conceptual framework as an industrial transformation pathway for SMEs. The subsequent sections of this essay will delve into a comprehensive analysis of the features outlined in the conceptual framework put out in this study.

A viable roadmap for industrial transformation towards a "Smart Factory" or "Smart Production" might be outlined as follows: The proposed initiative entails the design and approach for creating awareness using case study surveys. The objective is to identify the determining elements that contribute to the success of the initiative. Additionally, an implementation plan will be developed to guide the process of smart factory and supply chain management digitalization. Lastly, an evaluation will be conducted to assess the effectiveness and efficiency of the digitalization efforts.

2 Implementation Strategy and Design Approach

Having a strategy is an important aspect of any successful business. However, the journey towards digitalisation and Industry 4.0 is an uncertain path for most companies, especially SMEs. Defining the right strategy and ensuring the continuity of business is a challenging task, which is only increasing in complexity, as digitalisation is becoming a permanent bullet point on the strategic agenda. Managers and decision makers have to consider external as well as internal factors when defining their business strategy and creating an implementation plan. Failure to do so might have severe consequences for the company, leading to loss of business and in the worst-case, bankruptcy.

When implementing a strategy, managers and decision-makers have to go through a lot of considerations regarding internal as well as external factors. External factors: on one hand, digitalization efforts and the cost of investments in new digital capabilities are continuously decreasing, which is enabling SMEs to follow the trend and upgrade their facilities and products. On the other hand, competition is getting steeper, market trends are shifting at a higher rate, and customers are becoming more unpredictable, demanding better quality, faster delivery, and cheaper prices. Internal factors: identifying and setting the right objectives and estimating technical feasibility, as well as executing the strategies within the organisation based on the needs of the organization [2].

Hence, the organizational strategy is an essential part of the industrial transformation roadmap for digitalisation and smart factories that SMEs should not neglect ([1]; [2]; [4]). However, defining strategic objectives related to digitalization might be very challenging in itself and more so if a company wishes to quantify and monitor the objectives. It would be more beneficial to focus the company strategy on customer needs, market trends and company vision and use digital technologies as a means to achieve this. Additionally, it is equally important to prepare the organization to deal with the appertaining changes that will emerge as companies focus on digital technologies and ensure organizational buy-in.

Therefore, based on the above note it would be imperative that the awareness of digitalizing industrial SC processes is first sorted with the top management, executives and/or CEOs of organizations. This is a strategic top-down approach that would ideally work with very significant industrial transformation within the organizational operations setup. This approach could not also be realized without the entire work personnel on board the organizational "digital change management (DCM)" shift/movement. Furthermore, effective and deliberate relevant stakeholders' engagement of both customers and suppliers are expected in a co-design initiative.

2.1 Modes of Awareness Creation: Case Studies and Surveys

A good awareness creation procedure mostly begins with all of the relevant stakeholders coming together for a common goal, agenda or vision. The main purpose of awareness creation at the beginning of a digital transformation agenda is to quickly mobilise relevant and significantly transforming ideas about the digital transformation agenda by usually beginning with the top management team and then the operational staff. Therefore, awareness creation in this sense could be defined as a broadly organised effort to change routine operational practices or activities, policies or behaviours ([5]). Hence, a well-planned and orchestrated awareness creation is arguably one that would most effectively and efficiently seek to communicate to stakeholders detailed and pragmatic information. Therefore, this approach is about a particular mode of awareness creation to a large variety of groups or people with different backgrounds, skill sets, responsibilities and levels of education or assimilation rates such as that in manufacturing SMEs. On this note, this study would adapt Robinson's solution to identifying the seven steps to social change or transformation ([6]; [7]) which include:

- **Knowledge** - knowing there is a problem, thus, transforming legacy operational processes in a more digitalized transformed approach
- **Desire** - imagining a different future or transformational change agenda
- **Skills** - knowing what to do to achieve that expected future or transformational change
- **Optimism** - confidence or belief in success
- **Facilitation** - resources and support infrastructure (top management support and staff cooperation)

- **Stimulation** - a compelling stimulus that promotes action (requisite skill-set training & enhancement)
- **Reinforcement** - regular communications that reinforce the original message or messages – constant iteration of the digital change management processes until expected efficiency, effectiveness and productivity to boost return on investment (ROI) is achieved.

Fig. 1. The seven steps to social change or transformation Source: ([6]; [7]).

Figure 1, presented above, provides a sequential depiction of Robinson's seven steps towards societal change or transformation. Therefore, considering the aforementioned processes towards social and industrial change or transformation, this study aims to utilise a qualitative methodology by utilising surveys and interviews to gather and analyse data pertaining to the phase of raising awareness in this research.

3 Digital Transformation

The prevailing perspective on digital transformation is the gradual substitution of the automation pyramid with an interconnected system of nodes. These services are comprised of automated or semi-automated systems that communicate with one another through digital means ([8]).

3.1 The Digital Supply Chain Management Concept

According to [9], the digital supply chain can be characterised as an organisational structure consisting of interconnected systems. Its purpose is to facilitate and coordinate interactions among global partners ([10]), ensuring the synchronisation of various processes ([11]). The capabilities discussed in this context are derived from data created by machines, the interconnectedness among various participants in the supply chain, the implementation of choices on a broad scale, the automation of business processes, and the integration of information exchange across the whole supply chain ([12]). According to [13], transparency is identified as a crucial element within the digital supply chain. In the field of information management, the term under consideration is regarded as a synonymous concept to information transparency, as discussed by [14]. It pertains to the ability to make information visible within a given system. From a commercial perspective, this can be interpreted as the provision of information to facilitate decision-making processes ([15]; [16]; [17]; [14]). The competitive prospects associated with digital transformation [1] and, consequently, the shift towards a digital supply chain are contingent upon the attainment and utilisation of transparency throughout the supply chain.

3.2 Key Transformation Factors

While the genesis of this shift can be traced back to a technology-driven agenda, scholars and professionals alike have recognised certain key variables that revolve around it and must also be considered to facilitate this transition process. The concept under consideration has been characterised as a series of successive stages of increasing complexity [18], as outlined in various maturity models put out by researchers ([19]; [20]; [21]; [22]). The examination of the progression through these phases of maturity has underscored the necessity of addressing many deciding factors to effectively implement this transformation. The authors [23] have conducted an analysis and synthesis of these aspects in their publication titled "360 Digital Maturity Assessment," categorising them into five dimensions. The following items are [7]:

- **Governance:** clear company strategy, awareness concerning new technologies, both top-down and bottom-up innovation possibilities, lean management for innovation projects
- **Technology:** physical and digital assets that enable the generation, transmission, storage and analysis of digital data (e.g. CNC machines, getaways, cloud computing platforms) as well as physical and digital assets that base their functionalities on data (e.g. collaborative robots or autonomous guided vehicles)
- **Connectivity:** infrastructure needed for transmission inside the organization as well as across the supply chain value creation network: the ability to identify and capture value from new technologies and available data (e.g. business model shift towards the servitization paradigm, machine self-reconfiguration due to enabled communication between the product and the machine, predictive maintenance enabled by machine learning application on collected data from assets)
- **Competences:** cultural mindset and skills for the digital transformation (e.g. training and learning culture) as well as for capturing value out of digital technologies (e.g. competencies related to the use of digital technologies)

Despite the identification of these dimensions, further research is needed to examine the impact of these aspects on the digital transformation process and to determine the appropriate management practices required to handle them.

4 Process of Implementation

4.1 Implementation Benefits and Systematic Iterative Process

The primary objective of the implementation plan in this study is to facilitate the conversion of a company's strategic vision into concrete objectives at a tactical level, as well as delineate the precise operational measures to be undertaken. The digitalization strategy for small and medium-sized enterprises (SMEs) may not be as comprehensive as that of a large enterprise. Nevertheless, SMEs should still consider the potential benefits of implementing a digitalization plan. The efficacy of a rigid implementation strategy for small and medium-sized enterprises (SMEs) may be compromised due to the limited adoption of emerging digital technologies and the absence of actual evidence concerning potential challenges and prevalent errors. The implementation strategy for a small and medium-sized enterprise (SME) should prioritise flexibility and emphasise the alignment between decision-makers and production floor workers. This is because the workers are expected to have significant involvement in the design and implementation of any new solutions. Hence, an implementation plan for a small and medium-sized enterprise (SME) must be concise and focused on addressing key inquiries about the objectives, rationale, and methodology of the proposed actions. Responding to these inquiries will guarantee congruence between an organization's strategic vision and executed resolutions.

Further to the above, these concerns possess various significance for the next adventure. It is evident that Industry 4.0 represents a unique organisational or industrial trajectory that lacks a definitive endpoint and does not offer universally applicable solutions. Furthermore, it is evident that the proposed solutions must be firmly based on particular organisational or industrial circumstances and limitations that could equally be mitigated with the right technology enablers. Thirdly, it is evident that the process of testing, learning, evaluating and optimising plays a pivotal role in determining the optimal trajectory for each respective organization's progression.

The systematic iterative process model, often known as the iterative development model, is a structured approach to software development that involves repeating a series of steps in a systematic manner. Given the numerous uncertainties associated with engaging with novel technologies and the limited understanding of potential obstacles that may arise during the process, it is advisable to adopt a methodical iterative approach that prioritises ongoing learning and enhancements. At a macro level, we propose an implementation plan comprising four phases, as depicted in Fig. 2. The four processes encompassed in this framework are as follows: understanding, defining, prototyping and testing, implementing, and standardising. The model presented in this study is derived from the integration of the Design Thinking approach proposed by [24], which encompasses the Empathise, Define, Ideate, Prototype, and Test phases, and lean principles, which emphasise the significance of standardisation in new implementations [25]. The proposed model for the implementation plan offers a methodical and comprehensive approach to the adoption of novel and untested digital solutions.

At a granular level, specifically about operational and project management, it is recommended to adopt a straightforward Plan, Do, Check, Act (PDCA) strategy for the various tasks within each of the four stages outlined in the implementation plan. This method, as suggested by [26], facilitates an iterative process. The Plan phase is

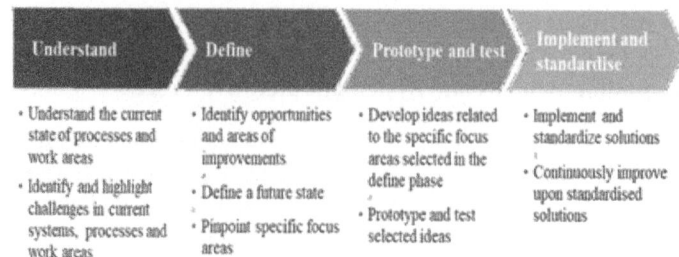

Fig. 2. Four-Phase Plan for Implementing New Digital Solutions, Inspired by Design- [24] and Lean Thinking [25].

centred on the establishment of the what, why, and how aspects, specifically in relation to the approach or design project. The implementation phase, often known as the Do phase, emphasizes executing and carrying out the planned actions. The Check phase is dedicated to the evaluation and verification of the actions that were carried out during the preceding Do phase. The Act phase is implemented to guarantee that appropriate measures are undertaken to adapt and enhance, or to establish a standard for the solution to simplify complexity and optimise responsiveness within the incremental digitalization transformational phase - Smart Factory / SCM Digitising Evaluation.

4.2 Human Ergonometric Factors

According to [27], the adoption of Industry 4.0 is projected to necessitate the implementation of design and engineering principles that prioritise the enhancement and augmentation of human employees' physical and cognitive abilities, as opposed to relying solely on unmanned automated factories. Therefore, this assertion underscores the need of taking into account human factors and ergonomics, as well as prioritising the welfare of workers. Although firms vary in their operations and practise, it is recommended that they consider incorporating or drawing inspiration from established standards such as human-computer-interaction (HCI) standards ([28]; [29]), which focus on Human Centred Design (HCD). When firms embark on the implementation of new digital technologies, it is advisable to take into account the following advice, particularly in situations where the adoption of these technologies has an impact on the duties and responsibilities of workers.

[30], propose several recommendations pertaining to the utilisation of collaborative robots. It might be contended that these concepts might also apply to other emerging digital technologies. In the context of adopting novel digital technologies, small and medium-sized enterprises (SMEs) should endeavour the creation of Standard Operating Procedures (SOPs) that delineate the allocation of tasks and responsibilities between human workers and digital technologies. Furthermore, it may be advantageous to formalise a concise job description for each worker, in addition to implementing Standard Operating Procedures (SOPs). The use of such standardisation measures will guarantee a high level of consistency and create a foundation for ongoing enhancements.

4.3 Transformational Roadmap: The Conceptual Framework for the Danish SMEs

The Industrial Transformational Roadmap refers to a strategic plan that outlines the steps and actions necessary for the transformation of an industrial sector. This roadmap serves as a guide for organisations. The local region of Aalborg in Denmark is where the designated Aalborg University (AAU) is located. Aalborg University Smart Manufacturing Lab was tasked to organise and created an ecosystem centred for the local Denish Manufacturing SMEs around the AAU Smart Lab. This ecosystem aims to provide support to local small and medium-sized enterprises (SMEs) by offering them information and activities that will help them recognise and capitalise on the opportunities presented by Industry 4.0 (I4.0) within their specific circumstances. Consequently, the establishment of the Innovation Factory North (IFN) project aimed to cultivate a regional network of small and medium-sized enterprises (SMEs), technology suppliers, and research and development (R&D) institutions to foster competencies in the realm of Industry 4.0 (I4.0) ([31]).

According to [31], the Innovation Factory North (IFN) served as a collaborative platform aimed at stimulating and expediting industry 4.0-driven innovations within the context of small and medium-sized manufacturing firms. The significant and widely acknowledged potential for small and medium-sized enterprises (SMEs) to enhance their intelligence is a subject of great interest. The IFN strategy, which has been formulated as part of an ongoing regional research and innovation initiative, is the result of a collaborative effort involving industry, academia, and the government. The aforementioned method facilitated the collaboration of proficient industries within the IFN ecosystem, intending to enhance awareness and foster innovation pertaining to Industry 4.0. Therefore, the process of achieving Industry 4.0 through digital transformation involved the strategic utilisation of information technology as a facilitator and objective within business transformation [31]. Hence, the majority of frameworks pertaining to industrial transformation predominantly use a hierarchical approach, guided by a robust management perspective and reinforced by substantial investments and initiatives aimed at facilitating progress, as depicted in Fig. 3. Despite the limited digital maturity of Danish manufacturing SMEs and their incongruity with the local industry.

structure, the conceptual framework depicted in Fig. 3 offers a viable roadmap for digital transformation in these SMEs.

Figure 3 depicted above presents the iteration sequence or model utilised in this study to develop the conceptual framework aimed at the Danish SMEs model. The framework focuses on the digitalization of industrial SMEs' transformation roadmap agenda.

5 SMEs Smart Factory Implementation and Evaluation

In order to realise the objective of shifting the value chain position closer to its end customers, a manufacturing firm with a product-centric approach must undergo a transformation. Hence, there is a shift towards adopting a product-service offering model as opposed to solely focusing on the provision of tangible things. It is contended by scholars that in the course of this transformation, organisations are inclined to modify

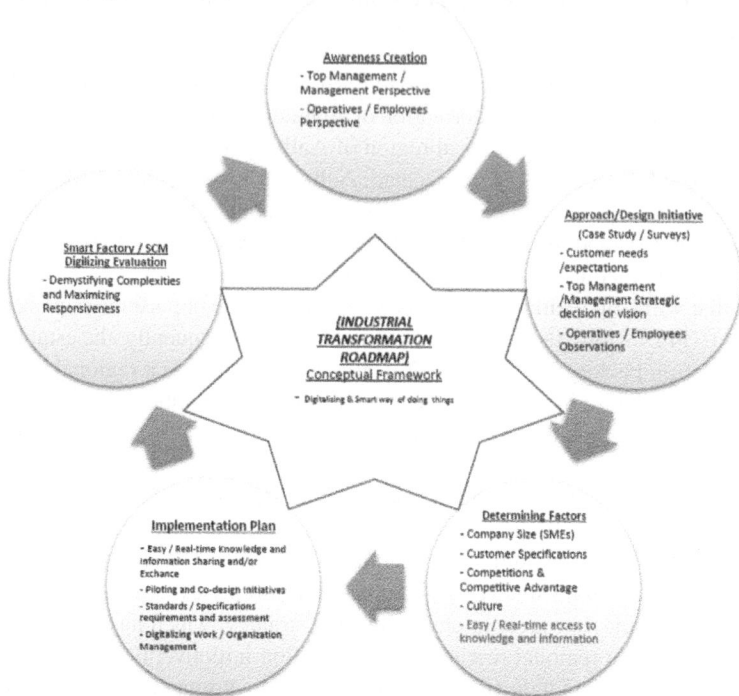

Fig. 3. Industrial Transformation Roadmap – A Conceptual Framework for Smart Factories [7].

their strategy, operations, value chains, technologies, human expertise, and system integration capabilities. The inquiry pertains to the distinctions between the current period of transformation and the preceding industrial revolutions. What are the key insights gained from the preceding industrial revolutions?

Undoubtedly, the corporate landscape of Industry 4.0 exhibits a significantly greater level of intricacy than any preceding era in history. A "product" is not exclusively manufactured for a singular functional purpose. The product, conversely, serves as a "bridge" to a business ecosystem. The following paper overview presents examples of Danish small and medium-sized enterprises (SMEs) in the smart factory domain that have endeavoured to incorporate smart production processes or elements thereof through the adoption of a digital transformation roadmap [31]. The collaboration between Maersk and IBM in the form of the Tradelens joint venture serves as an illustrative instance of a corporate entity implementing an Intelligent Supply Chain [32]. Maersk possesses comprehensive access to the entirety of the container logistics ecosystem through the utilisation of the Tradelens platform, which enables the company to potentially derive advantages from a well-maintained equilibrium between demand and supply. In a separate instance, a small and medium-sized enterprise (SME) underwent a transformation in its supply chain operations, transitioning from an Engineer-to-order approach to an Assembly-to-order approach. This shift was facilitated through the incorporation of digital technology into the company's supply chain framework [33].

The term "virtual manufacturing" is used to describe the integration of engineering tasks throughout the entire lifecycle. The possibility of concurrent engineering, verification, and validation of new items or modifications in products or manufacturing processes arises from the digital integration of engineering operations [34]. Vestas serve as an illustrative instance of the potentialities inherent in end-to-end digital manufacturing, as demonstrated by [35]. Vestas has the capability to provide virtual reality (VR) training to its staff prior to the completion of the actual factory, hence enhancing the speed at which products can be brought to market. The concept of Industry 4.0 is predicated on the cooperative integration of intelligent production facilities throughout the entirety of the manufacturing ecosystem [36]. In the context of Industry 4.0 and Smart Production, the presence of an empowered and adaptable organisation is of utmost importance. The optimisation of decision-making within an organisation can be facilitated by the strategic implementation and integration of individuals across all hierarchical levels, ranging from the operational staff to the executive leadership. This underscores the need of providing accurate and relevant information in a timely way to facilitate informed decision-making that can be effectively implemented. Arla serves as a prime example of how successful collaboration may enhance the capabilities of an organisation by distributing access to analytical data, hence facilitating localised data exploration and decision-making [37].

Therefore, the evaluation approach most likely encompasses perspectives from both practitioners [38] and researchers [39]. Evaluation and Innovation Factory North (EIFN): A Methodology for Enhancing Small-scale Enterprise's Reflection and evaluation are essential components in both viewpoints, and the outcome should result in the readjustment of the scope and strategy. From a research standpoint, this is the stage where the sense-making of the entire process is developed, resulting in an enhanced comprehension of both the method and the project or business case perspective.

6 Digital Transformation Approaches

The process of digital transformation can be broken down into several stages or methodologies. Industry 4.0 represents the most notable embodiment of the envisioned future of manufacturing. Based on the aforementioned concepts, researchers have developed a methodology to facilitate the transition to Industry 4.0, which has been termed as the Smart Factory approach [31]. The concept of Industry 4.0 was initially presented in 2011 at the Hannover Industry Fair in Germany by the Industry 4.0 Working Group, as documented by [18]. The working group comprised a consortium of prominent industry experts with the objective of altering public perception towards manufacturing and industry in Germany, while also providing recommendations for both national and industrial initiatives ([31]; [7]; [40]). Following its ten-year milestone, it is evident that Industry 4.0 transcends mere transitory trends. Despite the existence of other comparable concepts and efforts such as Supply Chain Management 4.0, Factories of the Future, Smart Industries, Smart Manufacturing, Manufacturing Execution Systems and others, Industry 4.0 has emerged as a prevailing and all-encompassing concept. According to [41], currently, it is utilised and extensively comprehended in various domains, including society, industry, and academia.

The process of adopting Industry 4.0 and the digital transformation approach in the manufacturing sector can present challenges for small and medium-sized enterprises

(SMEs). Small and medium-sized enterprises (SMEs) frequently encounter difficulties related to limited resources, including a dearth of financial tools and inadequate digital competencies. Moreover, the immediate efficacy of the change may provide challenges in terms of identification, while the specific actions required to facilitate the process remain uncertain. In order to showcase the capabilities of smart production, AAU has developed a laboratory dedicated to smart production, known as the Smart Lab [42]. The Smart Lab is a comprehensive manufacturing system that has been constructed using the FESTO CP Factory platform. The Smart Lab has been utilised as an educational facility [43] and can serve as a platform for constructing prototypes of diverse novel manufacturing applications and solutions within an authentic production environment [44]. Nevertheless, the ultimate goal is for this information to serve as a catalyst for advancements in the industrial sector.

The agile project management strategy would be one of the potential means to respond to and also be able to analyse those five deciding factors in Fig. 3 above ([7]; [23]) in the section that was described earlier. According to [45], it is commonly acknowledged that a suitable model for constructing project capabilities should contain two ways of complementary approaches. They had the impression that businesses that were equipped with two different levels of project management that interacted with one another were very successful in accomplishing competitive goals. On the one hand, a strategy known as "project-led learning" is working across the many layers of the organisation to facilitate learning from the ground up. The process begins with an experimental phase, during which the individual is unfamiliar with the technology, followed by a phase in which lessons are learned, during which experience is captured, and finally, a phase in which the individual is equipped, during which they have the ability to use the new technology.

On the other hand, a top-down approach that is taken place and called 'business-led' learning is taken place to support and lead the upcoming project activities with sufficient resources and the right competencies; Fig. 4 below gives a generic and simple illustration of these contextual perspectives of what this study also terms as digital change management (DCM). According to [23], the concept of operating a full project management circle generates checking points to echo the five variables that have been identified as contributing to the maturity of digitalization.

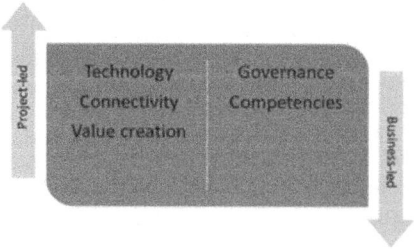

Fig. 4. Contextual evaluation framework towards digitalization [23].

Further to the move for digitalization of industrial production processes in smart production with Industry 4.0, it is approached in an industry-specific implementation process for SMEs; this has led the agenda of the European Council (EC) to come up with a new policy position on Industry 5.0 [46]. "It complements the existing Industry 4.0 approach by specifically putting research and innovation at the service of the transition to a sustainable, human-centric and resilient European industry" [47]. This is why the European Commission has positioned Industry 5.0 as its transformative vision for Europe in relation to Industry 4.0.

7 Practical and Academic Implications

Digital transformation in industries presents a range of complex and multifaceted trends that provide significant challenges for top-level management. Small and medium-sized enterprises (SMEs) are presently facing significant difficulties in fundamentally and swiftly restructuring and modifying their business operations. This situation is placing strain on their existing operations as they strive to maintain their competitive edge ([1]; [2]; [4]; [3]). Hence, the primary industrial implication identified in this study involves the establishment of a well-defined and achievable roadmap for what is referred to as the industrial transformation process. This process termed the "digital change management (DCM) process - Industry 4.0/Smart factory," is examined from the perspective of industrial small and medium-sized enterprises (SMEs) using the Danish Model, as depicted in Fig. 3.

Industrial digital transformation technologies can be characterised as a process of managing digital change, encompassing data/big data, information, computation, communication, and connection or networked technologies. The technologies encompassed in this study are cloud computing, big data value-chain management, big data analytics, and mobile and networking technologies [48]. Hence, digital transformation technologies offer small and medium-sized enterprises (SMEs) the opportunity to operate in open and adaptable environments, enabling them to overcome certain conventional operational limitations. The presence of organisational constraints, combined with previously separate networks that have been successfully and efficiently transformed through digitalization, creates a conducive atmosphere for innovations that result in the development of new customer experiences, relationships, and overall digital transformation within the organisation ([49]; [50]).

The present study trends in industrial digital transformation and innovation have shed light on the fundamental impact of the introduction of industrial digital transformation technologies, which are leading to a significant shift in industrial production processes. The utilisation of this technology has facilitated organisations in attaining significant levels of operational efficiency and effectiveness through the facilitation of novel business models or frameworks [51]. Moreover, it is widely acknowledged in the literature that innovation processes exhibit a certain degree of unpredictability. Previous scholarly investigations have elucidated the phenomenon wherein inferior technologies attain market dominance due to their higher adoption rates. Additionally, the persistent concern around cyber security issues further compounds the challenges associated with technological advancements. Hence, it is plausible to assume that less expensive and lower-quality technologies have the potential to disrupt the technologies of established suppliers [46].

According to [52], one potential solution for addressing cybersecurity concerns in smart manufacturing is the adoption of blockchain technology. The aforementioned computing paradigm is a novel and transformative concept that is now reshaping the digital landscape, offering a fresh tool to enhance the security and efficiency of systems [53]. Blockchain technology serves as a fundamental framework for distributed ledgers, providing a transparent and decentralised means of storing data and information. It functions as a system for executing authenticated computational transactions in several sectors, including commerce and industry [54]. According to [55], the utilisation of blockchain technology as a cybersecurity solution has the potential to augment confidence by means of promoting transparency and traceability in production and industrial transactions [57].

8 Research Originality and Contribution

This study aims to present a proposed roadmap for industrial digital transformation, with a focus on small and medium-sized enterprises (SMEs). The objective of this roadmap is to offer SMEs a distinct advantage by facilitating opportunities for value creation through the expansion of profit pools and the generation of return-on-investment (ROI). Additionally, the roadmap aims to enable SMEs to develop new revenue models, such as "servitization," within their operations management. As a result, this provides enterprises with a very advantageous and equitable opportunity to leverage digital projects in global marketplaces. Therefore, providing small and medium enterprises (SMEs) with the necessary capabilities to enhance their business operations more sustainably. Hence, this study aims to present a theoretical framework for the implementation of a smart factory roadmap within the context of Industry 4.0. The objective is to enable manufacturing small and medium-sized enterprises (SMEs) in Denmark to enhance the effectiveness and efficiency of their product transformation and/or servitization operations through the utilisation of digital transformation technologies [57].

9 Trends, Future Research and Benefits of Smart Factories Approach in Industrial SMEs Employing Industry 4.0

As earlier mentioned in the introduction section of this research, this study is a further and much more detailed study to our earlier research; [57], Addo-Tenkorang et al., (2023) published in ICSBT 2023. Therefore, this research approach was piloted with about 60 Danish SMEs engaged through industrial research collaborative projects over some time [31]. According to SBA Fact Sheet [58], SMEs play a vital role in Denmark, accounting for 60.8% of total value added and 64.1% of jobs. Between 2014 and 2018, SMEs and large enterprises increased their overall value added at a similar rate of roughly 18%. During this era, SME growth rates ranged from 3.6% for microenterprises to 14.4% for small corporations and 37.3% for medium-sized organisations [58]. Furthermore, in 2017–2018, SMEs increased their value contributed by 4.0% and employment by 2.0% [58]. SME value added is expected to expand by 10.6% between 2018 and 2020, with medium-sized firms leading the way with a 17.5% increase, their employment is predicted to increase by 5.1% from 2018 to 2020 [58].

The notion behind the Danish SME smart factory approach is that digitalization will enable a wide range of novel solutions to industrial difficulties and that these opportunities are waiting to be realised. Therefore, it is not possible to talk about Danish SMEs' smart factory Industry 4.0 without the technological layout ([59]; [60]). The introduction of Industry 4.0 is spurred by an exponential increase in computer power, which serves as the foundation for a wide range of new digital technologies such as Big Data, the Internet of Things, digital twins, cloud computing, artificial intelligence, sophisticated robotics, and so on [46]. The enabling power of data ubiquity and networking capabilities opens up an expanding number of new opportunities for the development of new products, processes, and services. On this note, a preliminary conclusion could be that there is no single technology that can be identified as Industry 4.0. Industry 4.0 technologies are the integration of various technologies into industrial applications and can thus be classified as networked technologies. Hence, interoperability could be a significant success element for both end users and vendors ([57]; [46]). Thus, this study in Fig. 5 below; recommends that future research looks into incorporating the stakeholder theory perspective in complimenting and enhancing Industry 4.0 in SMEs for effective, efficient and sustainable competitive advantage in SMEs' smart manufacturing activities. Additionally, as businesses migrate from technology to solutions, they must address adoption and use, which needs new knowledge, capabilities, and abilities. As a result, to realise the potential, the organisation must be activated, which will necessitate major managerial effort in staging the transition.

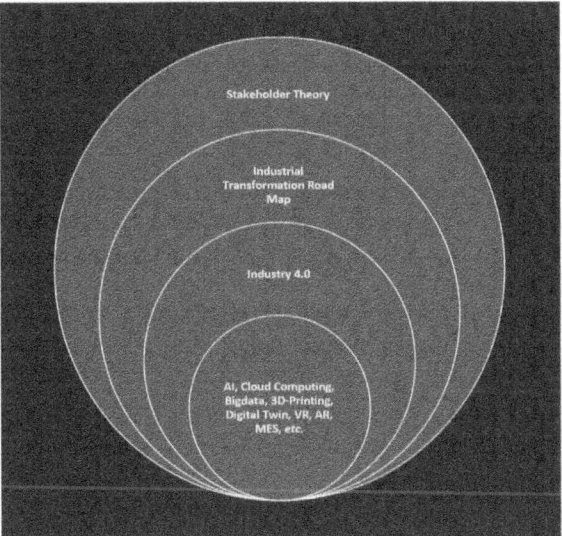

Fig. 5. Conceptual Framework for Future Research Trends in SMEs' Smart Factories.

10 Conclusion and Recommendation

The significance of recognising the collaborative power and worth of digital transformation technologies cannot be overstated. According to Parmar, et. al. 2010 [61] "stakeholder theory" or "stakeholder thinking" has emerged as a new narrative to understand and remedy three interconnected business problems—the problem of understanding how value is created and traded, the problem of connecting ethics and capitalism, and the problem of helping managers think about management such that the first two problems are addressed *(please,* Fig. 5 *above)*. Therefore, as digitalization plays a pivotal role as a prospective technical remedy for numerous difficulties faced by small and medium-sized enterprises (SMEs) in the present era, per the value-creating perspective of stakeholder theory or stakeholder thinking approach. This combination among others would propel the benefits and competitiveness of smart factories in SMEs with capabilities of digital technology enablers. Hence, it is imperative for small and medium-sized enterprises (SMEs) to be well-equipped and well-prepared to navigate increasingly innovative yet potentially extreme business upheavals [56]. This is intended to facilitate seamless integration and interaction with their pre-existing legacy systems together with active stakeholder engagement activities, as observed in a previous study on the effects of IT transformations ([4]; [57]).

Hence, future research endeavours will focus on conducting a comprehensive investigation of each individual block depicted in Fig. 3, which represents the conceptual pathway for industrial transformation. This paper will concentrate on the key problems and critical success factors related to the industrial digital transformation agenda among small and medium-sized enterprises (SMEs) in Denmark, specifically focusing on the Danish model. This research endeavour aims to contribute to the existing body of knowledge by conducting a comprehensive investigation into the phenomenon of digitalization and digital transformation within the context of industrial small and medium-sized enterprises (SMEs). The implementation of digitalization or digital transformation in the operational processes of small and medium-sized enterprises (SMEs) in Denmark has shown significant progress compared to previous studies on the emergence of Industry 4.0 activities and operations among large original equipment manufacturers (OEMs) in Germany ([56]; [46]; [31]; [57]).

Therefore, this study posits that the proposed conceptual framework (see Fig. 3) has the potential for generalisation and subsequent implementation in other analogous collaborations between academia and industry in research and development or pilot projects. The primary objective of such collaborations is to facilitate the advancement of Industry 4.0 – Smart Factories within small and medium-sized enterprises (SMEs).

Acknowledgements. Manufacturing Academy of Denmark (MADE) SPIR & Digital.

References

1. Mckinsey Digital, Industry 4.0: how to navigate digitization of the manufacturing sector. McKinsey and Company (2015)

2. Schuh, G., Anderl, R., Gauseimer, J., Ten Hompel, M., Wahlster, W.: Industrie 4.0 Maturity Index. Managing the Digital Transformation of Companies (acatech STUDY), Herbert Utz Verlag, Munich (2017)
3. Henfridsson, O., Mathiassen, L., Svahn, F.: Managing technological change in the digital age: the role of architectural frames. J. Inf. Technol. **29**(1), 27–43 (2014)
4. Piccinini, E., Hanelt, A., Gregory, R., Kolbe, L.M.: Transforming Industrial Business: the impact of digital transformation on automotive organizations. In: Thirty Sixth International Conference on Information Systems, Fort Worth, Texas (2015)
5. Sayers, R.: Principles of awareness-raising: Information literacy, a case study, Bangkok: Communication and information (CI), UNESCO Asia and Pacific Regional Bureau for Education, p. 124 (2006)
6. Giorgadze, K.: The Communication Initiative Network. 4 Nov (2003). [Online]. Available: http://www.comminit.com/content/social-marketing-7-step- approach
7. Addo-Tenkorang, R., Møller, C., Chen, K.: Industrial transformation roadmap for digitalisation and smart factories: the Danish SMEs model. In: Proceedings of the 20th International Conference on Smart Business Technologies - ICSBT; ISBN 978–989–758–667–5; ISSN 2184–772X, SciTePress, pp. 144–153 (2023). https://doi.org/10.5220/0012094300003552
8. Jeschke, S., Eds.: Industrial Internet of Things, Cybermanufacturing Systems, Springer, Cham (2017). https://doi.org/10.1007/978-3-319-42559-7
9. Porter, M.E., Heppelmann, J.E.: How smart, connected products are transforming competition. Harv. Bus. Rev. **92**(11), 64–88 (2014)
10. Bhargava, B., Ranchal, R., Othmane, L.B.: Secure information sharing in digital supply Chains. In: 2013 3rd IEEE International Advance Computing Conf. (IACC), Ghaziabad (2013)
11. Schmidt, R., Möhring, M., Härting, R.C., Reichstein, C., Neumaier, P., Jozinović, P.: Industry 4.0 -potentials for creating smart products: empirical research results. In: 18th International Conference on Business Information Systems (LNBIP), Poznań (2015)
12. Wu, L., Yue, X., Jin, A., Yen, D.C.: Smart supply chain management: a review and implications for future research. Int. J. Logistics Manage. **27**(2), 395–417 (2016)
13. Schrauf, S., Berttra, P.: Industry 4.0: How digitization makes the supply chain more efficient, agile, and customer-focused," PWC, 7 Sep. (2016). [Online]. Available: https://www.strategyand.pwc.com/reports/digitization-more-efficient
14. Turilli, M., Floridi, L.: The ethics of information transparency. Ethics Inf. Technol. **11**(2), 105–112 (2009)
15. Winkler, B.: Which Kind of Transparency? On the Need for Clarity in Monetary Policy-Making," European Central Bank (ECB) Working Paper, vol. 26 (2000)
16. Vaccaro, A., Madsen, P.: Firm Information Transparency: Ethical Questions in the Information Age. In: HCC7: IFIP International Conference on Human Choice and Computers, Social Informatics: An Information Society for All? In Remembrance of Rob Kling, Maribor (2006)
17. DiPiazza, J.S.A., Eccles, R.G., Granof, M.H., Granof, M.H.: Building public trust, the future of corporate reporting. Int. J. Acc. **38**(3), 391–394 (2003)
18. Kagermann, H., Wahlster, W., Helbig, J.: Recommendations for implementing the strategic initiative INDUSTRIE 4.0," Acatech – National Academy of Science and Engineering, Frankfurt (2013)
19. Lanza, G., Nyhuis, P., Majid Ansari, S., Kuprat, T., Liebrecht, C.: Befähigungs- und einführungsstrategien für Industrie 4.0. In: ZWF Zeitschrift fuer Wirtschaftlichen Fabrikbetrieb, vol. 111, pp. 76–79 (2016)
20. Leyh, C., Bley, K., Schäffer, T., Forstenhausler, S.: SIMMI 4.0 - a maturity model for classifying the enterprise-wide it and software landscape focusing on Industry 4.0. In: 2016 Federated Conf. on Computer Science and Information Systems (FedCSIS), pp. 11–14, 11–14 (2016)

21. Lichtblau, K., et al.: Industrie 4.0 Readiness, VDMA's IMPULS-Stiftung, Aachen (2015)
22. Schumacher, A., Erol, S., Sihn, W.: A maturity model for assessing industry 4.0 readiness and maturity of manufacturing enterprises. In: Procedia CIRP, vol. 52, pp. 161–166 (2016)
23. Colli, M., Madsen, O., Berger, U., Møller, C., Vejrum Wæhrens, B., Bockholt, M.: Contextualizing the outcome of a maturity assessment for Industry 4.0. In: IFAC- PapersOnLine, vol. 51, no. 11, pp. 1347–1352, 11–13 (2018)
24. Doorley, S., Holcomb, S., Klebahn, P., Segovia, K., Utley, J.: Design thinking bootleg, Accessed 12 Sep 2018
25. Womack, J.P., Jones, D.T.: Lean thinking: banish waste and create wealth in your corporation, New York: New York. Simon & Schuster, N.Y. (2003)
26. Andersen, B.: Business Process Improvement Toolbox, Second Edition, ASQ Quality Press, pp. 312 (2007)
27. Díaz, D.R., et al.: Towards an operator 4.0 typology: a human-centric perspective on the fourth industrial revolution technologies. In: 46th International Conference on Computers & Industrial Engineering, pp. 29–31 (2016)
28. BSI Group, Ergonomics principles in the design of work systems. In: ISO/TS 6385:2016, BSI Standard Publication (2010)
29. BSI Group, 2016. "Ergonomics principles in the design of work systems," in ISO/TS 6385:2016, BSI Standard Publication
30. Kadir, B.A., Broberg, O., Conceicao, C.: Designing human-robot collaborations in Industry 4.0: Explorative case studies. In: International Design Conference (2018)
31. Møller, C., et al.: Innovation Factory North: An Approach to Make Small and Medium Sized Manufacturing Companies Smarter. In: The Future of Smart Production for SMEs: A Methodological and Practical Approach Towards Digitalization in SMEs, pp. 113–126. Springer International Publishing, Cham (2022)
32. Moller, A., Maersk, P.: TradeLens blockchain-enabled digital shipping platform continues expansion with the addition of major ocean carriers Hapag-Lloyd and ocean network express. Accessed 22 Dec 2021, from https://www.maersk.com/news/articles/2019/07/02/hapag- lloyd-and-ocean-network-express-join-trade lens
33. Bejlegaard, M., Sarivan, I., Waehrens, B.V.: The influence of digital technologies on supply chain coordination strategies. J. Glob. Oper. Strateg. Sourcing **14**(4), 636–658 (2021). https://doi.org/10.1108/JGOSS-11-2019-0063
34. Addo-Tenkorang, R.: Concurrent engineering (ce): a review literature report. In Proceedings of the World Congress on Engineering and Computer Science, Vol. 2, pp. 19–21 (2011)
35. Yildiz, E., Møller, C., Bilberg, A.: Demonstration and evaluation of a digital twin-based virtual factory. Int. J. Adv. Manufact. Technol. **114**, 185–203 (2021)
36. Schou, C., et al.: Deconstructing Industry 4.0: defining the smart factory. In Towards sustainable customiza-tion: Bridging smart products and manufacturing systems Springer International Publishing, pp. 356–363 (2021). https://doi.org/10.1007/978-3-030-90700-6_40
37. Asmussen, C.B., Jørgensen, S.L., Møller, C.: Design and deployment of an analytic artefact–investigating mechanisms for integrating analytics and manufacturing execution system. Enterp. Inf. Syst. 1–30 (2021).https://doi.org/10.1080/17517575.2021.1905881
38. Lidón, I., Rebollar, R., Møller, C.: A collaborative learning environment for management education based on experiential learning. Innovations Educ. Teach. Int. **48**(3), 301–312 (2011)
39. Møller, C., et al.: Researching small and medium-sized enterprises—an action design research approach to study digital transformation in SME. In O. Madsen, U. Berger, C. Møller, A.H. Lassen, B.V. Waehrens, C. Schou (Eds.), The future of smart production for SME—A methodological and practical approach towards digitalization in SMEs. Springer International Publishing (2022c). https://doi.org/10.1007/978-3-031-15428-7_5

40. Addo-Tenkorang, R., Helo, P., Sivula, A., Gwangwava, N.: The Complexity of Data-Driven in Engineer-To-Order Enterprise Supply-Chains. In: Batako, A., Burduk, A., Karyono, K., Chen, X., Wyczółkowski, R. (eds) Advances in Manufacturing Processes, Intelligent Methods and Systems in Production Engineering. GCMM 2021. Lecture Notes in Networks and Systems, vol 335. Springer, Cham (2022). https://doi.org/10.1007/978-3-030-90532-3_39
41. Culot, G., et al.: Behind the definition of Industry 4.0: Analysis and open questions. Int. J. Prod. Econ. **226**, 107617 (2020). https://doi.org/10.1016/j.ijpe.2020.107617
42. Madsen, O., Møller, C.: The AAU smart production laboratory for teaching and research in emerging digital manufacturing technologies. Procedia Manuf. **9**, 106–112 (2017) Available at: https://doi.org/10.1016/j.promfg.2017.04.03
43. Abele, E., et al.: Learning factories for research, education, and training. Procedia CIRP, **32**, 1–6 (2015) Available at: https://doi.org/10.1016/j.procir.2015.02.187
44. Nardello, M., Madsen, O., Møller, C.: The Smart Production Laboratory: a Learning Factory for Industry 4.0 Concepts. In: CEUR Workshop Proceedings, **1898**(5) (2017)
45. Brady, T., Davis, A.: Building project capabilities: from exploratory to exploitative learning. In: Organization Studies, vol. 25, no. 9, pp. 1601–1621 (2004)
46. Møller, C., Madsen, O., Berger, U., Schou, C., Lassen, A.H., Waehrens, B.V.: The Smart Production Vision. In: The Future of Smart Production for SMEs: A Methodological and Practical Approach Towards Digitalization in SMEs, pp. 13–28. Springer International Publishing, Cham (2022)
47. European Commission. Industry 5.0: What this approach is focused on, how it will be achieved and how it is already being implemented (2021) Accessed May 25 2023, from https://researchandinnovation.ec.europa.eu/research-area/industrial-research-and-innovation/industry-50_en
48. Bharadwaj, A., El Sawy, O.A., Pavlou, P.A., Venkatraman, N.: Digital business strategy: toward a next generation of insights. MIS Q. **37**(2), 471–482 (2013)
49. Lucas, H., Agarwal, R., Clemons, E., El Sawy, O., Weber, B.: Impactful research on transformational information technology: an opportunity to inform new audiences. MIS Q. **37**(2), 371–382 (2013)
50. Yoo, Y., Boland, R.J., Jr., Lyytinen, K., Majchrzak, A.: Organizing for innovation in the digitized world. Organ. Sci. **23**(5), 1398–1408 (2012)
51. Fichman, R.G., Dos Santos, B.L., Zheng, Z.E.: Digital innovation as a fundamental and powerful concept in the information systems curriculum. MIS Q. **38**(2), 329–353 (2014)
52. Leng, J., et al.: Blockchain-secured smart manufacturing in Industry 4.0: a survey. In: IEEE Transactions on Systems, Man, and Cybernetics: Systems, vol. 51, no. 1, pp. 237–252 (2021). https://doi.org/10.1109/TSMC.2020.3040789
53. Ahram, T., Sargolzaei, A., Sargolzaei, S., Daniels, J., Amaba, B.: Blockchain technology innovations. In: Proceedings IEEE Technology Engineering Management Conference Santa Clara, USA, pp. 1–6. [5] (2017)
54. Yuan, Y., Wang, F.: Blockchain and cryptocurrencies: model, techniques, and applications. IEEE Transactions on Systems, Man, and Cybernetics: Systems, vol. 48, no. 9, pp. 1421–1428 (2018)
55. Abeyratne, S.A., Monfared, R.P.: Blockchain ready manufacturing supply chain using a distributed ledger. Int. J. Res. Eng. Technol. **5**(9), 1–10 (2016)
56. Adolph, L., et al.: German Standardization Roadmap: Industry 4.0. Version 2," The DIN/DKE Steering Group Industry 4.0, Berlin, (2016)
57. Addo-Tenkorang, R., Møller, C., Chen, K.: Industrial transformation roadmap for Digitalisation and smart factories: the danish SMEs model. https://doi.org/10.5220/001209430000 3552. In: Proceedings of the 20th International Conference on Smart Business Technologies (ICSBT), pp.144–153, (2023). ISBN: 978-989-758-667-5; ISSN: 2184-772X
58. European Commission 2019 SBA Fact Sheet: Denmark. Accessed 25th Mar 2024 at https://ec.europa.eu/docsroom/documents/38662/ attachments/8/ translations/en/ renditions/native

59. Oztemel, E., Gursev, S.: Literature review of Industry 4.0 and related technologies. J. Intell. Manuf. **31**(1), 127–182 (2018). https://doi.org/10.1007/s10845-018-1433-8
60. Zheng, T., Ardolino, M., Bacchetti, A., Perona, M.: The applications of industry 4.0 technologies in manufacturing context: a systematic literature review. Int. J. Prod. Res., **59**(6), 1922–1954 (2021). https://doi.org/10.1080/00207543.2020.1824085
61. Parmar, B.L., Freeman, R.E., Harrison, J.S., Wicks, A.C., Purnell, L., De Colle, S.: Stakeholder theory: the state of the art. Acad. Manag. Ann. **4**(1), 403–445 (2010)

Roadmap Proposal for the Implementation of Business Intelligence Systems in Higher Education Institutions

Nuno Sequeira[1(✉)], Arsénio Reis[1,3], Frederico Branco[1,3], and Paulo Alves[2]

[1] School of Science and Technology, University of Trás-os-Montes and Alto Douro, Quinta Dos Prados, Vila Real, Portugal
{nunosequeira,ars,fbranco}@utad.pt

[2] Research Centre in Digitalization and Intelligent Robotics (CeDRI), Instituto Politécnico de Bragança, Bragança, Portugal
palves@ipb.pt

[3] INESC TEC - Institute for Systems and Computer Engineering, Technology and Science, Porto, Portugal

Abstract. Nowadays, Higher Education Institutions (HEIs) are faced with the crucial challenge of establishing and supervising strategies and policies that are essential for decisions in various areas and at various levels. Within this context, the importance of Business Intelligence (BI) has increased significantly, emerging as an essential tool for analysing and managing data. This BI capability enables HEIs to make more informed choices in line with their global strategies. This research focuses on developing a roadmap for the effective implementation of BI systems in HEIs. Using a Design Science Research (DSR) methodology, this work proposes a structured and adaptable roadmap that covers the key factors from the design to the implementation of BI systems in HEIs. This roadmap includes not only a reference architecture for BI systems but also a set of dashboards. The roadmap was validated through a case study at the University of Trás-os-Montes e Alto Douro (UTAD), involving exploratory analysis and feedback from experts. This study stands out for its practical and theoretical approach, offering a strategic and practical guide for the adoption of BI systems in HEIs, thus responding to a need identified in the academic literature.

Keywords: Decision-making · Business intelligence · Higher education · Institutions

1 Introduction

Following the exploratory work described in the research carried out by the authors [1], this chapter presents a detailed roadmap to guide the implementation of BI systems in HEIs. This roadmap is intended to support decision-making in various areas and at various levels, providing critical information for key decision-making processes. The analysis focuses on the types of structured data that can help HEIs make more informed decisions.

The relevance of this study stems from the growing challenges faced by HEIs in the digital age, especially with the exponential increase in available data. The implementation of BI systems is therefore crucial for these institutions to be able to manage their data in a strategic and informed way. Our work focuses on creating a specific roadmap for implementing BI in the context of higher education, taking direct account of the sector's needs and particularities, and offering practical guidelines for HEIs to adopt these technologies effectively and efficiently.

The methodology adopted for this research is DSR, which stands out for its particular approach to HEIs. A critical point of the study is the validation of the proposed roadmap through the case study of the UTAD. This validation not only tested the roadmap's applicability in a real context but also allowed it to be adjusted and refined, ensuring its relevance and effectiveness in helping HEIs implement BI systems. The case study, complemented by interviews and focus groups, are the methods chosen for this research, representing a comprehensive and enriching approach to collecting data and understanding the object of the study.

Although there are numerous studies and projects on the implementation of BI in various sectors, it is crucial to recognise that HEIs have distinct characteristics, such as the complexity of their organisational structures and the diversity of data sources.

In short, this work aims to improve HEIs' ability to analyse and evaluate data and information from multiple systems and platforms, in line with two fundamental strategic objectives: in-depth knowledge of HEIs and support for decision-making in these institutions.

2 Roadmap for Implementation of a BI in HEIs

In an academic context, a roadmap for the implementation of a BI system outlines the various phases and activities inherent in this process, offering a structured method to guide and ensure the success of the implementation. The specific tasks and goals associated with each stage may vary depending on the particularities of each HEI, its available resources and the complexity inherent in implementing the BI system. This roadmap is an essential tool for promoting an organised and methodical approach to implementing a BI system, enabling HEIs to use data effectively for informed decisions and performance improvements [2–6].

The roadmap can be designed as a project template, serving as a reference or predefined structure that HEIs teams can adapt to develop their own BI system. Using a project roadmap template simplifies planning by providing an outline or structure that highlights the key elements and typical stages of a roadmap. Developing a roadmap in the form of a project template for the implementation of a BI system in a HEI involves establishing a set of structured steps that guide the institution from the design phase through to the implementation and subsequent optimisation of the solution.

2.1 Roadmap Proposal for Implementation in HEIs

Concerning this study, which centres on the development of a roadmap for the implementation of a BI system in HEIs in the form of a project template, the roadmap we propose is a structured model that offers both a visual representation and a logical sequence to guide an HEI through the process of successfully implement a BI solution. This roadmap can be a valuable resource for various HEIs, acting as a starting point that can be customised according to their specific needs and contexts.

Our roadmap proposal was the result of exploratory work and multiple meetings with various UTAD stakeholders, as well as a literature review, focusing on authors such as [7–10]. As illustrated in Fig. 1, the proposed roadmap includes twelve stages, grouped into several themes and identified as "ET": identifying the areas of activity and the strategic objectives; identifying and characterising the decision-making levels; identifying and describing the characteristic processes; identifying the Information System (IS); defining a decision matrix for the Key Performance Indicators (KPIs); identifying the KPIs to be systematised in the dashboards; identifying and characterising the contexts of information use; creating a set of dashboards; creating the information flows needed to feed the dashboards; validating the dashboards with user groups; defining the architecture of the BI system; and implementing the BI solution. In the following section, these activities are described in detail.

Table 1 shows the details of the "ET01" stage, which involves the detailed analysis and identification of the HEI's functional areas, as well as the definition of strategic objectives aligned with the institution's mission and vision.

Table 1. ET01 - Areas of Activity and Strategic Objectives: Identification of areas of activity and strategic objectives.

Objectives	HEIs need to undertake a detailed identification and understanding of their various functional areas. This analysis should be followed by the establishment of clear and far-reaching objectives and policies, in line with the mission and vision of the institution, to ensure a coherent and focused strategic direction
Description	To gain a full understanding of the activities and strategic goals of HEIs, it is essential to use a variety of sources and methods. Consultation with a wide range of stakeholders, including institutional leaders, academics and external partners, is key to gaining a holistic perspective. It is also important to ensure that both the areas of activity and the strategic objectives are aligned with the core values of the institution, thus ensuring that the strategy is consistent with the institutional mission
Expected results	It is vital to develop a comprehensive understanding of their areas of activity, which are essential to their effective operation. At the same time, it is essential to identify the priority strategic objectives that will guide the institution. Furthermore, it is essential to align BI activities with the guidelines of the institution's strategic plan, thus enriching the knowledge needed to effectively support the decision-making process

Table 2 shows the details of the "ET02" stage, which focuses on understanding the HEI's organisational structure, identifying the different decision-making levels and assessing their effectiveness.

Table 2. ET02 - Levels of Decision-Making: Identifying and characterising the levels of decision-making.

Objectives	HEIs need to understand their organisational structure, including governance mechanisms, leadership roles and the adoption of innovative approaches. This understanding enables the identification of the different levels of decision-making and their relevance to the effective governance of the institution. It is also important to analyse the effectiveness of decision-making at each level, taking into account the quality of information available, the clarity of communication and the ability to collaborate and integrate different perspectives
Description	For a comprehensive analysis of HEIs, it is essential to adopt a multifaceted approach that includes the review of official documents, semi-structured interviews with decision-makers at different hierarchical levels, and direct observation of decision-making meetings. This process also involves mapping the hierarchical structure of an HEI, identifying the different actors involved and analysing the complexity inherent in the institution, with a focus on operational efficiency at different decision-making levels
Expected results	It is essential to develop a clear understanding of the different levels of decision-making - strategic, tactical and operational - and of the specific roles of these levels in the management and operation of the institution. Improving decision-making involves ensuring that decisions at each level are based on clear information and are the result of a collaborative process. It is also important to facilitate the identification of problems and successes in each area of the institution, thereby contributing to greater accountability and operational efficiency

Table 3 shows the details of the "ET03" stage, which involves identifying and describing the key processes of the HEI.

Table 3. ET03 - Processes: Identification and description of characteristic processes.

Objectives	For effective management in HEIs, it is essential to understand and map in detail the systematic and organised processes that are implemented to achieve specific goals and objectives. This understanding must include an in-depth analysis of the activities, strategies and initiatives undertaken by the institution to improve outcomes and meet the needs of students, staff and the community. In addition, it is important to identify the mechanisms, procedures and steps by which the institution makes decisions on academic, administrative, financial and strategic matters
Description	To understand the processes and practices in HEIs, it is essential to carry out a literature review and content analysis of relevant documents. The study will also include the conduct of surveys and interviews with relevant members of the institution to gather information on the prevailing processes. In addition, it is important to gather detailed data on the mission, strategic objectives, organisational structure, courses and programmes offered, as well as internal policies and regulations. Process mapping in each identified area is carried out through interviews, direct observation and analysis of documents and workflows
Expected results	It is crucial to develop a clear understanding of their distinctive processes. This clarification is fundamental to improving the efficiency and quality of processes, ensuring the sustainability of the institution and the fulfilment of its mission. In addition, effective management of processes in each area helps to facilitate informed decision-making, promoting efficiency, transparency and alignment with the institution's specific goals and challenges

Table 4 shows the details of the "ET04" stage, which evaluates the HEI's existing IS, choosing those that best meet institutional needs and ensure data security.

Table 4. ET04 - IS: IS identification.

Objectives	When evaluating IS in HEIs, it is crucial to analyse existing systems to support processes, improve efficiency, facilitate decision-making and enrich the overall educational experience. The choice of systems must be aligned with the needs of the institution while ensuring the security and privacy of stored data. It is also essential to implement decision support systems that are appropriate, reliable and contribute to the quality management of the institution
Description	It is important to identify and categorise the different types of IS in use, ranging from academic management and Enterprise Resource Planning systems to systems for managing teaching, scholarly production and document management. To gain a detailed understanding of these systems, semi-structured interviews will be conducted with IT managers and other relevant staff. In addition, analysis of institutional documentation, such as annual reports and IT strategic plans, is fundamental to understanding the infrastructure and initiatives related to IS. The use of multiple sources and approaches is essential to obtain a complete and accurate picture of the IS in use at the institution
Expected results	It is essential to have a comprehensive understanding of the IS in use, including their functionalities, integrations and relevance to different areas of activity. This understanding enables the efficiency and quality of the services provided by the institution to be improved through the appropriate use of IS. In addition, it is essential to ensure the accuracy, security and accessibility of information to the various users within the institution, thereby contributing to more efficient management and informed decision-making

Table 5 shows the details of the "ET05" stage, which consists of creating a visual tool for prioritising and evaluating KPIs, based on specific criteria.

Table 5. ET05 - Decision Matrix: Definition of a decision matrix for the KPIs.

Objectives	The decision matrix is used in HEIs as an essential visual tool for prioritising decision-making processes. This method involves evaluating and comparing different KPI options or alternatives based on specific criteria. The aim is to provide a structured framework that allows the positive and negative aspects of each KPI option to be systematically assessed, helping to determine the most appropriate course of action
Description	When defining KPIs for HEIs, the first step is to identify the most relevant indicators for the institution's goals and objectives. Evaluation criteria are then established for these KPIs, taking into account factors such as alignment with strategic objectives, measurability, relevance and impact on decision-making. Weights are assigned to each criterion to reflect its importance, and the KPIs are scored against these criteria using rating scales or scoring systems. The scores for each KPI are calculated, culminating in an overall score that allows them to be ranked. Finally, the decision matrix is regularly reviewed and refined as necessary
Expected results	It is essential to identify the most important and effective KPIs. This process aims to facilitate informed decision-making by providing a clear and objective framework for evaluating alternatives and selecting the most appropriate options. It also improves the monitoring and analysis of KPIs, allowing comparisons to be made between expectations and actual results, thus contributing to more efficient and transparent management

Table 6 shows the details of the "ET06" stage, which selects KPIs to be monitored on dashboards, ensuring that these indicators are in line with the HEI's strategic objectives.

Table 6. ET06 – KPIs: Identification of KPIs to be systematized in dashboards.

Objectives	HEIs need to evaluate and quantify the performance of their processes, activities, projects, products and services about pre-defined objectives. The selection and implementation of KPIs that are aligned with the institution's mission, vision and strategic goals is fundamental. In addition, the regular monitoring of these KPIs through the use of dashboards and the use of the resulting analyses to support and guide the decision-making process is crucial
Description	In managing HEIs, it is crucial to identify strategic objectives and align KPIs with these priorities. The involvement of relevant stakeholders in the KPI selection process is essential to ensure an appropriate choice. The indicators selected must be measurable and capable of effectively assessing progress towards the strategic objectives. The availability and feasibility of data for the selected KPIs will also be assessed. Key indicators are prioritised based on their relevance, impact and feasibility, and a dashboard is developed to present the selected KPIs. Finally, the KPIs and the dashboard are regularly reviewed and updated
Expected results	When implementing BI systems in HEIs, it is essential to obtain KPIs that are aligned with the strategic objectives of the institution, reflecting its specificities and its specific context. Data-driven decision-making is promoted by encouraging stakeholders within the institution to use the dashboards and information provided by the KPIs. It also improves the monitoring and analysis of the institution's performance, allowing trends to be identified and providing key information for decision-making

Table 7 shows the details of the "ET07" stage, which comprises the specific contexts in which information is used at the HEI, ensuring that it is managed effectively.

Table 7. Use of Information: Identification and characterization of the contexts in which information is used.

Objectives	HEIs need to understand the specific contexts in which information is used, covering areas such as technological integration, knowledge management and innovation. This understanding will ensure that decisions are informed and that all stakeholders have access to relevant information. It is also essential to ensure that information is collected, processed and shared appropriately to support the success and mission of the institution
Description	Mapping institutional processes is essential for understanding how information is used in the different activities and processes of the institution. This process involves identifying the actors involved and analysing how they use information on a day-to-day basis. Interviews are conducted with key players to deepen this understanding and documents and IS are analysed to identify the areas in which information is used and the methods used to collect and store data. Mapping information flows between different processes and actors is crucial, as is identifying the specific information needs of each actor and process. This study makes it possible to characterise the contexts in which information is used, to classify information or types, and to assess the quality of the information available
Expected results	It is vital to develop a deep understanding of the contexts in which information is used. This knowledge enables processes to be optimised and the quality of services provided to be improved through efficient information management. It also promotes decision-making based on information that is accurate, up-to-date and relevant, thus ensuring more informed and effective decisions

Table 8 shows the details of the "ET08" stage, which involves the development of dashboards adapted to each context of use, focussing on the relevance and usefulness of the information presented.

Table 8. ET08 – Dashboards: Design and implementation of dashboards.

Objectives	It is essential to develop specific dashboards for each context in which information is used, adapting them to the needs and characteristics of each situation. These dashboards should provide relevant information to support decision-making processes in different areas of the institution. The aim is to increase the effectiveness of the actors involved by providing a clear and useful visualisation of data and information
Description	When designing dashboards for HEIs, a user-centred approach is taken to ensure that dashboards are adapted to meet their specific needs. This includes adapting existing dashboards based on detailed, contextual requirements. A low-fidelity UX approach is used to quickly and efficiently prototype dashboards. A pilot implementation is carried out to test the feasibility and effectiveness of the developed dashboards before a full-scale implementation
Expected results	For HEIs, the dashboards developed are efficient and tailored to each specific context, reflecting relevant information that supports informed decision-making. This approach significantly improves management and decision-making by providing detailed analysis and real-time monitoring of key metrics. In addition, the dashboards are interactive and easy to use, helping to improve internal communication and collaboration between different parts of the institution

Table 9 shows the details of the "ET09" stage, which concerns the creation of processes to collect and process the data that will feed the dashboards.

Table 9. ET09 - Information Flow: Creating the information flows needed to feed the dashboards.

Objectives	HEIs must develop a structured process that details how data is collected, processed, transformed and presented on dashboards. This process must ensure the accuracy, timeliness and relevance of data to meet the needs of dashboard users. It is also important to automate the creation of dashboards that are informative, personalised, effective and adaptable to different contexts and user profiles
Description	In higher education management, an information flow model is developed to illustrate the journey of data from its sources to its final visualisation on dashboards. This model includes mechanisms for collecting and integrating data from different sources, ensuring its consistency and quality. Advanced data processing and analysis techniques such as data cleansing, aggregation and statistical analysis are used to transform raw data into meaningful information. At the same time, interactive and easy-to-use dashboards are designed and developed to meet the needs of the institution's various stakeholders
Expected results	The dashboards developed are accurate and reliable, providing timely and pertinent information that is critical to making informed decisions. This approach significantly improves the efficiency and effectiveness of the institution's decision-making processes. In addition, the dashboards are tailored to the specific needs of different areas of the institution, promoting more informed and effective management throughout the institution

Table 10 shows the details of the "ET10" stage, which tests the dashboards with groups of users to ensure that they meet their needs and are effective in decision-making.

Table 10. ET10 - Dashboard Validation: Validation of dashboards with user groups.

Objectives	It is important to ensure that the dashboards developed meet the needs of their users by providing relevant and actionable information. To do this, it is important to improve the usability and effectiveness of the dashboards, thereby improving the decision-making process. Before launching the dashboards, any usability problems should be identified and corrected, and the relevance of the metrics and data presented should be checked to ensure that they are relevant to the target users
Description	In the process of validating dashboards, it is crucial to involve users directly in testing the dashboards in real-life situations to identify and correct any usability and relevance issues. This involvement helps to avoid costly post-launch adjustments and ensures that dashboards are aligned with user needs from the outset. This approach also encourages greater acceptance and regular use of the dashboards by the academic community
Expected results	Developing dashboards means creating intuitive and effective interfaces that facilitate efficient and informed decision-making. These dashboards must be trusted and valued by users. Identifying the need for training or additional support for users is also a critical step, as is ensuring consistency in the presentation and interpretation of data across different user groups

Table 11 shows the details of the "ET11" stage, which develops an integrated architecture for efficient data processing.

Table 11. ET11 – Architecture: Defining the BI system architecture.

Objectives	It is essential to develop an integrated structure that enables them to process and analyse data efficiently. This involves creating a centralised data repository that consolidates information from multiple sources. This approach supports informed decision-making at different levels of the institution's management by facilitating access to relevant and timely information
Description	IS architecture uses Extract, Transform and Load (ETL) processes to collect data from multiple sources, transform it into standardised information and store it in a central repository. This approach includes the implementation of data warehouses, data processing tools and BI dashboards, with a strong emphasis on data governance and security. The architecture developed must be flexible enough to adapt to varying volumes of data and the different operational needs of the institution
Expected results	Improving student outcomes and operational efficiency. This approach ensures that current and relevant data is made available, which is essential for making strategic decisions. There is also a strong focus on ensuring data integrity, security and compliance, increasing the reliability of information used in institutional management

Table 12 shows the details of the "ET12" stage, which consists of implementing the BI solution, collecting and analysing data from multiple systems to extract valuable insights.

Table 12. ET12 - Implementation: Implementation of the BI solution.

Objectives	Collecting and consolidating data from multiple internal systems and platforms is critical for HEIs. The use of modern analytical techniques, including artificial intelligence and big data, is key to extracting valuable insights. This process enables up-to-the-minute analysis, which is essential for making agile and informed decisions within the institution
Description	Data management uses tools such as Microsoft Power BI for data analysis, reporting and visualisation. This approach makes it possible to effectively manage and analyse large volumes of data, both structured and unstructured. In addition, BI platforms are integrated with the institution's existing infrastructure and tools to optimise the data management and information analysis process
Expected results	Detailed data analysis provides actionable insights that are key to improving processes. Quick and easy access to relevant information is critical to improving institutional processes. In addition, the adaptability of the systems is essential, allowing dashboards and reports to be customised to meet the specific needs of the institution

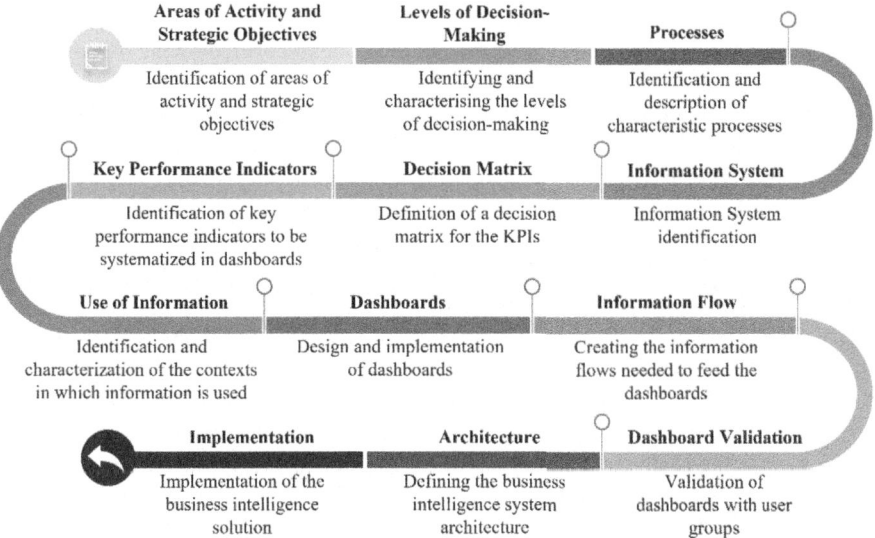

Fig. 1. Roadmap proposal for the implementation of a BI system in a HEI.

3 Roadmap Validation

Validating a roadmap involves a meticulous process of assessing and verifying its effectiveness, feasibility and accuracy. This stage is crucial to ensure that the roadmap fulfils the specific criteria or objectives established, thus guaranteeing its reliability and relevance in supporting decision-making and achieving the expected results. It is essential to recognise that the validation process can vary depending on the specific context and objectives of the roadmap, and this flexibility is essential for its applicability in different scenarios [11–14]. It is important to note that the validation process can vary depending on the specific context and objectives of a roadmap [12, 15–18].

Validating a roadmap by consulting experts involves gathering information, analyses and opinions from highly qualified and experienced professionals in the areas relevant to the plan being analysed. These experts have technical, strategic or domain-specific knowledge that can make a significant contribution to enriching, evaluating and improving the roadmap. The validation carried out with the collaboration of experts thus ensures that the plan is robust, realistic and in line with current best practices and trends in the relevant field [19, 20].

To validate a roadmap to confirm that it meets the stipulated requirements and contributes to solving the specified problem, it is imperative to adopt a structured and focused methodology. This systematic approach is essential to ensure that the roadmap not only meets initial expectations but also proves to be effective in practice, in the context of the problem addressed. The steps required to validate the roadmap with experts, taking these objectives into account, are as follows:

1. Expert selection - Identify and involve subject matter experts or stakeholders who have relevant knowledge and experience in the domain covered by the roadmap [21, 22].
2. Expert review - Share the roadmap with the selected experts and ask for their comments, opinions and recommendations regarding the content, structure, feasibility and alignment of the roadmap with the intended objectives [21–23].
3. Expert evaluation criteria - Define evaluation criteria or guidelines to assess the roadmap's validity, effectiveness and potential for success. These criteria can include factors such as clarity, completeness, relevance, practicability and alignment with industry standards or best practices [16].
4. Gathering Feedback - Carry out interviews, surveys or workshops with experts to gather their comments, opinions and suggestions on the roadmap. This can involve structured questionnaires, open discussions or specific evaluation forms [15, 24].
5. Iterative refinement - Incorporating the feedback and recommendations provided by experts into the roadmap, making the necessary adjustments, revisions or additions to improve its quality, accuracy and usability [14, 25].
6. Consensus building - Facilitating discussions and collaborative sessions between experts to reach a consensus on the validity, feasibility and potential impact of the roadmap. This may involve resolving contradictory opinions, addressing concerns and refining the roadmap based on collective expertise [26].

7. Documentation and reporting - Document the feedback received from the experts, along with any modifications made to the roadmap based on their input. This documentation serves as proof of the validation process and provides transparency and accountability [14, 26].

3.1 Validation of Dashboards with User Groups

Validating dashboards through collaboration with user groups is a crucial step in ensuring that the BI solution effectively aligns with the needs of its users, providing relevant and actionable information. Involving users in the validation process allows HEIs to confirm that dashboards meet their specific needs while promoting usability and optimising decision-making processes based on accurate and relevant information [27–31].

Bearing in mind the UTAD case study, the approach chosen for the validation of this work comprised a set of semi-structured interviews divided into three phases to obtain detailed and valuable information from the experts, to validate the dashboards and to obtain information on their applicability and effectiveness. Below is a more detailed explanation of each of the phases.

- Phase 1: Presentation of the research and demonstration of the dashboards - The presentation of the research and demonstration of the dashboards framed the experts about the context of the research and the dashboards that were developed, providing a comprehensive overview of the purpose of the study and the functionality of the BI solution. This initial interview phase aimed to lay a solid foundation for the subsequent validation steps and ensured that the experts fully understood the purpose and objective of the research.
- Phase 2: Testing the dashboards by the experts - The experts explored and interacted with the dashboards that had been developed. They were allowed to use the dashboards as real end users, to navigate through the different views, apply filters, analyse data and try out the interactive features. This phase made it possible to assess usability, user experience, the effectiveness of the dashboards and the relevance of the information presented, allowing impressions to be gathered and problems or improvements to be identified by the experts.
- Phase 3: Answers to Questions from the Experts - The phase of answering questions from the experts was the third and final stage of the interview. In this phase, the experts provided detailed and structured answers to a set of predefined questions that were developed as part of the questionnaire, which served as a guide for validating the dashboards. The main aim of this phase was to gather specific information from the experts on various aspects of the dashboards.

Following the interviews conducted during the validation process, it was realised that there was a need to implement several changes relating to the presentation of the dashboards. This observation emerged as a crucial aspect for improving the effectiveness and efficiency of the dashboards in question.

4 Conclusions

This study focused on the development of a roadmap for the efficient implementation of BI systems in HEIs, based on the premise of the importance of a strategic approach to the adoption of such technologies. The research followed a methodology that incorporated exploratory analysis and interaction with various stakeholders, culminating in the development of a practical guide for the implementation of BI systems in HEIs, with the aim of optimising decision-making at various levels and areas. The methodology adopted, DSR, stands out for its effective contribution to formulating the proposed roadmap. This work it has a practical applicability, providing HEIs with a clear path to adopting BI systems, thus filling a significant gap in academic literature.

The roadmap developed in this study is based on a theoretical foundation, supported by an extensive literature review and consultations with experts. In addition to its theoretical value, the roadmap suggests a reference architecture for BI systems, including decision-support dashboards that are intuitive, informative and aligned with the specific needs of HEIs. These components have been designed to ensure that the roadmap is practical and adaptable to the diverse requirements and capabilities of HEIs.

The roadmap validation phase included consultation with a panel of experts and was complemented by a practical case study carried out at a HEI, specifically UTAD. This crucial step confirmed the viability of the roadmap and demonstrated how effectively the BI system, as outlined in the roadmap, can be implemented.

The study recognises that the roadmap's applicability may vary depending on the specific characteristics of each HEI. However, the proposed roadmap offers flexibility and detail, allowing for adaptations to the specific needs of different HEIs.

5 Future Work

Although the proposed roadmap has an important contribution for BI implementation in HEIs, is considered to explore various areas in future research. A key initiative would be to carry out a longitudinal study to assess the sustained effectiveness of the proposed roadmap. This study should focus on how the roadmap adjusts to technological and organisational changes in HEIs, identifying the adjustments needed to ensure its relevance and effectiveness over time.

In addition, it is proposed to investigate the applicability of this roadmap in a variety of educational contexts, particularly in HEIs of different profiles, sizes and resources. This research would make it possible to understand the extent of the roadmap's flexibility and adaptability to different institutional environments.

Another area of interest is the integration of the roadmap with new emerging technologies in the BI field, such as artificial intelligence and machine learning. A study in this area could provide crucial information on how HEIs can use these advanced technologies to improve decision-making and institutional management.

Finally, comparative case studies on different HEIs that have implemented the roadmap would also represent a valuable approach.

Acknowledgments. The study was developed under the project A-MoVeR – "Mobilizing Agenda for the Development of Products & Systems towards an Intelligent and Green Mobility", operation n.º 02/C05-i01.01/2022.PC646908627–00000069, approved under the terms of the call n.º 02/C05-i01/2022 – Mobilizing Agendas for Business Innovation, financed by European funds provided to Portugal by the Recovery and Resilience Plan (RRP), in the scope of the European Recovery and Resilience Fa-cility (RRF), framed in the Next Generation UE, for the period from 2021 -2026. The authors acknowledge the work facilities and equipment provided by CeDRI (UIDB/05757/2020 and UIDP/05757/2020) to the project team.

References

1. Sequeira, N., Reis, A., Branco, F., Alves, P.: Roadmap for implementing business intelligence systems in higher education institutions: exploratory work. In: Proceedings of the 20th International Conference on Smart Business Technologies, SCITEPRESS - Science and Technology Publications, Rome, Italy, pp. 162–169 (2023). https://doi.org/10.5220/0012118000003552
2. Gaol, F.L., Abdillah, L., Matsuo, T.: Adoption of business intelligence to support cost accounting based financial systems — case study of XYZ company. Open Eng. **11**(1), 14–28 (2020). https://doi.org/10.1515/eng-2021-0002
3. Jahantigh, F.F., Habibi, A., Sarafrazi, A.: A conceptual framework for business intelligence critical success factors. Inter. J. Bus. Inform. Syst. **30**(1), 109–123 (2019). https://doi.org/10.1504/IJBIS.2019.097058
4. Mathrani, S.: Critical business intelligence practices to create meta-knowledge. IJBIS **36**(1), 1 (2021). https://doi.org/10.1504/IJBIS.2021.112413
5. Montero, J.N., Lind, M.L.: Determining business intelligence usage success. IJCSIT **12**(6), 45–67 (2020). https://doi.org/10.5121/ijcsit.2020.12604
6. Rezaie, S., Mirabedini, S.J., Abtahi, A.: Identifying key effective factors on the implementation process of business intelligence in the banking industry of Iran. JISIB **7**(3) (2017). https://doi.org/10.37380/jisib.v7i3.276
7. Ma, X., Xiong, F., Olawumi, T.O., Dong, N., Chan, A.P.C.: Conceptual Framework and roadmap approach for integrating BIM into lifecycle project management. J. Manage. Eng. **34**(6), 05018011 (2018). https://doi.org/10.1061/(ASCE)ME.1943-5479.0000647
8. Mannina, G., Gulhan, H., Ni, B.-J.: Water reuse from wastewater treatment: the transition towards circular economy in the water sector. Biores. Technol. **363**, 127951 (2022). https://doi.org/10.1016/j.biortech.2022.127951
9. Skoumpopoulou, D., Robson, A.: Systems change in UK HEIs: how do culture, management, users and systems align? JEIM **33**(6), 1627–1645 (2020). https://doi.org/10.1108/JEIM-03-2019-0091
10. Wollny, S., et al.: Students' expectations of learning analytics across Europe. Comput. Assisted Learn. **39**(4), 1325–1338 (2023). https://doi.org/10.1111/jcal.12802
11. Castro, B.M., Reis, M.D.M., Salles, R.M.: Multi-agent simulation model updating and forecasting for the evaluation of COVID-19 transmission. Sci. Rep. **12**(1), 22091 (2022). https://doi.org/10.1038/s41598-022-22945-z
12. Jalundhwala, F., Londhe, V.: A systematic review on implementing operational excellence as a strategy to ensure regulatory compliance: a roadmap for Indian pharmaceutical industry. IJLSS **14**(4), 730–758 (2023). https://doi.org/10.1108/IJLSS-04-2022-0078
13. Kerr, C., Phaal, R.: Roadmapping and roadmaps: definition and underpinning concepts. IEEE Trans. Eng. Manage. **69**(1), 6–16 (2022). https://doi.org/10.1109/TEM.2021.3096012

14. Ozcan, S., Homayounfard, A., Simms, C., Wasim, J.: Technology roadmapping using text mining: a foresight study for the retail industry. IEEE Trans. Eng. Manage. **69**(1), 228–244 (2022). https://doi.org/10.1109/TEM.2021.3068310
15. Ekenna, C., Thomas, S., Amato, N.M.: Adaptive local learning in sampling based motion planning for protein folding. BMC Syst. Biol. **10**(S2), 49 (2016). https://doi.org/10.1186/s12918-016-0297-9
16. Juaristi, M., Konstantinou, T., Gómez-Acebo, T., Monge-Barrio, A.: Development and validation of a roadmap to assist the performance-based early-stage design process of adaptive opaque facades. Sustainability **12**(23), 10118 (2020). https://doi.org/10.3390/su122310118
17. Mitchell, S.-L., Clark, M.: Reconceptualising product life-cycle theory as stakeholder engagement with non-profit organisations. J. Mark. Manag. **35**(1–2), 13–39 (2019). https://doi.org/10.1080/0267257X.2018.1562487
18. Sareminia, S., Hasanzadeh, A., Elahi, S., Montazer, G.: Developing technology roadmapping combinational framework by meta synthesis technique. Int. J. Innovation Technol. Manag. **16**(02), 1950019 (2019). https://doi.org/10.1142/S0219877019500196
19. Chofreh, A.G., Goni, F.A., Klemes, J.J.: A master plan for the implementation of sustainable enterprise resource planning systems (part iii): evaluation of a roadmap. Chem. Eng. Trans. **52**, 1105–1110 (2016). https://doi.org/10.3303/CET1652185
20. Münch, J., Trieflinger, S., Lang, D.: The product roadmap maturity model deep: validation of a method for assessing the product roadmap capabilities of organizations. In: Hyrynsalmi, S., Suoranta, M., Nguyen-Duc, A., Tyrväinen, P., Abrahamsson, P. (eds.) Software Business. LNBIP, vol. 370, pp. 97–113. Springer International Publishing, Cham (2019). https://doi.org/10.1007/978-3-030-33742-1_9
21. Claessens, F., et al.: A co-creation roadmap towards sustainable quality of care: a multimethod study. PLoS ONE **17**(6), e0269364 (2022). https://doi.org/10.1371/journal.pone.0269364
22. Zuo, G., Li, M., Yu, J., Wu, C., Huang, G.: An Efficient motion planning method with a lazy demonstration graph for repetitive pick-and-place. Biomimetics **7**(4), 210 (2022). https://doi.org/10.3390/biomimetics7040210
23. Rust, P., Flood, D., McCaffery, F.: Creation of an IEC 62304 compliant software development plan: IEC 62304 compliant SDP. J. Softw. Evol. Proc. **28**(11), 1005–1010 (2016). https://doi.org/10.1002/smr.1826
24. Baranowski, P., Damaziak, K.: Numerical simulation of vehicle-lighting pole crash tests: parametric study of factors influencing predicted occupant safety levels. Materials **14**(11), 2822 (2021). https://doi.org/10.3390/ma14112822
25. Damasco, J.A., Ravi, S., Perez, J.D., Hagaman, D.E., Melancon, M.P.: Understanding nanoparticle toxicity to direct a safe-by-design approach in cancer nanomedicine. Nanomaterials **10**(11), 2186 (2020). https://doi.org/10.3390/nano10112186
26. Horry, R., Booth, C.A., Mahamadu, A., Manu, P., Georgakis, P.: Environmental management systems in the architectural, engineering and construction sectors: a roadmap to aid the delivery of the sustainable development goals. Environ. Dev. Sustain. **24**(9), 10585–10615 (2022). https://doi.org/10.1007/s10668-021-01874-3
27. Laurent, G., Moussa, M.D., Cirenei, C., Tavernier, B., Marcilly, R., Lamer, A.: Development, implementation and preliminary evaluation of clinical dashboards in a department of anesthesia. J. Clin. Monit. Comput. **35**(3), 617–626 (2021). https://doi.org/10.1007/s10877-020-00522-x
28. McCoy, C., Rosenbaum, H.: Uncovering unintended and shadow practices of users of decision support system dashboards in higher education institutions: uncovering unintended and shadow practices of users of decision support system dashboards in higher education institutions. J. Am. Soc. Inf. Sci. **70**(4), 370–384 (2019). https://doi.org/10.1002/asi.24131

29. Roberts, L.D., Howell, J.A., Seaman, K.: Give me a customizable dashboard: personalized learning analytics dashboards in higher education. Tech Know Learn **22**(3), 317–333 (2017). https://doi.org/10.1007/s10758-017-9316-1
30. Schall, M.C., Cullen, L., Pennathur, P., Chen, H., Burrell, K., Matthews, G.: Usability evaluation and implementation of a health information technology dashboard of evidence-based quality indicators', CIN: Comput. Inform. Nursing **35**(6), 281–288 (2017). https://doi.org/10.1097/CIN.0000000000000325
31. Weggelaar-Jansen, A.M.J.W.M., Broekharst, D.S.E., De Bruijne, M.: Developing a hospital-wide quality and safety dashboard: a qualitative research study. BMJ Qual. Saf. **27**(12), 1000–1007 (2018). https://doi.org/10.1136/bmjqs-2018-007784

A Study Partner Recommender System Using a Community Detection Algorithm

Chukwuka Victor Obionwu[1(✉)], Devi Prasad Ilapavuluri[1], David Broneske[2], and Gunter Saake[1]

[1] University of Magdeburg, Magdeburg, Germany
`obionwu@vgu.de`
[2] German Centre for Higher Education Research and Science Studies, Hannover, Germany

Abstract. The potential for an individual's interaction to be limited by an underlying inclination has significant implications when overlooked in situations where group contact is crucial. In university course projects, the absence of synergy among a project team often leads to failure. In order to provide students enrolled in our course projects with an optimal team recommendation, we have devised a highly efficient strategy. This strategy involves utilizing their personalities and assessing their collaborative effectiveness through individual personality questionnaires. Additionally, we employ community detection using the Leiden algorithm. In order to assess the soundness of our recommendation technique, we conducted an evaluation of current algorithms that have been employed for this purpose, taking into account their modularity scores and the decision to establish preferred team sizes. The assessment section presents results that demonstrate how the Leiden algorithm outperforms competing algorithms and techniques that rely on clustering coefficients. Specifically, the Leiden algorithm is capable of recommending study partners that possess many personality features that match the user and their respective teams.

Keywords: Community detection · Social network analysis · Recommendation system · Collaboration in teams

1 Introduction

Collaboration is a vital component of university education as students unite to pursue shared goals, such as acquiring knowledge in certain subjects or engaging in team projects and group assignments. In a fruitful collaboration engagement, they exchange knowledge, achieve their goals, and also enhance their technical and interpersonal abilities, among other things. Conversely, a failed collaboration results in a failure to achieve these goals and is specifically regarded as a bad encounter, perhaps influencing their future partnerships. According to the study conducted by [14], students who engage in cooperation achieve greater personal achievements in comparison to those who do not cooperate. Additionally, they emphasized the factors that impact collaboration, including the profiles of the students, the group dynamics, and the nature of the work. Therefore, it is crucial to enhance certain components, such as synergy among group members, in order to prevent unfavorable consequences. Moreover, students may encounter challenges in locating compatible study companions for cooperation and may opt for arbitrary individuals or those with contrasting personalities. Consequently, the collaboration may be unproductive or give rise to confrontations, ultimately culminating in an abrupt termination of their joint efforts.

A strategy we adopted to improve the membership of project groups leveraged the personality traits of potential team members and a community detection algorithm. Puga et al. also employed this strategy in their quest to identify the phenotypes, or characteristics, of people with tinnitus using community detection algorithms and health data questionnaires of those individuals [22]. Their work on generating communities using questionnaires provides scope for us to apply community detection methods to personality questionnaires to form cohesive student communities of desired sizes. Communities are groups of strongly connected nodes with similar properties local to their group [13]. Suitable community detection algorithms are used to identify such communities in a network. A large collection of literature is present on various algorithms used over the years for different purposes. Some of the extensively used algorithms are Edge Betweenness [16], Fast Greedy [4], Walktrap [21], Label Propogation [23], Infomap [25], Multilevel or Louvain [2], Leiden [28]. All these algorithms identify communities based on a metric named Modularity that was first mentioned by [16]. Although, in recent years, new metrics such as Surprise, Significance, and Conductance have been proposed, limited applications are seen based on them, as most of the works being carried out today in community detection are still based around the Modularity metric only [3].

Compared to the state-of-the-art efforts on project partner recommendation, our strategy provides an approach that leverages multiplex partitioning to create collaboration groups of desired sizes. We further show the effectiveness of graph pruning in improving the effectiveness of community detection algorithms. Thus, we are able to generate more precise and meaningful partner recommendations for course projects.

This work is an extension of [17], which focused on the strategy we adopted towards structuring and administering student teams in our course projects. This work

1. focuses on the improvement of our partner recommendation system, where we devised two strategies for grouping similar students based on their questionnaire responses. Recommendations from both of these come under the collaborative filtering method, as student communities are formed based on personality similarities.
2. We further describe two approaches. The first approach is based on community detection. Our second approach is an alternate one for grouping students through their clustering coefficients and serves as an additional option to suggest study partners different from the first approach.

The subsequent sections of the study have been delineated as follows: Sect. 2 provides an overview of the related works, and Sect. 3 gives a background on community detection measures. In Sect. 4, we describe the Leiden algorithm, and in Sect. 5, we describe the graph pruning technique. The questionnaire transformation strategy is described in Sect. 6 and in Sect. 7, we describe the implementation process. Our strategy is evaluated and discussed in Sect. 8 and in Sect. 9, we conclude and indicate directions for future efforts.

2 Related Work

In this section, works that are closely related to recommending study partners for students are briefly discussed. [30] worked on recommending partners to collaborate on patent partner recommendation in enterprise social networks. The underlying important aspects of their approach include recommending high-ranked partners from a pool of probable partners generated through similarity, closeness, etc. Additionally, feedback from the researcher is considered, and a learning model tends to generate new recommendations. Another work that is aimed at recommending courses to students instead of partners is [26] which utilizes the concept of community detection through the K-Means algorithm to group similar users for recommending courses to the students of the group. Their approach primarily considers the students' interactions that occur in discussion forums to form the links between student nodes. Next, similarities between students in terms of their skills, preferences, and performances on one side and interactions on the other side are used to group them with the K-Means algorithm.

An approach to recommending study partners for Massive Open Online Course students that, besides considering their engagement in the discussion forum of the course, also takes into account students' behavior is [31]. Basically, their approach relies on the data gathered from the forum of the course and the data from the profiles of students. Through these, similarities among the students are identified, and all of them are separated into three groups based on the tasks carried out and their knowledge of that particular course.

In comparison, our approach identifies similarities among the students by considering their personality traits, which are not limited to a course but apply to any task they carry out on a daily basis. Further, there is flexibility to form any number of groups of desired sizes. [24] deals with considering Twitter data for grouping students and assigning projects through the DBSCAN clustering algorithm and softmax function, respectively. They used data about tweets related to domains of computer science. Further, project leaders were decided through the identification of highly influential students for all the clusters based on their Twitter engagement level in the particular domain.

All these works comprised some form of similarity matching or clustering, but with data other than personality traits to be used for recommendation. In contrast, in our approach, we placed weight on the significance of personality traits for group students and recommended them in order to work efficiently. We could find only a couple of works [18, 27] that adapted personality questionnaires or traits closely matching ours to build recommendation systems for students.

In [27] personality, factors such as communication, interests, profile data, and preferences of students are considered by their system to generate recommendations for study partners. They begin by gathering data through questionnaires and interviews, then compute matching scores between students, take into account all the factors with different weights, and finally present recommendations to the students along with the scores. Finally, [18] is a recent work that is intended to recommend partners for projects at the university based on personality questionnaire data. Primarily, they built a model that calculates academic scores to be used for the recommendation of matching the mean academic scores of students by setting a threshold score for each questionnaire and taking the personality questionnaire scores of students. While conducting our research, we did not see any work that used community detection on a multiplex network of personality questionnaires with equal consideration and significance for building a study partner recommendation system for students like ours.

3 Background: Community Detection Measures

Community detection measures are metrics used to evaluate the quality of the communities identified within a network. These communities, also called clusters, represent groups of nodes (data points) that are highly connected to each other but have weaker connections to nodes outside the group [7]. They fall under the category of intrinsic measures. While another category of measures called extrinsic measures also exists, all these metrics are intended to verify the essence of the communities, but in different contexts, as specified below.

Intrinsic Measures. The process of evaluation using these metrics is focused on the internal community structure, specifically to assess the kind of connections within the structure. An algorithm designed for partition detection aims to identify communities within a network by optimizing a specific metric to generate an optimal solution that represents a derived community. It must be noted that other potential solutions may exist but remain unknown [3]. The next section provides a concise overview of the metrics employed in our study.

Modularity. The concept of modularity can be interpreted in several ways. According to Gates et al., modularity in the context of a weighted network refers to the quantification of the relative strength of connections within a community compared to connections outside of that community [8, 11, 12]. Essentially, modularity measures how well a community detection algorithm separates the network into distinct and meaningful modules. If we depict modularity as Q, it can either be:

1. Positive Modularity ($Q > 0$): This is the desired outcome. It indicates that the identified communities have a higher number of connections within themselves compared to the number of connections expected by random chance. In other words, nodes within a community are well-connected to each other, suggesting a strong internal structure.
2. Modularity Close to Zero ($Q \approx 0$): This suggests that the communities are not well-defined, and the network might not have a clear community structure. The identified communities might not be significantly different from what you would expect by chance.
3. Negative Modularity ($Q < 0$): This is generally not desirable. It might mean that the community detection algorithm is inappropriate for the given network or that the network itself lacks a distinct community structure that modularity can effectively capture.

Surprise. The Surprise metric, in the context of network analysis, measures how statistically surprising the observed distribution of edges within and between communities is. It aims to spot communities that significantly deviate from what one might anticipate by chance. It's pretty hard to figure out the surprise metric because you have to compare the chance of seeing the real edge distribution under a null model (random chance) to the chance of seeing the real edge distribution in the network with communities that have been detected [1]. This metric is particularly useful in identifying hidden patterns or structures within complex networks that may not be immediately apparent. By quantifying the level of surprise in community structure, researchers can gain insights into the underlying organization and relationships within the network. In general, communities with a high surprise score suggest a more unexpected and potentially more meaningful structure within the network [1,29]. The surprise metric can either be:

1. High Surprise ($Q > 0$): This indicates that the observed community structure is highly unexpected based on random chance. The nodes within communities are significantly more connected to each other than would be expected by random shuffling, suggesting a strong and potentially meaningful community structure.
2. Low Surprise ($Q \approx 0$): This suggests the observed community structure is not very surprising. The distribution of edges is not much different from what you might expect by chance, indicating the communities might not be well defined.
3. Negative Surprise ($Q < 0$): This is not a typical outcome and can be interpreted as a less informative community structure compared to random chance.

Extrinsic Measures. These metrics evaluate the correctness of the detected communities by performing a comparison in terms of similarity with the actual communities. So, the evaluation is not based on the internal network structure; hence, the name extrinsic measure. For the comparison, the actual communities that correspond to the ground truth are to be available. Alternatively, these metrics are applicable for similarity checking for the derived communities from a couple of algorithms. For our purpose, the latter scenario is applicable. Several metrics are available for comparing two sets of communities, and among them, adjusted mutual information is the metric that has been considered in our evaluation, as even with the absence of ground truth, adjusted mutual information still returns us the correct similarity score between the two sets irrespective of their internal arrangement of community labels. [20].

Adjusted Mutual Information (AMI). Adjusted mutual information is a metric that checks the similarity between two clusterings or memberships of communities. It's particularly useful for evaluating the performance of clustering algorithms in unsupervised learning tasks. It builds upon the concept of mutual information, which measures the mutual dependence between two variables, in this case, the cluster labels assigned by two different clustering algorithms [10,15]. However, mutual information can be high even for random clusterings due to the inherent structure of the data. AMI involves calculating the following components:

1. Mutual Information: This measures the information shared between the two clusters. A higher MI indicates a stronger relationship between the cluster labels assigned by the two algorithms.
2. Expected Mutual Information: This represents the expected level of agreement between random clusters with the same number of clusters and data distribution.
3. Entropy: This measures the uncertainty associated with the cluster assignments in each cluster.

Adjusted mutual information values range from −1 to 1, with 1 indicating perfect agreement between the two clusters and 0 suggesting no agreement beyond what is expected by chance. Negative values are uncommon and can indicate very poor agreement [32].

4 The Leiden Algorithm

The Leiden Algorithm is a community detection algorithm that uses a modularity optimization technique to identify densely connected groups of nodes within a network. It has been shown to be effective in identifying communities in large networks with millions of nodes and edges. While identifying the right community detection algorithm, the Leiden [28] has been considered for our first approach due to its efficiency and ability to handle large and complex. The workings of the Leiden algorithm in the paper [28] follows three-step: as shown in Fig. 1, local moving shown in Fig. 1(b), refinement shown in Fig. 1(c), and aggregation shown in Fig. 1(d).

Local Moving. Local moving is a step wherein communities occur by moving the graph nodes so as to increase the value of the graph's modularity. In the Leiden algorithm, all the nodes shown in Fig. 1(a) are randomly chosen to be put in a queue, one at a time. Once the nodes are available in the queue, a node from the front is taken and assigned to a randomly selected community if the modularity increases with that addition. If that

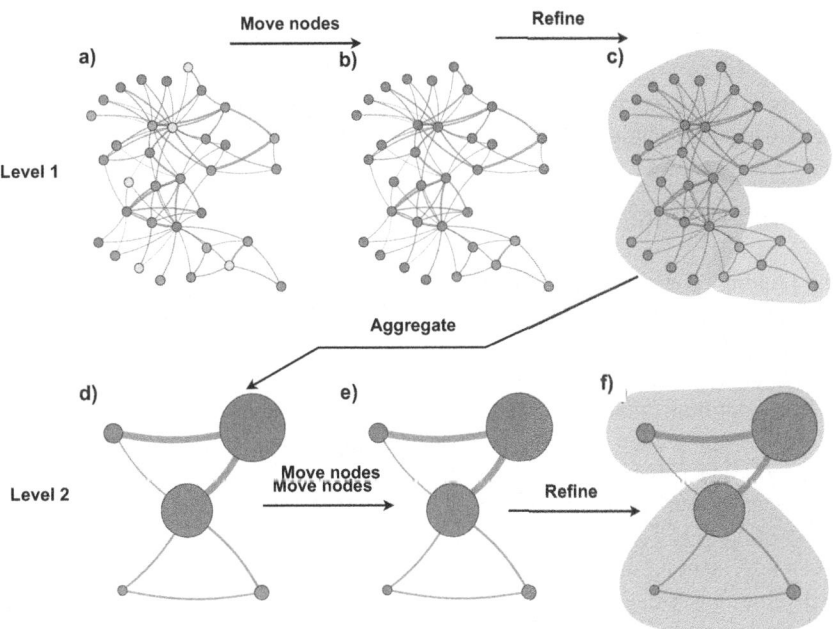

Fig. 1. Illustration of Working of Leiden Algorithm (taken from [28]).

node gets added to an unknown community, nodes beside that moved node get shifted to the queue's rear end. This is done if the neighboring nodes are not already part of the new community and if they are not present in the queue. The process is carried out for all the nodes in the queue. After this, the process of moving nodes is again carried out, except that only those nodes are considered for moving into new communities where their neighborhood has changed. The remaining nodes remain undisturbed.Once this step ends, a partition or set of communities is returned by the Leiden algorithm, which represents Fig. 1(b), and it is used in the next step [28].

Refinement. The refinement step begins by considering all the nodes in the partition as singletons, or individual communities. Next, a node is selected randomly and merged with another community, also selected randomly, only if the modularity value increases. However, this merge occurs based on two conditions: both nodes should have previously been part of the same community in the local moving partition, and they should also have been strongly connected. Considering these aspects, the step is executed for all eligible nodes, resulting in a refined version of the partition that may have some additional communities compared to the previous step, as shown in Fig. 1(c) [28].

Aggregation. In this step, for the initial formation of an aggregated graph, the first partition derived in the local moving step is considered. Later, an aggregated graph is formed by taking the refined partition obtained in the previous step. This graph is shown in Fig. 1(d), where all three communities are aggregated as three nodes. It is to be observed from this figure that we have two nodes, each in red and green. This is because, in the refinement step, the red and green communities got broken down into new communities while the blue community remained the same. For this graph again, the local moving and refining steps are carried out, as presented in Fig. 1(e) and Fig. 1(f), respectively. These repetitions take place until an improvement in the partition's modularity value is no longer possible, and the algorithm returns the final partition [28].

5 Graph Pruning

Graph pruning refers to a technique that is used to discover important regions hidden by edges that are considered to be noisy or less significant to the graph and need to be removed [6]. In our case, the graphs built from personality questionnaires become complete weighted graphs that are highly dense in nature, due to which the possibility of identifying optimal communities or clusters by the algorithms reduces. To handle this problem, the application of graph pruning is a necessity. In this case, the Maximum Likelihood Filter (MLF) pruning method proposed by [6] is the best because it works quickly and efficiently, and it was used in both of our methodologies.

According to [6], MLF works by using a null model graph to figure out a p-value for each edge using a marginal probability distribution. Once this is done, only edges with p-values lower than a chosen threshold are considered statistically significant and are retained in the pruned network. Setting the threshold for p-values can impact the number of edges removed. A stricter threshold might remove too many edges, while a loose threshold might retain less informative ones. Edges with p-values higher than the threshold are considered less informative and might be removed as they can introduce noise and mask true underlying relationships in the network [6].

Extracting Questionnaires. All the questionnaire responses are extracted from the SQL-Validator database. These questionnaires can be found in the Appendix. We used the Likert scale method for surveys, which consists of a personality questionnaire based on the Big Five personality model. Each questionnaire consists of 25 questions. The corresponding number of the option selected by the student is stored in the database, and the same is extracted as a dataframe. The administrator, while triggering the program, selects the particular semester from which the data has to be extracted for carrying out the succeeding steps of the implementation process.

Transformation. For carrying out the transformation of the obtained responses, numpy and pandas libraries were used. Also, the values derived from the responses are transformed in order to maintain the correlation between the different personality traits. The exact transformation criteria considered are undisclosed in order to ensure that the questionnaires are genuinely answered, representing their personalities. If an empty response occurs for any question, then that particular value is deleted, as we do not want to score an unanswered question. While the answered responses are replaced with new value scores wherever necessary, after that, for each student, all the scores are summed up uniquely for every questionnaire. So, in this way, we get six new dataframes with transformed scores of students for six personality questionnaires. Finally, all these dataframes are merged or appended to form a single dataframe.

6 Transformation of Questionnaire Scores

6.1 Weights Assignment

In the assignment of the weights part, as previously mentioned, the split of two paths for two approaches begins. All the steps followed in the implementation process are discussed together for both approaches.

Normalization and NMF. Due to the variance in the nature of scores in questionnaires, instead of building edge-weighted graphs directly from the transformed scores in the previous step, normalization is applied for both the first and second approaches. For the implementation, existing methods from the scikit-learn library [20] have been used. Further, for implementing the Non-negative Matrix Factorization technique on the normalized data in the clustering coefficients approach as well, a method from the same library [20] is considered. Adding the NMF technique to the pipeline is an unavoidable task to reduce dimensions from six (six questionnaires) to one. Thus, the resulting dataframe for one component is used for the calculation of weights. Likewise, the dataframe of normalized data is also used for weight calculation in the community detection approach.

Edge Weights Calculation. The next step in the pipeline for both approaches has been to calculate edge weights between two students at a time by considering their scaled scores. As we intend to build undirected weighted graphs, for assigning an edge between two nodes, any of those can be taken as a source, and the other node becomes the target.

Firstly, the scaled scores are transposed to suitable datatypes. Next, a combination function is executed on a pair of selected scores. This operation results in the elicitation of the edge weight between two selected sores, which represents two students [22]. Also, during the computation of edge weights, it is possible for scenarios to occur where the calculation results in an infinite edge weight or cases where the scores of two students are the same. As such, additional data preprocessing steps may be required to handle these exceptional cases and ensure the accuracy of the final results. It is important to carefully monitor and address any instances of infinite edge weights to maintain the integrity of the network analysis. Once all computations are done, we obtain the dataframes with the final edge weights.

Personality Weighted Graphs. Graphs are the final data structures that we use to detect communities and calculate clustering coefficients. In this implementation step, we generate six weighted graphs corresponding to six questionnaires that represent the different personality traits of students for the community detection approach. Similarly, for the clustering coefficients approach, we generate a single weighted graph. The edge weights dataframe from the previous step has the first column, which has the ids of two students, and the remaining column(s) are the weights corresponding to personality traits. So, in order to build a graph, we take the first column from the dataframe and use the split method to obtain source and target nodes for the graphs. In the next step, we merge a weight column with the source and target columns. Lastly, a graph will be created representing the ties between students and the variation in the strength of ties through the weights assigned to them. This procedure is repeated for all the personality graphs. For creating the weighted graphs efficiently, networkx [9] with extensive available documentation has been used to create graphs. However, for carrying out graph pruning and community detection, it was found that the igraph [5] is the most supported package. Hence, from these graphs, corresponding igraph graphs are created.

7 Implementation

In this section, all the steps carried out in the implementation of this work are explained. Also, the recommendation system was tested and deployed on the SQLValidator [19] learning management system. Now given that personality questionnaires have been filled out by students, the raw questionnaire responses are transformed into scores that can potentially be used for grouping students.

After this step, as can be observed from Fig. 2, there is a split into two paths that lead to the two approaches we consider for the recommendation system. In the case of the main approach, the transformed scores are normalized. The calculation of the edge weights using the normalized scores of students is done. The edge-weighted graphs are created from the calculated edge weight. Later, the graphs are pruned by

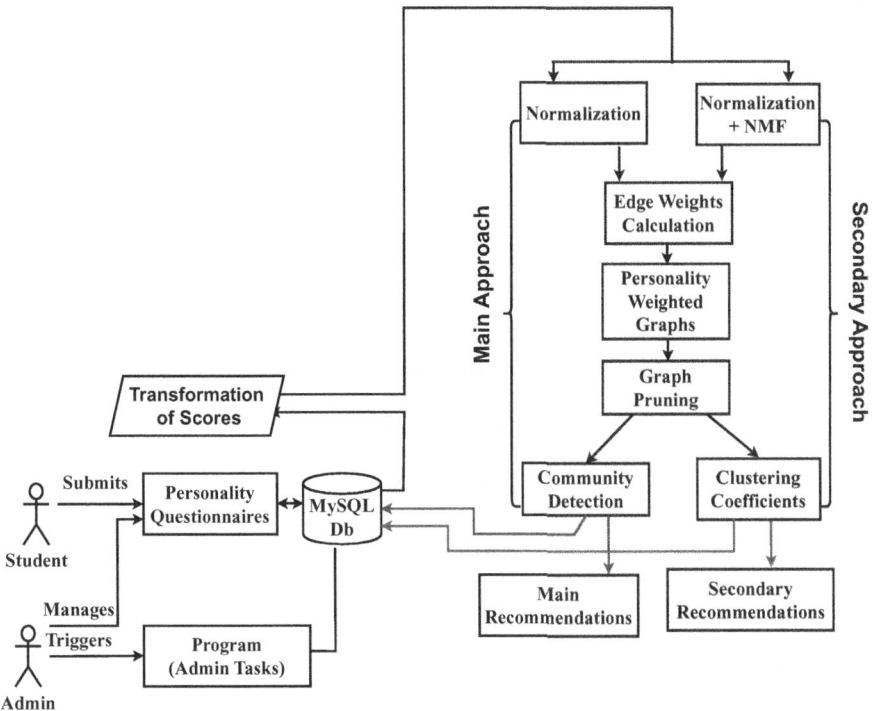

Fig. 2. Workflow of the partner recommendation system.

removing the least significant edges, and then, through the Leiden community detection algorithm [28], students are grouped into communities. In the alternate approach, the transformed scores are normalized, and Non-Negative Matrix Factorization (NMF) is applied to reduce the dimensions of the questionnaire data. The succeeding three steps in this approach are similar to the previous approach. For the pruned graph, the clustering coefficients of students are calculated. Finally, both communities of students are detected through the Leiden algorithm, and the clustering coefficients of students are stored in the database, which is recommended separately for each student through two different pages as the main and alternate recommendations, respectively. For the purpose of generating recommendations, we employ the "find_partition_multiplex" method available in the Leiden algorithm. This method accepts a list of graphs as input and detects communities that are based on all the provided graphs. Alternatively, the find_partition method is also available and can be used to get separate communities for each graph. Furthermore, in order to have the flexibility of forming groups of different sizes, parameters such as max_comm_size and partition method were included as options for selection inside the web application. We considered having options for community sizes between 3 and 6, while the partition methods were modularity vertex partition and surprise vertex partition. A variety of partition methods are available in the package, but considering the nature of graphs, these two are relevant for use in this setting. The six personality graphs, which were derived and trimmed in the previous steps, were used for testing. Communities are detected by considering the method for single-layer graphs as well as the method for multiplex networks. A detailed analogy of the results derived through the application of these methods and different parameters is presented in Sect. 8.

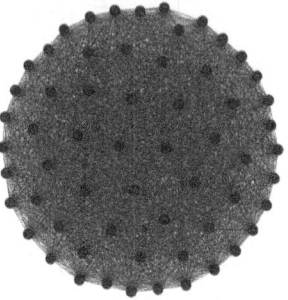

Fig. 3. Without Graph Pruning Technique.

8 Evaluation and Discussion

For the recommendations of study partners to be efficient, the underlying community detection algorithm should create communities of decent quality. To carry out the evaluation, the questionnaire data filled by 60 students were considered for the study. This chapter discusses the evaluation process carried out in two phases: one is comparing the community detection results without applying the graph pruning technique to the data, and another is applying it.

In general, the Leiden algorithm's [28] vertex partition generates the communities for each phase's individual questionnaire graphs, and its comparison to the outcomes of other algorithms through modularity scores comes first. This step helps to decide and justify the suitable and efficient community detection algorithm whose communities can be recommended. Next, we look at the modularity scores of the communities made by the Leiden algorithm through modularity vertex partition and surprise vertex partition for graphs of different sizes. We do this for each individual graph. Additionally, for the multiplex network or combined questionnaire graphs, similar to the previous case, the communities generated by the Leiden algorithm through modularity vertex partition and surprise vertex partition for different sizes are compared, but through their improvement scores. Lastly, only in the second phase with graph-pruned data is a similarity check carried out through adjusted mutual information between the communities generated through different algorithms and also different vertex partition methods. It is to be noted that the modularity metric is one of the most widely used metrics to evaluate communities, and its value ranges between -1 and 1, with 1 being the highest, and every community detection algorithm is intended to maximize this value. On the other hand, adjusted mutual information ranges between 0 and 1, where 1 means the communities generated with different algorithms or methods are identical or the same.

8.1 Without Graph Pruning Technique

The first phase of the evaluation without applying the graph pruning technique essentially means considering the questionnaire graphs with all their existing weighted edges. In this regard, the graphs consisted of 60 nodes, 1770 edges, average and max degree values of 59, and a density of 1, as shown in Fig. 3. Even though such densely connected graphs make it difficult to identify strong community structures, it will be a useful step to examine the way Leiden algorithm performs on both noisy graphs and noiseless graphs.

8.2 With Graph Pruning Technique

The graph pruning technique through a maximum likelihood filter with different edge retention percentages has been applied separately to all the noisy graphs, and after analyzing the results, it was found that when 15% significant edges were retained, the algorithms showed the best possible modularity and adjusted mutual information scores. Hence, all the results discussed in this section are applicable to our 15% significant edge retained graphs. As can be observed in the figures below, the graph pruning step retains the most significant edges from all six questionnaire graphs and drops the least significant edges, thereby improving the cohesiveness of the detected communities. Figures 4, 5, 6, 7, 8 and 9 show the questionnaire graph after applying the graph pruning technique.

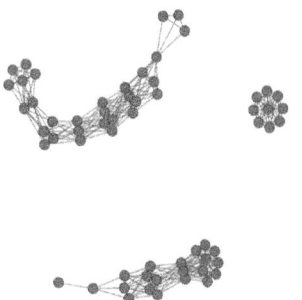

Fig. 4. Communicating and Role questionnaire graph

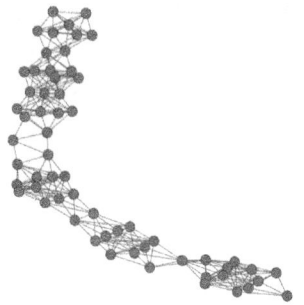

Fig. 5. Optimist or Pessimist questionnaire graph.

Table 1 shows the properties of all six questionnaire graphs after the application of graph pruning to retain 15% significant edges. Consequently, in comparison to the previously stated properties of graphs in Sect. 8.1, the edges are reduced thereby the degrees are also significantly lowered, and overall the graphs are less densely connected. For the graph in Fig. 3, the modularity score and the number of detected communities for the Leiden algorithm is shown in Table 2.

 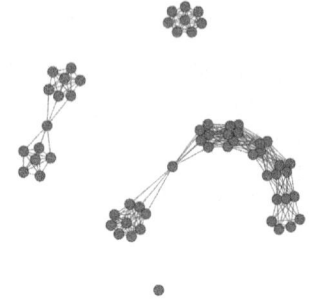

Fig. 6. Tough and Tender questionnaire graph

Fig. 7. Success and Risk questionnaire graph

Table 1. Properties of individual questionnaire graphs after applying graph pruning technique.

Questionnaire	Nodes	Edges	Average Degree	Max Degree	Density
Extrovert or Introvert	60	274	9.133	15	0.154
Optimist or Pessimist	60	269	8.966	13	0.151
Tough-minded or Tender-minded	60	266	8.866	15	0.150
Managing People and Resources	60	293	9.766	16	0.165
Communicating and Role	60	266	8.866	15	0.150
Success and Risk	60	266	8.866	14	0.150

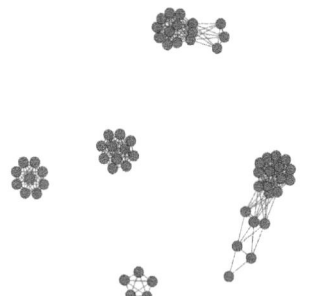

Fig. 8. People and resource management questionnaire graph

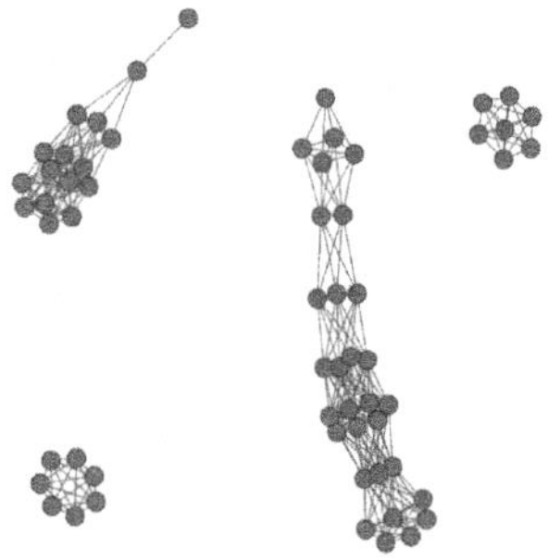

Fig. 9. Extrovert and Introvert questionnaire graph

Table 2 makes it clear that the Leiden algorithm through modularity vertex partition did not get the best modularity scores for all six questionnaire graphs. Also, the total number of communities detected portrays the same pattern, as the system is not able to detect communities properly. However, in Table 3, it is clearly observable that the application of graph pruning improved the modularity scores. The Leiden algorithm achieved an optimum modularity score for all six questionnaire graphs. Analogous to the changes in the modularity scores, the detected communities count also displayed

Table 2. Modularity scores for Leiden algorithm on individual questionnaire graphs before applying graph pruning technique and respective number of detected communities.

Questionnaire	Leiden Modularity scores	Number of detected communities
Extrovert or Introvert	0.336	4
Optimist or Pessimist	0.373	3
Tough-minded or Tender-minded	0.299	3
Managing People and Resources	0.322	3
Communicating and Role	0.280	3
Success and Risk	0.320	4

Table 3. Modularity scores for Leiden algorithm on individual questionnaire graphs after applying graph pruning technique and respective number of detected communities.

Questionnaire	Leiden Modularity scores	Number of detected communities
Extrovert or Introvert	0.733	6
Optimist or Pessimist	0.694	5
Tough-minded or Tender-minded	0.621	6
Managing People and Resources	0.752	6
Communicating and Role	0.705	7
Success and Risk	0.710	7

positive changes, as presented in Table 3. It is evident from this table that there is an increase in the detected communities. It seems that the graph pruning has removed all the least significant edges present previously, which made the Leiden algorithm form weakly connected and lesser communities with low modularities. Consequently, the communities now have strong internal ties and weak external ties, and thereby, the changes in the community structure led to more communities. Next, an attempt to understand the similarities between the communities generated by the algorithms is discussed.

8.3 Comparison of Modularity Scores of the Leiden Algorithm for Different Community Sizes Before and After Graph Pruning

The results achieved so far after the application of the graph pruning technique on the questionnaire graphs demonstrated significant improvements in communities detected by all the algorithms. Table 4 shows the pre-graph pruning phase, where negative modularity scores were obtained for all the graphs, irrespective of the size and the poste-graph pruning phase where modularity scores of the Leiden algorithm through modularity vertex partition for different community sizes improved significantly.

Also, we further observe from Table 4 that the Leiden algorithm managed to achieve positive modularity scores for all the specified community sizes between 3 and 6. For every graph, when a community size of 6 is specified, the algorithm gives a high mod-

Table 4. Comparison of Modularity scores of Leiden algorithm through Modularity Vertex Partition for different community sizes on individual questionnaire graphs before and after applying graph pruning technique.

	Pre-Graph Pruning				Post-Graph Pruning			
Questionnaire	Size 3	Size 4	Size 5	Size 6	Size 3	Size 4	Size 5	Size 6
Extrovert or Introvert	−0.015	−0.015	−0.015	−0.015	0.150	0.226	0.286	0.354
Optimist or Pessimist	−0.015	−0.015	−0.015	−0.015	0.162	0.243	0.302	0.353
Tough-minded or Tender-minded	−0.015	−0.015	−0.015	−0.015	0.153	0.222	0.312	0.377
Managing People and Resources	−0.015	−0.015	−0.015	−0.015	0.138	0.209	0.276	0.333
Communicating and Role	−0.016	−0.016	−0.016	−0.016	0.161	0.234	0.293	0.368
Success and Risk	−0.015	−0.015	−0.015	−0.015	0.150	0.232	0.305	0.381

ularity score compared to the other three sizes. We can directly say by observing the table that when a high community size is specified, the modularity scores will possibly be higher than the sizes lower than it. Also, an indirect inference is that when community sizes are not specified, the algorithm tries to freely group more nodes into each community based on the strength of their cohesion. Therefore, Table 3 about the Leiden algorithm without a specified community size has better modularity values than the Leiden algorithm for all the specified community sizes in Table 4.

However, for the purpose of recommending study partners to a student for team formation, a tradeoff is to be made between the modularity score and communities of desirable sizes. In this regard, obtaining communities of desirable sizes is prioritized over achieving the highest possible modularity scores. It is also to be highlighted that obtaining negative modularity values is not desirable. Another aspect of the comparison in the Leiden algorithm besides the community sizes is the type of vertex partition method. Both modularity vertex partition and surprise vertex partition are compared in this phase again, as mentioned previously, to decide the best method to use in our pipeline.

Results of the Leiden algorithm's surprise vertex partition method are mentioned in Table 5. As observed before in the pre-graph pruning phase, the surprise vertex partition method achieved positive modularity scores that are close to the modularity vertex partition method's scores in the post graph pruning phase. Furthermore, the surprise vertex partition method also achieved a high modularity score for all the graphs when a community size of 6 was specified. Both methods performed equally well in terms of modularity scores.

Observation

An important observation when the communities formed by both strategies were analyzed is that the surprise vertex partition method formed more singleton communities than the modularity vertex partition method. This is because the surprise algorithm is a greedy algorithm that iterates over each operation until it exhausts all possible improvements, and no further improvements can be found. Thus, the detection of communities

Table 5. Adjusted Mutual Information score similarity of communities formed by Leiden algorithm's Modularity Vertex Partition with Surprise Vertex Partition on individual questionnaire graphs before and after applying graph pruning technique.

	Pre-Graph Pruning				Post-Graph Pruning			
Questionnaire	Size 3	Size 4	Size 5	Size 6	Size 3	Size 4	Size 5	Size 6
Extrovert or Introvert	0.143	0.221	0.295	0.367	0.530	0.561	0.552	0.554
Optimist or Pessimist	0.155	0.245	0.311	0.374	0.272	0.256	0.393	0.464
Tough-minded or Tender-minded	0.141	0.238	0.291	0.350	0.274	0.373	0.457	0.551
Managing People and Resources	0.137	0.205	0.288	0.333	0.716	0.586	0.784	0.918
Communicating and Role	0.161	0.217	0.303	0.370	0.631	0.633	0.777	0.752
Success and Risk	0.152	0.225	0.305	0.367	0.361	0.489	0.655	0.590

through surprise vertex partition, which is based on the asymptotic surprise metric, creates many differences in the community structure in comparison to modularity vertex partition, which is based on the modularity metric. This is an important consideration to be mentioned again, as another possible reason for the differences is the high number of singleton communities that occur through the surprise vertex partition method. In other words, the surprise vertex partition method did not group some nodes into any communities and left each of them as an individual community. Additionally, the surprise vertex partition method formed many communities smaller than the specified community size. Such deviations are not desirable, as we prefer that the optimum number of students be grouped into communities of specified sizes, thus avoiding students being singled out or being part of small groups. As a result, the modularity vertex partition method is a more preferable choice for our community detection system. In this regard, we prefer to consider detecting communities through the modularity vertex partition method as the best applicable method for our work.

9 Conclusion and Future Efforts

The agenda of this work was to develop a recommender system that helps students find suitable study partners for group assignments or projects. To this end, we have devised two approaches for grouping similar students based on their questionnaire responses. Recommendations from both of these come under the collaborative filtering method, as they group the students based on personality similarities in their answers. For deciding the algorithm for the first approach, which is the main focus in this work, our primary one, varied algorithms designed to achieve detection of communities, is evaluated through their modularity scores alongside the choice to form preferred-size teams. The results confirmed that Leiden is the best community detection algorithm for grouping students.

In the implementation process, as mentioned in previous sections, graph pruning through the maximum likelihood filter showed significant improvement in the Leiden algorithm. We evaluated our results by comparing the modularity scores for the detected communities or groups before and after the pruning. Regarding reliability, the Leiden algorithm provides an option through the multiplex partition method to form groups of desired sizes, considering the responses to all six personality questionnaires.

Limitations

Although, through the evaluation of the Leiden algorithm on the questionnaires, it was shown that this approach to detecting communities is comparatively better than the other algorithms, it is not a perfect detection. This is because optimizing the modularity metric is an NP-Hard problem, which makes it impossible to find out the correctness of the communities. Multiple intrinsic metrics can possibly be applied in the process of detecting communities, and the results can be analyzed to approximately estimate their correctness. Another limitation in both approaches is the trade-off between attaining high modularity and the level of graph pruning. The level of pruning is decided manually only through multiple trials on the questionnaire graphs and the resulting modularity scores. The second limitation can be tackled to an extent as mentioned in the future scope.

Acknowledgement. We thank all reviewers for their constructive feedback.

Appendix

A Extrovert or Introvert Survey

1. Enter your Group and Role
2. Do you prefer to work alone, or as part of a team?
3. How much do you enjoy social gatherings?
4. What is your ideal way of celebrating your birthday?
5. Are you more comfortable when talking to people on a one-to-one basis or in a group discussion?
6. How quickly do you become bored and restless when performing routine tasks?
7. When travelling alone on a long train journey would you be likely to strike up a long conversation with a complete stranger sitting next to you?
8. How often do you like to let your hair down, let yourself go and have a real good time?
9. If you were asked to give a speech at a function, would you feel happy about doing this?
10. How easily do you make friends?
11. If you need to approach someone in high authority for a favor, would you prefer to ask them:
12. How quickly are you on the dance floor at a social function?
13. Would you describe yourself as a leader or a follower?
14. What would be your reaction if someone asked you to sell some raffle tickets for charity?
15. Do you think people see you as a fun person?

16. What would be your reaction if the position of chair suddenly became vacant on a committee on which you were sitting?
17. How often do you let your opinions be known?
18. Do you enjoy being the centre of attention?
19. Which of the following words would you say is the most applicable to you?
20. Do you enjoy making small talk at buffet lunches?
21. Do you prefer to discuss things face-to-face or over the telephone?
22. Would you go out of your way to meet 'the right people'?
23. Which of the following words would you say is the most applicable to you?
24. Do you enjoy performing your party piece at Christmas parties and other occasions?
25. Would you appear naked on a charity calendar?
26. Do you ever run out of things to say when talking to someone you have just met?

B Tough or Tender Survey

1. Enter your Group and Role
2. I always seem to find myself rooting for the underdog.
3. I admire people who are prepared to admit they were wrong.
4. I feel great sympathy for street beggars.
5. I believe that there is such a thing as love at first sight.
6. I always feel some sympathy for celebrities who are having a bad time in the press.
7. I am turned off completely by vulgar jokes and sexual innuendo.
8. After a serious argument with my partner all I want to do is make up as quickly as possible.
9. If someone does me a bad turn I don't waste time thinking of revenge.
10. My heart rules my head more than my head rules my heart.
11. I would put in a good word for a work colleague who I thought deserved my support.
12. I detest watching movies that contain excessive violence.
13. I feel very sorry for people who always seem to be the butt of other people's jokes.
14. I would encourage anyone to talk over their troubles with me.
15. I have always ensured that I put aside some quality time to spend with my partner.
16. I always buy my partner a card or present on St. Valentine's Day.
17. On occasions my eyes have filled up with tears when watching a movie, be it happy or sad.
18. Do you enjoy being the centre of attention?
19. I would always go out of my way to help someone who is going through an emotional trauma.
20. I would find it extremely difficult to tell anyone some real home truths.
21. I have never found it difficult to forgive and forget.
22. I like stroking cats and=or dogs.
23. I find it difficult to say 'No' when asked for a favor.
24. I am as supportive of others as I am ambitious for my own aspirations.
25. I often feel happy for other people.
26. People should be much more concerned about other people.

C Success and Risk Survey

1. Enter your Group and Role
2. Getting on in business requires ruthlessness.
3. I might lack some of the years of experience offered by other candidates but my success comes from the energy and determination that I have to make things happen.
4. My success is due to my ability to think strategically while overseeing day-to-day activities.
5. Success comes to a great team empowered by exemplary management.
6. My success is due to my strong interpersonal skills.
7. Drive and determination are the keys to my success.
8. My success is due to my ability to think laterally and outside of the box.
9. My success is due to my full understanding of the marketplace and competitors' trends.
10. The higher the risk, the higher the potential return.
11. The importance of avoiding loss is often underestimated.
12. Regulations stifle creativity.
13. Success belongs to the bold.
14. Provided the customer is happy, everything else should bode well.
15. A problem shared is a problem halved.
16. It is better to double margins than the customer base.

D Optimist or Pessimist Survey

1. Enter your Group and Role.
2. I believe that superstitious beliefs, e.g. 'breaking a mirror brings 7 years' bad luck', are bunkum.
3. I never even notice the fire regulations when staying in a hotel, let alone read them.
4. I believe in keeping my aspirations high at all times.
5. You must speculate to accumulate.
6. When one door closes another one always opens.
7. I never lose sleep through worrying.
8. I am constantly on the lookout for opportunities to move on to new and exciting ventures.
9. In life, there is an ideal partner for everyone.
10. Every dog has his day.
11. In the long run, things always turn out for the better.
12. If I lent money to a friend, it would never occur to me that I might not get it back.
13. I fully expect that one day I will be a big winner on the lottery or premium bonds.
14. I never worry about my health.
15. Things are never quite as bad as they appear.
16. It is a waste of time going to the doctor with minor complaints such as a mild dose of 'flu.
17. If at first you don't succeed, you should try, try and try again.

18. I rarely or never worry about my financial situation.
19. I am always hopeful that the next stroke of good fortune is just around the corner.
20. It is always possible to find a silver lining to every cloud if you look hard enough and long enough.
21. Ultimately, good will always triumph over evil.
22. I look forward to the post arriving in the morning.
23. I very rarely carry an umbrella around with me.
24. I always look forward to the future with high expectations.
25. Something positive always comes from adversity.
26. I am all in favor of taking calculated risks.

E Managing People and Resources Survey

1. It is better to focus on selling a few more products rather than worry about how much we are spending on stationery.
2. Everyone makes mistakes so it is best if we report them immediately.
3. I would feel uncomfortable in a situation where resources were being used that did not represent best value for money.
4. I understand the importance of effective listening.
5. To manage people well you have to get fully involved in the detail.
6. Above all else, good management includes trusting people to do the job.
7. Yes, managing people is important but it must come second to fulfilling the client's expectations.
8. I wish more credit was given to all the positive outcomes that you can't put numbers on.
9. I would not normally expect to be part of the important decision making process.
10. I could make recommendations that went against my personal beliefs.
11. Only those qualified in a subject area should contribute to a debate.
12. I feel happiest when I can implement defined regulatory processes.
13. I expect to take joint responsibility for important decisions and am comfortable to provide a justification for the conclusions reached.
14. I would expect most decisions to be based predominantly on numerical information.
15. When painful choices have to be made I find it difficult to commit myself.
16. When information is incomplete a decision is best deferred.
17. The decisions that really shape an organization or policy are best handed down from senior management.
18. The views of someone who has been in an organization only a short time are not as valid as those of someone with long service.
19. If you know something is right then it is important to keep telling people no matter how repetitive it becomes.
20. A compromise is rarely good for business.

F Communicating and Role Survey

1. Above all else my success to date is due to my ability to build and maintain business relationships.
2. If a colleague is performing below par then they can expect honest, constructive feedback from me.
3. When all the hard work has been done, the key points identified and the recommendations formulated then I feel comfortable if others have the job of selling the policy.
4. I pride myself in being able to do a high-pressure job while dealing sensitively with people and issues.
5. I have a very direct approach.
6. Knowledge is a commodity and so I prefer to keep it to myself.
7. I am happiest producing written material and much prefer that role to one that involves presenting an argument orally.
8. Being opinionated is not always a bad thing.
9. I am used to presenting recommendations to groups of people drawn from all levels of an institution or organization.
10. I do not consider it a part of my current job to suggest ways in which something could be done more efficiently.
11. Being personable can make up for many potential pitfalls.
12. If you can get people to buy into a set of objectives or targets then everyone will work that bit harder towards a shared goal.
13. I wish I could more often make novel links between previously unconnected issues.
14. I want a job where my cool-headed approach will serve me well.
15. I like nothing better than to get my teeth into a challenge.
16. I work best when I can get on with my job with the minimum of distractions.
17. I feel I perform best in a job where I need to be copied into every e-mail.
18. My current job is 24/7 and my next one will be - it goes with the territory.
19. I feel resentment if my working life starts to impinge on my home life.
20. I prefer a high degree of order and tend to get stressed if things do not go to plan.

References

1. Al-Sharoa, E.M., Bara'M, A., Alkhassaweneh, M.A.: Robust community detection in graphs. IEEE Access **9**, 118757–118770 (2021)
2. Blondel, V.D., Guillaume, J.L., Lambiotte, R., Lefebvre, E.: Fast unfolding of communities in large networks. J. Stat. Mech: Theory Exp. **2008**(10), P10008 (2008)
3. Chakraborty, T., Dalmia, A., Mukherjee, A., Ganguly, N.: Metrics for community analysis: a survey. ACM Comput. Surv. (CSUR) **50**(4), 1–37 (2017)
4. Clauset, A., Newman, M.E., Moore, C.: Finding community structure in very large networks. Phys. Rev. E **70**(6), 066111 (2004)
5. Csardi, G., Nepusz, T., et al.: The igraph software package for complex network research. Int. J. Complex Syst. **1695**(5), 1–9 (2006)
6. Dianati, N.: Unwinding the hairball graph: pruning algorithms for weighted complex networks. Phys. Rev. E **93**(1), 012304 (2016)

7. Fortunato, S., Hric, D.: Community detection in networks: a user guide. Phys. Rep. **659**, 1–44 (2016)
8. Gates, K.M., Henry, T., Steinley, D., Fair, D.A.: A Monte Carlo evaluation of weighted community detection algorithms. Front. Neuroinform. **10**, 45 (2016)
9. Hagberg, A.A., Schult, D.A., Swart, P.J.: Exploring network structure, dynamics, and function using networkx. In: Varoquaux, G., Vaught, T., Millman, J. (eds.) Proceedings of the 7th Python in Science Conference, pp. 11 – 15. Pasadena, CA USA (2008)
10. Huang, X., Chen, D., Ren, T., Wang, D.: A survey of community detection methods in multilayer networks. Data Min. Knowl. Disc. **35**, 1–45 (2021)
11. Jiang, H., Liu, Z., Liu, C., Su, Y., Zhang, X.: Community detection in complex networks with an ambiguous structure using central node based link prediction. Knowl.-Based Syst. **195**, 105626 (2020)
12. Jie, Y., Zhishuai, L., Qiu, X.: Community detection in complex networks: algorithms and analysis. In: Lu, Y., Wu, X., Zhang, X. (eds.) ISCTCS 2014. CCIS, vol. 520, pp. 238–244. Springer, Heidelberg (2015). https://doi.org/10.1007/978-3-662-47401-3_31
13. Kanawati, R.: Multiplex network mining: a brief survey. IEEE Intell. Informatics Bull. **16**(1), 24–27 (2015)
14. Lai, E.R.: Collaboration: A literature review. Pearson Publisher. Retrieved November **11**, 2016 (2011)
15. Lazarenko, D., Bonald, T.: Pairwise adjusted mutual information. arXiv preprint arXiv:2103.12641 (2021)
16. Newman, M.E., Girvan, M.: Finding and evaluating community structure in networks. Phys. Rev. E **69**(2), 026113 (2004)
17. Obionwu, C.V., Karl, M., Broneske, D., Hawlitschek, A., Blockhaus, P., Saake, G.: A strategy for structuring teams collaboration in university course projects. In: ICSBT (2023). https://api.semanticscholar.org/CorpusID:259874711
18. Obionwu, C.V., Walia, D.S., Tiwari, T., Ghosh, T., Broneske, D., Saake, G.: Towards a strategy for developing a project partner recommendation system for university course projects. In: 2023 6th World Conference on Computing and Communication Technologies (WCCCT), pp. 144–151. IEEE (2023)
19. Obionwu, V., Broneske, D., Hawlitschek, A., Köppen, V., Saake, G.: SQLValidator – An Online Student Playground to Learn SQL. Datenbank. Spektrum, pp. 1–9 (2021)
20. Pedregosa, F., et al.: Scikit-learn: machine learning in Python. J. Mach. Learn. Res. **12**, 2825–2830 (2011)
21. Pons, P., Latapy, M.: Computing communities in large networks using random walks. In: Yolum, I., Güngör, T., Gürgen, F., Özturan, C. (eds.) ISCIS 2005. LNCS, vol. 3733, pp. 284–293. Springer, Heidelberg (2005). https://doi.org/10.1007/11569596_31
22. Puga, C., Niemann, U., Unnikrishnan, V., Schleicher, M., Schlee, W., Spiliopoulou, M.: Discovery of patient phenotypes through multi-layer network analysis on the example of tinnitus. In: 2021 IEEE 8th International Conference on Data Science and Advanced Analytics (DSAA), pp. 1–10. IEEE (2021)
23. Raghavan, U.N., Albert, R., Kumara, S.: Near linear time algorithm to detect community structures in large-scale networks. Phys. Rev. E **76**(3), 036106 (2007)
24. Rani, P., Shokeen, J.: Designing a project leader recommender system using twitter feed analysis. In: 2019 International Conference on Machine Learning, Big Data, Cloud and Parallel Computing (COMITCon), pp. 56–60. IEEE (2019)
25. Rosvall, M., Bergstrom, C.T.: Maps of random walks on complex networks reveal community structure. Proc. Nat. Acad. Sci. **105**(4), 1118–1123 (2008)
26. Sankar, A., Kiruthikaa, K., et al.: Community based recommendation in e-learning systems. J. e-Learning Knowl. Soc. **10**(1) (2014)

27. Thanh, T.N., Morgan, M., Butler, M., Marriott, K.: Perfect match: facilitating study partner matching. In: Proceedings of the 50th ACM Technical Symposium on Computer Science Education, pp. 1102–1108 (2019)
28. Traag, V.A., Waltman, L., Van Eck, N.J.: From louvain to leiden: guaranteeing well-connected communities. Sci. Rep. **9**(1), 5233 (2019)
29. Traag, V.A., Aldecoa, R., Delvenne, J.C.: Detecting communities using asymptotical surprise. Physical review. E, Statistical, nonlinear, and soft matter physics **92 2**, 022816 (2015) https://api.semanticscholar.org/CorpusID:6995134
30. Wu, S., Sun, J., Tang, J.: Patent partner recommendation in enterprise social networks. In: Proceedings of the sixth ACM International Conference on Web Search and Data Mining, pp. 43–52 (2013)
31. Xu, B., Yang, D.: Study partners recommendation for xmoocs learners. Comput. Intell. Neurosci. **2015**, 15–15 (2015)
32. Zhang, P.: Evaluating accuracy of community detection using the relative normalized mutual information. J. Stat. Mech: Theory Exp. **2015**(11), P11006 (2015)

Exploring the Impact of Innovation and Competition on Profitability in Internet-Based SMEs: A Survey Analysis

Nabil Mohammad Abu Bakar(✉) and Mahady Hasan

Department of Computer Science and Engineering, Independent University Bangladesh, Dhaka, Bangladesh
{2010797,mahady}@iub.edu.bd

Abstract. The aim of this paper is to explore the interaction between innovation and competition in internet-based SMEs and to identify key factors influencing innovation. The author investigates how competition impacts industry innovation by analyzing product market dynamics and conducting a comprehensive survey asking industry experts about the challenges that hinder innovation and competition. Additionally, the study reviews various models and case studies to understand how competition drives innovation. The findings suggest that increased competition enhances productivity across multiple industries. The author also provides policy recommendations to support innovation and competition, which are crucial for regulators aiming to boost these elements in small and medium-sized internet-based enterprises. This paper offers valuable insights into the relationship between innovation and competition and proposes actionable policies to promote both.

Keywords: Innovation · Competition · Sustainable development · Policy recommendation · Business process

1 Introduction

Competition plays a pivotal role in driving innovation across industries, and its impact can be understood through two primary channels [1,2]. The first channel pertains to the reduction in the number of firms engaging in research and development (R&D), which, while keeping product market profits constant, has the potential to slow down the pace of innovation within the industry. The second channel is closely tied to the direct influence of competition on product market outcomes, thereby affecting the profit differential between the industry leader and its competitors. Consequently, the level of competition in the product market has a significant bearing on the incentives motivating firms to innovate. The specific dynamics of the product market game determine whether a decrease in competition within the product market will result in an expansion or contraction of the profit gap between industry leaders and followers [3,4].

The influence of competition on innovation has captured substantial attention within the realm of economic literature. On one hand, certain studies assert that competition serves as a catalyst for innovation by motivating firms to allocate resources toward research and development (R&D) and by preventing monopolistic entities from stifling innovative endeavors. Conversely, an opposing viewpoint suggests that intense competition might impede innovation by discouraging firms from assuming risks and making substantial R&D investments [5]. Notably, industries characterized by diminished competition often exhibit lower innovation rates, whereas firms with commanding market shares are typically driven to engage in preemptive innovation initiatives [6]. Nevertheless, some research indicates a modest positive correlation between the intensity of R&D activities and market concentration, signifying that in markets marked by high fixed costs attributed to R&D competition, only a limited number of firms can viably participate [7]. Despite these nuances, it remains evident that competition remains a pivotal driver in the realm of R&D, with firms channeling their efforts into R&D to secure a competitive edge within the market [8].

The relationship between competition, R&D investment, and innovation remains far from settled. While some research suggests that competition serves as a catalyst for innovation, conflicting studies propose the opposite viewpoint. It is apparent that further investigation is necessary to unravel the intricate dynamics of this relationship and to comprehend its implications for both businesses and policymakers [9].

Prominent figures in the business world, such as Michael Porter [10], and research teams like the one at McKinsey Global Institute [11], have independently observed that heightened competition within product markets among firms in a given nation correlates with increased productivity for companies within that country. In contrast, the post-publication version, which is the focus of this paper, delves into a comprehensive analysis of how innovation and competition interact in the context of internet-based SMEs, identifying influential factors and proposing policies to address challenges related to maintaining innovation and competition within this specific business landscape.

In today's complex business landscape, organizations encounter formidable obstacles in the realms of innovation and competition, often navigating these challenges without adequate regulatory support.

To delve deeper into these challenges and gain a comprehensive understanding of their nuances, The author executed an online survey involving 22 small and medium-sized internet-based firms. This survey featured participation from key personnel. The survey was thoughtfully constructed, employing tailored questionnaires meticulously designed to delineate the intricacies of the landscape pertaining to innovation and competition, while also scrutinizing their interplay with product market outcomes.

The primary objective of this paper is to conduct a comprehensive analysis of the relationship between competition and innovation in the context of small internet-based firms. This analysis aims to identify the crucial factors that promote both competition and innovation. Additionally, the study seeks to propose policy recommendations that can be employed to foster innovation and competition within this specific business landscape. The key questions for this research are given below,

Q1. What strategies and measures can be implemented to facilitate partnerships and enhance cooperation among businesses engaged in research and development ?

Q2. What regulatory frameworks are currently in place to establish a fair and competitive environment, with a particular focus on minimizing entry barriers for new players, such as the implementation of net neutrality for internet-based firms?

In pursuit of these research objectives and questions, author approach encompassed a multifaceted methodology. The author initiated the research process with an exhaustive review of existing literature to understand the current state of knowledge in the field. Subsequently, The author conducted a survey involving 22 small internet-based firms, aiming to uncover gaps and challenges in the existing literature. Our survey findings illuminate that many companies within this sector grapple with analogous regulatory hurdles. While some have made partial strides in overcoming these challenges, start-ups, in particular, face significant obstacles that hinder their ability to compete effectively in the market. In response to these identified issues, The author propose a policy guideline that takes into account the dynamics of product market payoffs, with the ultimate goal of optimizing both innovation and competition.

2 Research Background

Public policies encompassing regulatory, monetary, tax, procurement, standards, human capital development, and market access play a pivotal role in shaping an environment that either fosters or hinders innovation, as noted in previous research [29]. These policies can exert a profound influence on the innovative capabilities of firms and their ability to compete effectively in the market.

The potential profitability stemming from innovation stands out as another critical determinant of a firm's motivation to engage in innovation activities. The magnitude of the expected rewards associated with innovation hinges on various factors, including the scale of the innovation itself, the size of the target market, and the extent to which the act of innovating erodes the profits derived from the firm's pre-innovation technology [26]. A larger potential for profit from innovation can serve as a potent incentive for firms to channel resources into research and development endeavors.

However, firms that encounter limited pre-innovation competition, characterized by a steeply declining demand curve, may enjoy substantial ongoing economic profits. In such cases, these firms might be motivated to safeguard their existing profits by slowing down their innovation efforts [26]. This underscores the pivotal role of competition in stimulating firms to innovate and invest in research and development. Competitive pressures often act as a catalyst, compelling firms to continuously improve and innovate in order to maintain or enhance their market positions.

Peter Howitt [12] contends that it is unwise to relax competition policy with the expectation of promoting innovation, as increased competition often serves as a powerful motivator for innovation. Nevertheless, certain studies have identified a modest positive correlation between R&D investment intensity and market concentration [13]. This correlation can be attributed to the fact that fewer firms can viably participate in markets characterized by substantial fixed costs stemming from R&D competition.

In a study conducted by Lin and Wu [14], they delve into the impact of competition on firm innovation and unearth evidence pointing towards a non-linear relationship. Their research suggests that moderate levels of competition can act as a catalyst for innovation, whereas excessive competition might have an adverse effect.

In a deterministic R&D model outlined by Dasgupta and Stiglitz [15], they explore the role of product market competition in a scenario where firms are symmetric, meaning they have identical cost structures and capabilities. These firms compete in a manner reminiscent of Cournot competition, where each firm chooses its output level assuming the output levels of its competitors are fixed. While developing process innovations and assuming an isoelastic demand function, the authors demonstrate that an increase in the number of firms leads to decreased individual firm investments but results in an overall increase in aggregate investment.

Reinganum introduces a dynamic element into this [1] research by investigating a series of patent races in which firms engage in competition across a progression of innovation levels. Her findings parallel those of Dasgupta and Stiglitz [15] in a scenario where the outcomes in the product market remain unaffected by the number of competing firms.

Aghion et al., in their series of studies [16, 17], along with subsequent research, have explored the influence of product market competition on innovation choices within duopolistic markets. In these models, the duopoly competition centers around pricing strategies, with the intensity of competition being determined by the level of substitutability between the products offered by the firms. The researchers have noted that innovation tends to be driven by what they term the "escape competition" effect. This effect hinges on the disparity between the benefits firms experience before and after introducing an innovation. When there are significant advantages to be gained by "escaping" the existing competitive landscape, the likelihood of innovation taking place increases.

Numerous studies have provided evidence supporting the existence of an "inverted U" relationship between market competition and innovation. In particular, these studies have shown that industries characterized by oligopolistic market structures, where only a few dominant firms operate, tend to demonstrate higher levels of innovation when compared to industries with either highly competitive or monopolistic structures [18, 19].

Indeed, Baumol [20] posits that oligopolistic industries stimulate firms to innovate due to the intense competitive pressures and the imperative to distinguish their products from those of their competitors. Conversely, monopolistic industries may not experience the same competitive drive, and highly competitive markets can sometimes result in a "race to the bottom" in terms of innovation, as companies prioritize cost-cutting over product differentiation [19].

An intriguing example from a study [34] in the tobacco industries of the United States and United Kingdom suggests that periods of heightened competition were linked to more rapid technological innovation, even though both industries were monopolistic at different times in their history. Nevertheless, it's important to acknowledge that case studies like these face challenges in establishing causality and isolating the sole effect of competition [21].

Despite these complexities, research indicates that greater product market competition among firms within a nation can lead to enhanced productivity across various industries, encompassing both manufacturing and services [22].

The relationship between market competition and innovation is indeed multifaceted, and its dynamics can vary significantly across industries and contexts. Contrary to Schumpeterian theories, which suggest that monopolistic or less competitive markets foster more innovation due to larger firms having more resources for R&D, some researchers have argued that strengthening competition policy could have an overall positive impact on innovation [17]. This complexity underscores the fact that the level of competition in a market plays a pivotal role in influencing firms' incentives to invest in Research and Development (R&D). Firms undertake R&D investments with the aim of gaining a competitive advantage in the product market, a goal that is directly affected by the level of competition and the subsequent product market payoffs [8].

Numerous studies have reported a positive and noteworthy correlation between R&D activities conducted by businesses, public institutions, and higher education institutions, and innovation outcomes [23, 24]. Business R&D, in particular, is considered instrumental in the development of novel and innovative products and services [25].

However, it's essential to recognize a potential downside of competition, which is the prospect of excessive R&D expenditures in a patent race [8]. This scenario implies that companies may engage in costly R&D efforts primarily to secure patents and thwart their competitors, rather than focusing on developing innovative products that ultimately benefit consumers.

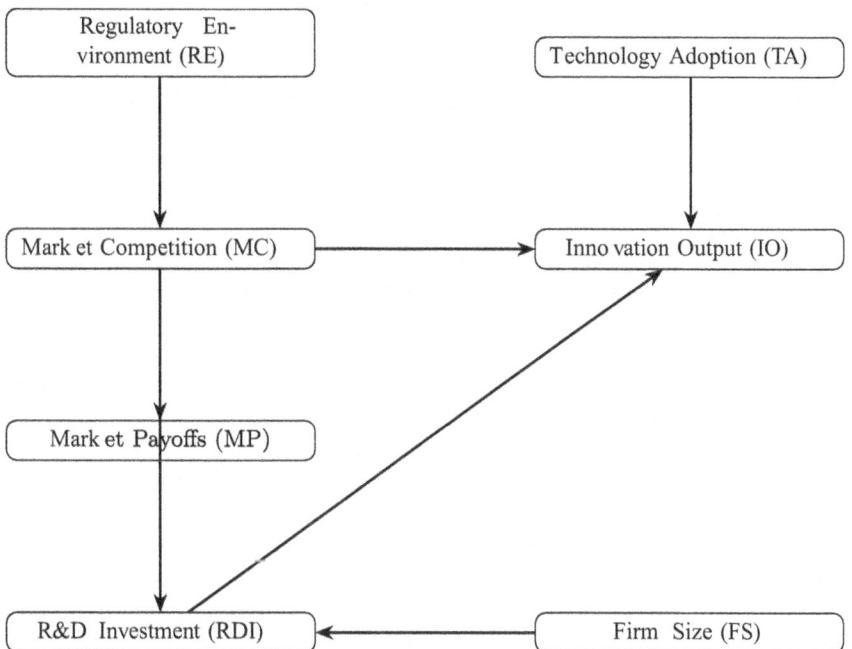

Fig. 1. Causal model showing the relationships between market competition, R&D investment, and innovation output for internet-based firms.

The causal model depicted in Fig. 1 illustrates the relationships between key factors influencing innovation in internet-based firms. Regulatory Environment (RE) impacts Market Competition (MC), which in turn affects Market Payoffs (MP) and R&D Investment (RDI). Increased competition drives firms to invest in R&D to gain a competitive edge, leading to higher Innovation Output (IO). Firm Size (FS) and Technology Adoption (TA) also play crucial roles, with larger firms typically investing more in R&D and rapid technology adoption enhancing innovation outcomes. This model helps understand the complex interplay between these variables in fostering innovation.

3 Research Design

The study endeavors to explore the intricate relationship between innovation and competition within internet-based firms, particularly focusing on those situated in developing countries. It aims to propose policies aimed at enhancing their growth trajectory. Given the pivotal role of internet-based firms in driving economic progress, their rapid digital innovation, and significant contribution to job creation, it's imperative to address their unique challenges with tailored policy interventions. These firms possess distinctive characteristics such as agility, global reach, and digital dependence, necessitating nuanced policy formulations to navigate challenges like platform monopolies and regulatory barriers effectively [21]. This research seeks to shed light on the specific hurdles and potentials inherent in internet-based firms concerning competition and innovation, thereby laying the groundwork for tailored policy interventions.

To address the specific challenges confronting internet-based firms in Bangladesh, the study conducted a survey involving 22 firms, with participants ranging from CEOs to legal advisors. These firms were meticulously categorized based on various metrics such as age, size, and nature of projects or services offered. Through data analysis, the author identified key challenges and crafted policy recommendations that consider constraints like budget limitations, resource availability, and innovation timelines, with the overarching goal of offering a comprehensive understanding of the primary obstacles faced by internet-based firms and suggesting policy interventions to overcome them.

The data collection process encompassed both online and offline surveys, with subsequent evaluation utilizing Factor Analysis, Reliability Analysis, and Regression Analysis. Factor analysis enabled the assessment of performance-related variables, condensing a large volume of observations into manageable factors. The use of a 3-point scale facilitated the evaluation of organizations and gap identification. Reliability analysis assessed the consistency and reliability of the measurement, particularly regarding the survey questionnaire. Subsequently, regression analysis was employed to analyze the relationships between identified factors, innovation, and competition. This analysis aimed to test hypotheses based on the theoretical framework and the causal model outlined in Sect. 2, providing insights into the factors influencing innovation and competition dynamics within internet-based firms.

3.1 Characteristics of Firms Towards the Topic

In the conducted research, 22 small and medium-sized companies were evaluated based on multiple criteria, including work experience, company size, location, and job positions. Table 1 provide valuable insights into the characteristics of the surveyed companies and their respective workforces. According to the data collected, the distribution of job positions within these companies was as follows: CEO and Project Manager(PM) each accounted for 50% of the workforce, CTO for 20%, and Business Analyst(BA), Legal Advisor(LA), and Product Owner(PO) each for 30%.

Table 1. Survey profile characteristics [35].

Title	Measure
Total Number of company	22
Respondent Experience	50% 5–10 years 45% 2–5 years 5% 0–1
Product Types	100% internet based
Product market place	Bangladesh
Respondent Location	Bangladesh
Respondent Role	CEO & PM 50%, CTO 20%, BA,LA & PO 30%
Company Size	20-70 employees

4 Findings

4.1 Trend Followed by Company

In our research, a total of 44 responses were collected from individuals representing the 22 companies involved in the study. These responses encompassed various roles within the companies and were gathered in response to a set of 25 questions covering a range of factor areas. The study focused on nine specific factor areas, which were identified and discussed in prior research studies [8, 26–30]. These factor areas provided the framework for our analysis and enabled us to examine various aspects related to innovation and competition in the context of small and medium-sized internet-based companies.

The primary objective of this study was to gain insights into the trends among small and medium-sized internet-based companies. To achieve this objective, a survey was administered, and the average values of responses to each question were calculated based on the respective factor area. Table 2 presents the percentage distribution of these factor areas, offering valuable insights into the prevailing trends within firms.

Analyzing the average values within each factor area allowed the authors to identify the challenges confronted by internet-based firms regarding innovation and competition. This analytical approach provided a comprehensive understanding of the trends and shed light on the underlying reasons for fluctuations in product market payoffs. Such understanding is crucial for devising strategies and policies to support the growth and sustainability of these firms in a competitive landscape.

Table 2. Percentage of following Factor Area [35].

Factor no.	Factors	Responses
F1	Competition among rivals	43.5
F2	less incentive to invest in R&D	62.5
F3	Antitrust intervention	18.75
F4	First movers gain	32.5
F5	Companies preventing new entrants	37.5
F6	Regulatory, monetary, tax policy.	62.5
F7	Procurement, workforce, market access	43.75
F8	Potential profit	70
F9	Pre-innovation competition.	25

4.2 Reliability Analysis

eliability analysis is a valuable method employed to evaluate the properties of measurement scales and the individual items that comprise those scales, as highlighted in prior research [31]. In this study, the author utilized reliability analysis to assess the extent to which our questionnaire aligned with the nine factor areas concerning innovation and competition. The questionnaire encompassed a total of 25 questions, and the reliability analysis allowed the author to gauge the internal consistency and reliability of these questions in measuring the intended constructs related to innovation and competition.

To evaluate the reliability of our questionnaire, the author employed the Cronbach's Alpha method, a widely used coefficient of reliability that assesses internal consistency based on the average inter-item correlation. As a general guideline, the acceptable level of reliability alpha typically falls within the range of 0.6 to 1.0, as referenced in prior literature [31].

Table 3. Reliability Analysis Results.

Factor no.	Cronbach Alpha	No. of Items
F1	0.85	3
F2	0.78	4
F3	0.92	2
F4	0.81	3
F5	0.89	3
F6	0.88	3
F7	0.84	3
F8	0.90	2
F9	0.82	2

In Table 3, the author present the Cronbach Alpha values for each factor scale, along with the number of items included in each scale. These results demonstrate the internal consistency and reliability of the questionnaire items within each factor scale. Overall, the high Cronbach Alpha values indicate robust levels of internal consistency among the items in our survey questionnaire, reinforcing the trustworthiness of our research findings.

4.3 Regression Analysis

Based on the causal model Fig. 1, author set up a regression model to predict Innovation Output (IO) as follows:

$$IO = \beta_0 + \beta_1 \times F1 + \beta_2 \times F2 + \ldots + \beta_9 \times F9 + \epsilon \quad (1)$$

IO denotes the Innovation Output, F1 to F9 represent the responses from Factor Areas F1 to F9, β_0 serves as the intercept, β_1 to β_9 are the coefficients indicating the effect of each factor on the Innovation Output, ϵ stands for the error term. The coefficients β_0 to β_9 were estimated through regression analysis, allowing us to discern the relationship between the factors and the Innovation Output. Additionally, to assess the reliability and internal consistency of our measurements, the author utilized Cronbach's alpha, a measure commonly employed for scale reliability assessment. This ensured the robustness of our findings and enhanced the validity of our regression model.

5 Survey Result Analysis

5.1 Factors that Affect Innovation

The graph in Fig. 2 visualizes the results of a regression analysis, examining the relationship between various factors (independent variables) and their coefficients in predicting innovation output (dependent variable).

- **Potential Profit:** With a high coefficient of 0.90, potential profit is a significant influence on innovation output. This suggests that expected rewards from innovation strongly impact these companies.
- **Less Incentive to Invest in R&D:** This factor has a coefficient of 0.78, highlighting its importance. It may be closely linked to potential profit.
- **Regulatory, Monetary, Tax Policy:** This factor has a substantial impact, with a coefficient of 0.88, indicating that government policies significantly affect these companies' innovation efforts.
- **Competition Among Rivals:** With a coefficient of 0.85, competition among rivals is a notable challenge, though relatively lower compared to other factors.
- **Companies Preventing New Entrants:** The coefficient for this factor is 0.89, showing its significant impact on innovation output. Barriers posed by existing companies strongly affect industry dynamics.
- **Procurement, Workforce, Market Access:** This factor has a coefficient of 0.84, indicating its significant role in influencing innovation output.

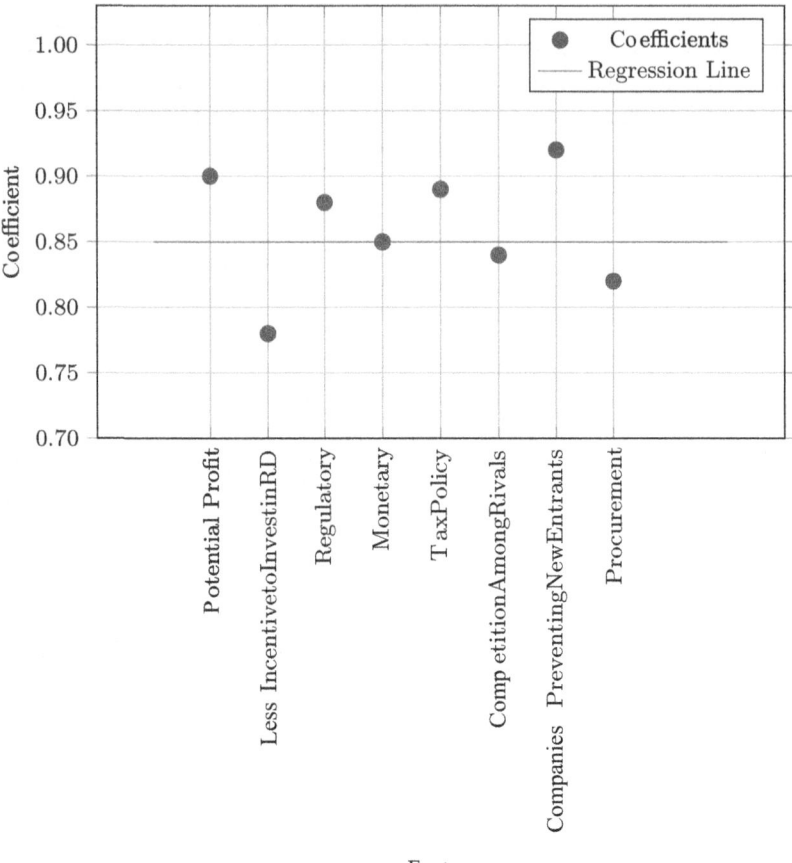

Fig. 2. Regression Analysis: Relationship between Factors and Coefficients.

- **Antitrust Intervention:** With a coefficient of 0.92, antitrust intervention, though less influential, still warrants attention as a potential challenge.
- **Pre-innovation Competition:** This factor has a relatively lower impact, with a coefficient of 0.82.

6 Policy Recommendation

Based on analysis of the data, the authors suggest policy recommendations that take into account factors such as innovation, competition, budget constraints, and available resources, with the ultimate goal of maximizing product market returns. These policies recommended to address the particular obstacles to innovation and competition encountered by internet-based companies.

6.1 Antimonopoly and Merger

Based on the survey and analysis conducted, it becomes evident that small and medium-sized internet-based firms are grappling with substantial competition from large corporations. To address this issue and foster an environment conducive to innovation and competition, the authors recommend the implementation of anti-monopoly and merger policies. These recommendations are in alignment with existing research and literature [26, 31]. These policies should encompass:

a. Reversing Past Mergers Reducing Competition: An effective strategy involves undoing mergers that have previously diminished competition. This can entail breaking apart merged entities or mandating divestiture of certain assets.
b. Enacting Regulations to Prevent Dominant Companies Impeding New Entrants: Implementing laws and regulations that curb dominant companies from leveraging their market power to deter new entrants fosters a climate of competition and innovation. Measures may include prohibiting exclusive agreements, tying arrangements, and predatory pricing.
c. Restricting Horizontal Shareholdings by Shareholders: Preventing shareholders from amassing significant stakes in multiple companies within the same industry curbs the formation of interlocking ownership structures that can stifle competition.
d. Imposing Limits on Shareholders' Holdings in Competing Companies: Instituting limits on individual shareholders' ability to acquire more than 5% of competing firms in the same industry deters ownership concentration and promotes competition.
e. Accelerating Antitrust Trials for Timely Enforcement: Speedy resolution of antitrust trials ensures the timely enforcement of laws, preventing companies from engaging in anti-competitive practices over prolonged periods.
f. Streamlining the Appeals Process with Due Safeguards: Rationalizing the appeals process reduces the time and cost associated with antitrust trials, which in turn facilitates a climate of competition and innovation. However, safeguards should be maintained to protect defendants' rights.

6.2 Regulation

This research indicates that the focus of small and medium businesses revolves around market payoff. Enforcing the suggested regulations could foster equitable competition in the market, thereby potentially enhancing product market payoff for all businesses, particularly the smaller ones.

a. Establishing a level playing field that minimizes barriers to entry for new players, akin to the benefits observed with the enforcement of net neutrality for internet-based companies [32].
b. Formulating regulations that reduce switching costs and prevent customer lock-in, thereby fostering a competitive environment through the elimination of entry barriers [33].

By implementing these regulatory measures, policymakers can help create an environment where small and medium sized companies can thrive, compete effectively, and contribute to innovation and market dynamism.

6.3 Patents and Copyright

Promoting healthy competition post-patent expiration, for instance, by expediting the approval process for generic products and facilitating the importation of generics from developed nations into underdeveloped countries, can stimulate innovation and effectively serve the public interest.

7 Conclusion

The central aim of this investigation is to bolster the product market payoff for small and medium internet-based enterprises by examining the interplay between innovation and competition. To accomplish this objective, the researchers conducted a comprehensive survey to delineate the key areas of innovation and competitive factors, offering policy recommendations based on their findings.

Focusing on innovation and competition, the study identified specific areas detailed in Table 1. Through diverse research methodologies, the authors assessed the prevailing practices and policies of these enterprises, drawing comparisons with standard procedures to propose measures that could enhance competition and product market payoff. A total of 24 responses were collected from 22 internet-based firms, providing valuable insights into their activities and the gaps they encounter concerning innovation and competition. Analyses of the results shed light on the factors influencing innovation and competition in internet-based products. Subsequently, the authors put forward policy suggestions that took into account financial constraints and available resources, aiming to maximize product market payoff.

Future investigations in this domain should prioritize the identification and remediation of the most impactful factor areas and any existing gaps. Examining trends in greater depth can offer a more profound understanding of the reasons behind fluctuations in specific factors. Moreover, conducting additional surveys to validate product market payoffs and performing comprehensive comparative evaluations of internal processes within companies could prove beneficial. It is imperative to implement standard policies alongside existing ones to ensure a continuous improvement process. To enhance specific factors, a comprehensive analysis of the relevant domain and the identification of all associated tasks are essential. Such an approach can significantly contribute to fostering competition and encouraging innovation.

References

1. Reinganum, J.F.: Innovation and industry evolution. Q. J. Econ. **100**(1), 81–99 (1985)
2. Li, M.: Nguyen, Bang: When will firms share information and collaborate to achieve innovation? a review of collaboration strategies. The Bottom Line **30**(1), 65–86 (2017). https://doi.org/10.1108/BL-12-2016-0039
3. Shimomura, K.-I.: Thisse, Jacques-François: Competition among the big and the small. Rand J. Econ. **43**(2), 329–347 (2012). https://doi.org/10.1111/j.1756-2171.2012.00149.x
4. Bresnahan, T.F., Reiss, P.C.: Entry and competition in concentrated markets. J. Polit. Econ. **99**(5), 977–1009 (1991)

5. Griffith, R., Van Reenen, J.: Product market competition, creative destruction and innovation. CEPR Discussion Paper No. DP16763 (2021)
6. Bloom, N., Griffith, R., Van Reenen, J.: Do R&D tax credits work? Evidence from a panel of countries 1979–1997. J. Public Econ. **85**(1), 1–31 (2002)
7. Sutton, J.: Market structure: theory and evidence. In: Handbook of Industrial Organization, vol. 3, pp. 2301–2368 (2007)
8. Marshall, G., Parra, A.: Innovation and competition: the role of the product market. Int. J. Ind. Organ. **65**, 221–247 (2019)
9. Bessen, J., Maskin, E.: Sequential innovation, patents, and imitation. Rand J. Econ. **40**(4), 611–635 (2009)
10. Porter, M.E.: Competitive advantage of nations: creating and sustaining superior performance. Simon and Schuster (2011)
11. Manyika, J., et al.: How to compete and grow: A sector guide to policy. McKinsey Global Institute (2010)
12. Howitt, P.: Innovation, Competition, and Growth: Schumpeterian Ideas for the 21st Century. 1st edn. MIT Press (2007). https://doi.org/10.7551/mitpress/9780262083565.001.0001
13. Sutton, John: Technology and Market Structure: Theory and History, 1st edn. MIT Press (1999). https://doi.org/10.7551/mitpress/5594.001.0001
14. Lin, C.-H., Wu, Y.-L.: Competition and firm innovation: a non-linear perspective. Int. J. Ind. Organ. **78**, 102930 (2021). https://doi.org/10.1016/j.ijindorg.2021.102930
15. Dasgupta, P., Stiglitz, J.E.: Uncertainty, industrial structure, and the speed of R&D. Bell J. Econ. **11**(1), 1–28 (1980). https://doi.org/10.2307/3003322
16. Aghion, P., Harris, C., Howitt, P., Vickers, J.: Competition, imitation, and growth with step-by-step innovation. Rev. Econ. Stud. **68**(3), 467–492 (2001). https://doi.org/10.1111/1467-937X.00172
17. Howitt, P.: Competition and innovation: an inverted-U relationship. Q. J. Econ. **120**(2), 701–728 (2005). https://doi.org/10.1093/qje/120.2.701
18. Baumol, William J.: The Free-Market Innovation Machine: Analyzing the Growth Miracle of Capitalism, 1st edn. Princeton University Press (2002). https://doi.org/10.1515/9780691182244
19. Sutton, John: Sunk Costs and Market Structure: Price Competition, Advertising, and the Evolution of Concentration, 1st edn. MIT Press (1991). https://doi.org/10.7551/mitpress/9742.001.0001
20. Baumol, W.J.: The free-market innovation machine: analyzing the growth miracle of capitalism. J. Entrepreneurial Financ. Bus. Ventures **7**(1), 1–18 (2002). https://doi.org/10.7916/D8FJ4PWR
21. Howitt, P.: Endogenous growth, productivity and economic policy: a progress report. Canadian J. Econ./Revue canadienne d'économique **37**(3), 587–710 (2004). https://doi.org/10.1111/j.0008-4085.2004.00214.x
22. Syverson, C.: Product substitutability and productivity dispersion. Rev. Econ. Stat. **86**(2), 534–550 (2004). https://doi.org/10.1162/003465304323031067
23. Cabral, Luís, M.B.: On the dynamics of innovation and competition: An investigation of the interactions between market structure, technology, and competition. Massachusetts Institute of Technology (2000)
24. Gavil, A.I., Kovacic, W.E., Baker, J.: Antitrust law in perspective: Cases, concepts and problems in competition policy. West Publishing Co. (2002)
25. Wei, Z., Liu, Z., Song, L., Romilly, P.: Productivity, innovation and R&D in Chinese enterprises. Int. J. Innov. Manag. **5**(3), 363–386 (2001)
26. Baker, Jonathan B: Beyond Schumpeter vs. Arrow: Antitrust fosters innovation. Antitrust Law J. **74**, 575 (2007)

27. Carayannis, E.G., Campbell, D.F.J.: Mode 3 and quadruple helix: toward a 21st century fractal innovation ecosystem. Int. J. Technol. Manage. **46**(3-4), 201–234 (2009)
28. Carayannis, E.G., Rakhmatullin, R.: The quadruple/quintuple innovation helixes and smart specialisation strategies for sustainable and inclusive growth in Europe and beyond. J. Knowl. Econ. **5**(2), 212–239 (2014)
29. National Science Foundation: The science of science and innovation policy (SciSIP) program solicitation (2012). https://www.nsf.gov/pubs/2012/nsf12556/nsf12556.htm
30. Merges, R.P., Nelson, R.R.: On the complex economics of patent scope. Berkeley Technol. Law J. **22**(2), 567–607 (2007)
31. Gemino, J., Horner Reich, C., Serrador, P.: Project management and its effects on innovation. Proj. Manag. J. **52**(1), 6–21 (2021)
32. Vandal, S.: The battle for net neutrality: a case study of activism and the Internet as a public sphere. Media Cult. Soc. **39**(2), 238–255 (2017)
33. Brynjolfsson, E., Hu, Y.J., Rahman, M.S.: Competing in the age of omnichannel retailing. MIT Sloan Manag. Rev. **54**(4), 23–29 (2013)
34. Zitzewitz, E.W.: Competition and innovation in the United States and United Kingdom tobacco industries, 1900–1990. Rev. Ind. Organ. **22**(3), 179–197 (2003). https://doi.org/10.1023/A:1026202410166
35. Bakar, N., Hasan, M., Rokonuzzaman, M.: Enhancing product market payoff in small and medium internet-based firms: a survey-based analysis of innovation and competition factors. In: Proceedings of the 20th International Conference on Smart Business Technologies, ISBN 978-989-758-667-5, ISSN 2184-772X, pp. 154–161 (2023). https://doi.org/10.5220/0012096600003552

Evolution and Comparative Analysis of Enterprise Architecture Tools

Federico Heras[✉]

Universitat Pompeu Fabra, Barcelona, Spain
federico.heras@upf.edu

Abstract. The discipline of Enterprise Architecture (EA) involves the creation and maintenance of essential artifacts, including documents and architectural diagrams, to deliver tangible benefits to stakeholders. This paper examines the historical evolution of Enterprise Architecture and the tools associated with it. As we will explore further, EA tools have evolved from being tools for a small audience reliant on complex notations and visualizations to becoming more collaborative and user-friendly tools accessible to all stakeholders. Then, a high-level assessment and comparison of the different types of EA tool is presented. Finally, we examine the practical application of these tools for different common relevant artifacts commonly used within the Enterprise Architecture discipline.

Keywords: Enterprise architecture · Enterprise architecture tools

1 Introduction

Enterprise Architecture (EA) is a discipline that plays an important role in many organizations today [24]. EA is involved in strategic planning, design, and management of an organization's overall structure and operations, aligning its business objectives with its technology and resources. Enterprise Architecture offers a structured approach to optimizing processes, improving decision-making, and ensuring efficient resource allocation. It provides a comprehensive view of the organization, fostering transparency and facilitating informed decisions to drive growth and innovation. Enterprise Architecture is typically guided by established frameworks [20], such as TOGAF (The Open Group Architecture Framework) [25] and Zachman [27], which provide methodologies and best practices for creating, implementing, and maintaining an effective EA structure.

Each of these frameworks presents its own unique set of advantages and disadvantages, making it challenging to identify a one-size-fits-all solution [11]. Depending on the organization's size, level of maturity in the discipline and other factors, a more lightweight version of one of these frameworks may be preferable to facilitate the onboarding of new EA members and other teams [21]. Besides, the traditional EA practices and framework have been evolving to on board recent software and infrastructure architecture advances led by recent digital transformation including cloud services providers, very granular services (i.e. Internet of Things, Microservices, etc.) [14,29] and other recent trends like DevSecOps, Artificial Intelligence, Low-Code Development etc.

Enterprise Architects typically produce outputs in the form of documents and other artifacts [17], such as application landscapes or architectures, regardless of the specific EA framework they use. Therefore, it is crucial for Enterprise Architects to select Enterprise Architecture tools that align with their organization's approach to transformation, modernization, and innovation processes. This paper is an extension of [12] where several types of EA Tools were compared with emphasis on a single EA artifact called *application landscape management*.

In this paper, we additionally present various artifacts frequently created and maintained by Enterprise Architects, categorized into four primary domains: foundation, vision, solutions and designs, as well as landscapes. Subsequently, we examine the transformation of Enterprise Architecture over the past two decades, transitioning from an IT-centric approach with a limited technical audience to a more collaborative practice that actively engages business stakeholders with a focus on providing tangible business value. Organizations sometimes find it challenging to justify their investment in Enterprise Architecture due to a poor understanding of its value. Demonstrating the value of enterprise architecture can be challenging [7,9], but transitioning to simplified and collaborative environments can streamline processes, enhance communication, and make it easier to showcase the direct impact of architectural improvements on business outcomes.

Such EA evolution has transformed EA tools from desktop installed applications that required a remarkable understanding of IT concepts or EA Frameworks or concepts, into *Software as a Service (SaaS)* solutions that emphasize flexibility, a centralized repository of data, streamlined models that can be accessed by stakeholders throughout the organization, and improved collaboration for the collection and to keep up-to-date data. Then, we compare each type of EA Tools and provide recommendations when to use them with regards to the artifacts presented before.

This paper is structured as follows. First, some preliminary concepts are introduced including usual Enterprise Architecture artifacts and the usual roles in a company using EA Tools. Second, a discussion on the evolution of EA and its related tools in the last two decades is presented. Then, the various types of EA tools are presented, along with a comparison of them. Next, we discuss how to use the various types of tools for the several artifacts based on our experience. Finally, some closing remarks and future work are presented.

2 Preliminary Concepts

Some preliminary concepts are introduced in this section. Essentially, the common artifacts developed by EA teams and other collaborators, as well as the typical roles in organizations that use Enterprise Architecture tools.

2.1 Enterprise Architecture Usual Artifacts

Enterprise architects play a crucial role in guiding an organization's strategic technology decisions and ensuring alignment between business objectives and IT capabilities. To achieve this, they create various artifacts that fall into distinct categories. These artifacts help in planning, designing, and governing the enterprise's architecture effectively. They also provide a structured and strategic approach to managing the complexity of modern IT landscapes while driving innovation and efficiency. In what follows, an expanded explanation of the common artifacts [16] created by enterprise architects grouped in 4 categories.

Foundation. Enterprise architects begin their work by establishing foundational principles, policies and related documents that will guide decision-making throughout the organization. Those artifacts include:
Principles: These are high-level guidelines that articulate the organization's architectural philosophy and standards. They ensure consistency and alignment in technology decisions.
Policies: Enterprise architects create policies that define the rules and standards for various aspects of the IT landscape, such as security, data management, and technology procurement.
Data Models: A data model represents the organization's data architecture at an abstract or logical level, defining key data entities and their relationships. It helps in understanding data flows and dependencies.
EA Gaps: This artifact identifies gaps between the current state of the enterprise architecture and the desired future state. It outlines strategies and plans to address these gaps, ensuring that the architecture evolves as needed. Once a strategy or solution is found for a GAP it is usually documented to ensure that for future similar situations the same approach is taken.
Technology Reference Model: It used to categorize the various technologies that can be used in building IT systems.

Note that some of those artifacts may have an Enterprise-wide version and a IT-focused version. For example, an Enterprise principle may refer to *prefer or enforce globalized business processes*, while an IT Principle may refer to *prefer SaaS and off-the-shelf products*. Those principles could be documented in the same document or in separated ones, depending on the authors' preferences.

Vision. The vision category is formed by artifacts that provide a clear roadmap for how the organization's architecture will evolve to meet business needs and add value. Such roadmap outlines the strategic initiatives and solutions that will drive transformation.
Architecture Roadmaps: This artifact outlines the sequence and timeline of business initiatives and projects with underlying IT changes/impacts that will be undertaken to achieve the desired future state. Roadmaps typically cover a multi-year horizon.
IT Roadmaps: Similar to the architecture roadmap, IT roadmaps focus on the evolution of specific technology domains. They outline plans for retiring legacy systems, adopting new technologies, and ensuring alignment with the overall architecture vision.

Usually, those roadmaps are intrinsically interrelated.

Solutions and Designs. In this category, enterprise architects provide the detailed design and assessment of solutions. They evaluate various options and create designs that align with the established principles, policies, etc.

Option Assessments: Used to conduct assessments of different technology options or approaches to solve specific business problems. These assessments consider factors such as cost, feasibility, and alignment with IT reference technologies and architecture principles.

High-Level Solution Design: This document outlines the overall structure and components of a solution. It provides a high-level view of how a particular technology or system will meet business requirements.

Low-Level Solution Design: Building on the high-level design, this artifact provides detailed specifications and technical plans for implementing a solution. It includes information about data models, interfaces, process changes, and integration points.

Landscapes. Understanding the current state of the IT landscape is essential for making informed architectural decisions. Enterprise architects create artifacts that capture the existing architecture and help plan for its evolution:

Application and Assets Inventories: Detailed inventories list all applications, systems, and assets within the organization. This inventory is critical for managing and rationalizing the application portfolio.

Landscape Diagrams: These visual representations provide a comprehensive view of the organization's IT assets, including hardware, software, networks, and data centers. Landscape diagrams help identify areas for optimization and consolidation.

2.2 Application Landscape Management

This is a particular case of a Application Inventory plus Landscape Diagram mainly focused on applications/software and their relations. *Application landscape management* is used to document applications and the interconnections (integrations) between them. We will refer to an application landscape that covers *all* applications in the organization as *full application landscape*. We will refer to an application landscape that covers just a partial subset of the applications in the organization as *partial application landscape*. The latest ones are usually used to describe a specific architecture or a subset of applications from a particular domain.

Application landscape management enables companies to take control of their evolving IT landscape, rationalize their existing applications, and tackle major transformation initiatives like cloud migration [6, 13]. With this information and potentially additional data, several use cases can be covered like *Application Portfolio Management, landscape optimization/rationalization, Technology Risk Management, AS IS vs TO BE change impact analysis* etc.

According to our experience in several organizations, application landscapes are extensively used by various stakeholders such as technical teams, business teams, and vendors. The main advantage is that they are not very technical, making them understandable regardless of technical expertise of the audience. See Fig. 1 for an example of a partial application landscape.

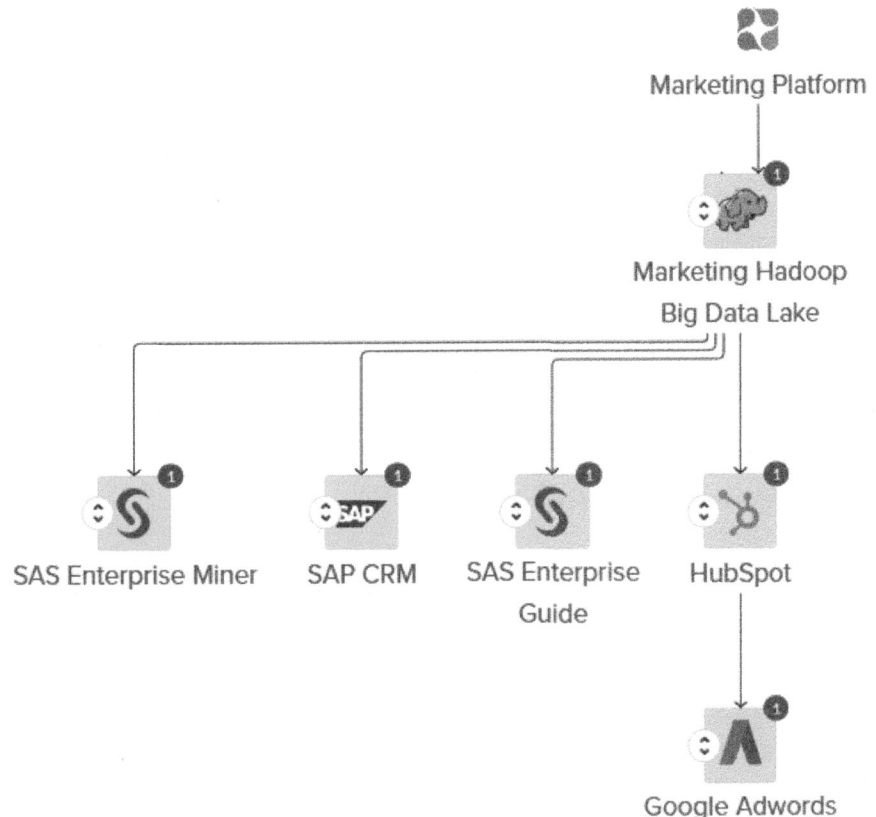

Fig. 1. Partial Application Landscape example.

2.3 Roles

In what follows, the most common roles that contribute to Enterprise Architecture or related functions are introduced informally. It should be noted that many of these roles may be played by the same person in a company, or they may be understood differently depending on the company.

Business analysts focus on business needs, requirement gathering, business process documentation and solution delivery. As an example, they may use *Business Process Model and Notation* (BPMN) [5, 10] to document business processes, use case diagrams for requirements gathering, etc. Process modelling might be part of High-level and Low-Level design artifacts.

Technical architects are the most hands-on and have in-depth knowledge of one or a few technologies. They typically lead a technical team responsible for very low level architecture definition, UML class and sequence diagrams [1] for software systems, infrastructure and networking diagrams, etc.

Enterprise architects ensure that an organization's information technology strategy is in sync with its business objectives. Enterprise architects are responsible for using this knowledge to ensure IT and business alignment, and they collaborate closely with many different stakeholders from IT and business, including senior management. They have a holistic view of all enterprise applications and the role they play in achieving the business strategy. Enterprise Architects typically document the artifacts described before and regarding Application Landscape Management they usually care of full application landscapes.

Solution architects are responsible for developing and documenting solutions for specific architectural issues that are intended to enable a specific business outcome. Solution Architects are experts in one or more domains of knowledge and define high-level architectures for a subset of applications in their areas of expertise, always adhering to the strategy defined in collaboration with Enterprise Architects. Solutions architects sometimes contribute in the different EA artifacts or at least take them into account to ensure their outputs are aligned with EA. Partial application landscapes are typically documented by solution architects.

3 Considered Types of Tools

There are numerous EA tools on the market, but we propose a classification into three major types. This classification may be somehow artificial and oversimplified, but it is done for simplicity's sake.

Diagramming tools (for example, Lucidchart) are extremely simple to use for quickly sketching a design to understand your own thoughts or to share with others. *Modelling tools* (for example, Sparx Enterprise Architect) have a higher barrier to entry, but the extra effort pays off when creating multiple, linked views or inferring information across many linked components. Finally, *Enterprise Architecture Management tools* (for example, Ardoq) are intended to handle the Application Landscape Documentation case and are a combination of other tools. *Gartner Magic Quadrant* for EA Tools is shown in Fig. 2[1]. *Gartner* is an organization that does technology research and communicates to their clients that data through private consultation and conferences. Gartner's recommendations are based on the size of the organization and the maturity of its clients on the topics consulted. In general, all of these tools typically include shapes and arrows that connect the shapes. Depending on the context, the arrows may represent relations, interconnections, integrations, etc.

3.1 Diagramming Tools

Some examples of tools are: *Lucidchart* [19], *Microsoft Visio* or even *Microsoft PowerPoint*.

They enable the rapid creation of diagrams from predefined shapes. But, the shapes on a screen have no *identity*. You must draw the same shape again if you want it in multiple diagrams or even the same diagram. However, just because two shapes share a name does not imply that they represent the same thing. As a result, changing one shape in one diagram will not be reflected in any other diagram that contains the same component or line.

---

[1] Image publicly available at https://www.softwareag.com/en_corporate/platform/alfabet/ea-tools-gartner.html.

Fig. 2. Gartner Magic Quadrant for Enterprise Architecture tools 2022.

3.2 Modelling Tools

Some examples of tools are: *Sparx Enterprise Architect* [23] and *Archi* [28].

They enable you to create shapes and relations with unique identities, allowing the same shape to be represented in multiple diagrams. If you change the shape in one place, it will be reflected everywhere it is referenced. Shapes can also have fields/attributes that allow them to hold more information. In these tools, diagrams can be created by arranging shapes and references (such as arrows) from a toolbar to create a custom layout. These tools typically support a wide range of modelling standards, such as the TOGAF and Zachman EA Frameworks, *Business Process Model and Notation* (BPMN)

[5,10], UML, etc. In the case of UML, some of those tools can generate an *scaffolding* of code for an actual implementation, which could be useful for technical architects.

3.3 Enterprise Architecture Management Tools

Some examples of tools are: *Ardoq* [2] and *LeanIX* [18].

They can support similar frameworks like modelling tools. They are also widely used for *Application Landscape Management*. They enable the documentation of each application and their integrations with other applications. Each application, integration, and other component will have a unique identity that allows it to be reused in various diagrams or visualizations, maximizing re-usability. These tools include predefined components and relationships between components based on industry best practices. Furthermore, the user can add custom components to model new concepts. EA Management tools also include their own visualization, reporting, and querying engines, allowing for the creation of useful dashboards, reports, and visualizations. Enterprise Management Tools can be understood as a combination of modelling tools enhanced with a powerful visualization engine.

While there are automated methods for getting the data from the applications into those tools, manual data collection is still the most common practice today. Typically, automation is accomplished through the use of connectors for *IT Service Management tools*, cloud providers like Azure or Amazon Web Services (AWS) and other mechanisms [4,22].

4 Enterprise Architecture Evolution

Enterprise architecture (EA) has indeed evolved significantly over the past two decades [15], moving away from a traditional IT Centric approach to a more collaborative and dynamic practice. This transformation can be attributed to various factors, including technological advancements, changing business needs, need for explicit value realization, etc.

In the early 2000s and before, enterprise architecture was often seen as a technical discipline practised by a few specialized individuals or teams within organizations. It was considered somewhat isolated from the broader business strategy. In the mid-2000s, a shift began towards aligning enterprise architecture with broader business goals. The emphasis moved from pure technology considerations to how technology could support and drive business objectives.

Digital transformation (2010s) is another critical area where EA has played a relevant role. It included major transformation programmes like migrations from legacy on-premises setups to cloud and SaaS products, migrations from multiple legacy ERPs or CRMs to a single one, etc. Technology evolution including cloud providers' services, very granular services (i.e. Internet of Things, Microservices, etc.) [14,29] and other recent trends like DevSecOps, Artificial Intelligence, Low-Code Development have had a relevant impact on digitalization [14,29]. As organizations embrace digital technologies to streamline processes, enhance customer engagement, and create new business models, EA guides and supports these initiatives by aligning technology with strategic goals.

As technology has evolved some frameworks like TOGAF have been adapted to consider some of these concepts. Additionally, in February 2009 The Open Group published the first version of *ArchiMate* [28] as an open standard for enterprise architecture modelling language to support the description and visualization of several EA artifacts.

In addition to these changes, EA now actively participates in business process optimization, recognizing that improving operational effectiveness is crucial. It involves identifying inefficiencies, automating workflows, and using technology to drive business process improvements. Data is at the heart of modern businesses, and EA has adapted accordingly. It emphasizes data architecture, data governance, and data management to name a few.

Lastly, EA has improved its communication and visualization skills to effectively convey complex architectural concepts to business stakeholders. Visual models and diagrams are used to facilitate better understanding and decision-making, ensuring that EA's recommendations are transparent and accessible to non-technical leaders. This is where Enterprise Architecture artifacts and EA tools play an important role.

5 Enterprise Architecture Tools Evolution

In this section we see As Enterprise Architecture has evolved, the same has happened with the EA Tools. In what follows, we will refer as Software as a Service (SaaS) to products that are licensed in a subscription model (i.e. usually per user, per feature, usage etc.), that are centrally hosted by the vendor and that have a web-based interface with no need of installed clients.

As suggested in [21], many enterprise architecture initiatives start by creating an information model that addresses the EA-related concerns of several stakeholders. During the design of this model, enterprise architects frequently follow established frameworks (i.e. TOGAF) but may create what is often called an "ivory tower" model, restricting contributions from other stakeholders who have relevant knowledge and EA value is not appreciated or understood [7,9]. Such research offers a different way to develop information models by using the wisdom of a diverse group. These included standards tools, wikis, and an open templating system to bring all the important enterprise architecture information together. The proposal was designed to be easy for both people and computers to use, and to ensure all subject matter experts could collaborate with their information. While EA frameworks are useful, they does not fit every company. Picking an enterprise architecture approach should consider things like the company's size, how complex it is, EA maturity, the resources available, and what it wants to achieve. Sometimes, this means tweaking or simplifying EA frameworks like TOGAF to match the company's unique needs.

In the same way, pioneering tools for Enterprise Architecture used to be very focused on modelling technical and EA frameworks standards. Usually, they were software you had to install, and with steep learning curve as the EA user needed to fully understand such standards. The resulting artifacts would be very difficult to understand by business stakeholders and cannot be shown in such state, thus requiring creating separated presentations understandable by them. Finally, those tools did not make it easy for EA teams to collaborate due to its installed software and sometimes single user nature.

But modern tools from recent years are different. First, they are cloud based solutions and they come with lots of features to make easy collaboration and understanding. They have user-friendly ways to model concepts and visualize them on screen, so they are understandable for all kinds of stakeholders (IT or business). Those new models and representations are still inspired in EA frameworks like TOGAF and ArchiMate, and indeed they still support them. They usually come with additional features that allow non IT users to provide data on a controlled and simplified way (i.e. easy to use online surveys or views). Some of the pioneering tools have transitioned their products into Software as a Service (SaaS) offerings, aligning with the contemporary trend toward cloud-based solutions and improved their collaboration capabilities. See below the evolution of some well-known Enterprise Architecture tools in Table 1. Most of them support ArchiMate modelling, but not all of them have transitioned to a SaaS offering with the characteristics described before. A few pioneering applications, dating back to the early 2000s, still operate mainly as desktop applications (i.e. Visual Paradigm, Sparx Enterprise Architect). Additionally, Archi Software is a relatively new and free tool, but it is only available as a desktop-installed application.

However, note that Sparx now offers a similar desktop-installed product that can connect to a centralized database, enabling collaboration among multiple users still using the installed client. Additionally, Sparx has a more recent SaaS offering (Prolaborate). Visual Paradigm online offer a number of productivity products as a SaaS offering and they include a diagramming tool to handle several scenarios and notations including ArchiMate.

Bizzdesign Enterprise Studio, originally was primarily a desktop-installed application. However, during the years its product evolved to be a SaaS offering.

Vendors that emerged in the 2010s like Ardoq and Lean IX have typically started with a SaaS product right from the beginning. They have integrated numerous features to facilitate collaboration and make data collection and maintenance more accessible to a broader audience (i.e. the so-called *democratize enterprise architecture*).

Concerning diagramming tools such as Microsoft Visio and LucidChart, it is worth mentioning that Visio has traditionally been a desktop-installed software product, but it has more recently undergone adaptation and improvement to include Visio Online, a web-based version. In contrast, LucidChart has consistently been available as a Software as a Service (SaaS) offering, providing collaboration features from its early versions.

Another significant aspect to consider of a EA Tool is its integration capabilities of systems. Traditional installed applications typically create project files, which are then saved in a designated folder or shared folder. These traditional applications can handle various file formats, primarily for manual import and export functions. In contrast, modern cloud-based tools often offer additionally seamless connectors to other SaaS products, facilitating the synchronization of valuable data. As an example, connectors with cloud providers like Azure or Amazon Web Services to gather all the infrastructure resources and their relationships.

Enterprise Architecture (EA) tools that depend on storing artifacts in local or online folders, such as a shared folder or SharePoint, often encounter challenges related to data being scattered in many places. This can lead to difficulties in tracking and accessing files, especially when an employee leaves the company. The current trend in modern EA tools is the adoption of a (1) unified repository for all users or (2) alternatively, each user may maintain their individual artifacts in the cloud, and when they leave the company, a seamless transfer of their artifacts to a colleague, even post-departure, is facilitated.

It is important to note that even though certain products have transitioned from being installed software to Software as a Service (SaaS), it does not necessarily mean that they have now embedded the collaborative, simplified user experience and unified repositories dimensions we previously discussed. On the other hand, it is important to remember that desktop installed products offer the benefit of offline editing capabilities.

Finally, note that it is out of the scope of this paper to include any detailed and low-level comparison of products' setups and features. If the reader is interested, it is advisable to conduct their own evaluation and seek information or proposals independently.

Table 1. EA Tools deployment method and first release year (or company foundation year).

Tool	SaaS	1st version	Type
Microsoft Visio	Desktop, now also SaaS	1992	Diagramming
LucidChart	SaaS	2008	Diagramming
Sparx Enterprise Architecture	Desktop, now also SaaS	2000	Modelling
Visual Paradigm	Desktop, now also SaaS	2002	Modelling
Archi Software	Desktop	2013	Modelling
Bizzdesign Enterprise Studio	Desktop, now also SaaS	2004	Mix
Ardoq	SaaS	2013	EAM Tool
Lean IX	SaaS	2012	EAM Tool

5.1 Comparison of Tools

In this subsection, the different types of tools are compared considering several high-level characteristics including learning curve, re-use, layout, and so on.

Learning Curve and Re-use. The main advantage of diagramming tools is that they allow you to quickly create diagrams of an Architecture or any other artifact, provided you have all relevant information. Its main disadvantage is that the shapes/arrows cannot be reused in subsequent exercises. In general, we can say that diagramming tools are the easiest to use, modelling tools are slightly more complex, and EA Management Tools have the steepest learning curve. In terms of re-use, EA Management Tools, in general, maximize re-use, modelling tools provide some degree of reuse, but diagramming tools do not.

Shape Libraries. Shape libraries are collections of related shapes used to create a specific artifact. Simple shapes, application integration, UML, BPMN notation, stream value mapping, flow charts, network infrastructure or ArchiMate are a few examples. Diagramming tools, in general, have the most libraries, followed by Modelling Tools. EA Management Tools are much more limited in this regard, but they may allow you to create your own library sets.

Layout. Most primitive diagramming tools have a very limited area in which to place shapes and references. In Microsoft PowerPoint, for example, the area is limited to a single slide. In general, this is an exception because current tools theoretically allow for unrestricted areas.

Most CASE (Computer Aided Software Engineering) tools, as described in [26], require manual corrections, which means that a significant portion of time is spent dragging shapes and arrows to form an understandable diagram. This is a significant disadvantage for diagramming tools and, to a lesser extent, modelling tools. Typically, EA Management tools do not require manual corrections because the software displays the shapes and arrows automatically. On the other hand, this restricts the ability to see the shapes in a specific order.

Consider shapes to be nodes and arrows to be arcs in a graph. There are several techniques for optimizing node placement, such as *Force-Directed Layouts (FDLs)*, which have a variety of implementations, including the Fruchterman-Reingold algorithm [8]. This technique is used by some modelling tools and enterprise architecture management tools. Figure 3 illustrates an example in which we may observe applications, technical and business owners of such applications, and a variety of additional relationships that result in a complex graph.

Access to Artifacts. Another pertinent topic is the location and accessibility of the tools' artifacts. Several diagramming and modelling tools save the artifacts as files, either in local folders or in shared repositories such as shared folders or collaborative platforms (i.e. Sharepoint, Confluence, etc.). As time passes, the files become dispersed in various locations in local or shared repositories, complicating their management (High data/file scattering). Similarly, in the case of software as a service offerings of diagramming and modelling tools, many artifacts are difficult to access because only the creator or the people with whom the artifact was shared have access to it. Some SaaS offer the possibility of re-assigning the artifacts of a user leaving the company to a colleague, even post-departure. Although we do not have a single repository, this feature ensures that access to the artifacts is preserved and minimizes the document dispersion issue (Low data/file scattering).

Recent EA Management Tools, on the other hand, are generally Software as a Service based, and the modelling and data are centralized (no data scattering), even if users only have access to a portion of the data and model.

Query and Reporting. As previously stated, shapes and arrows in EA Management tools and Modelling tools are uniquely identified. The pre-built reporting and querying functionality in EA Management tools allows you to create reports, dashboards, and visualizations based on the centralized data repository. Modelling tools are more focused

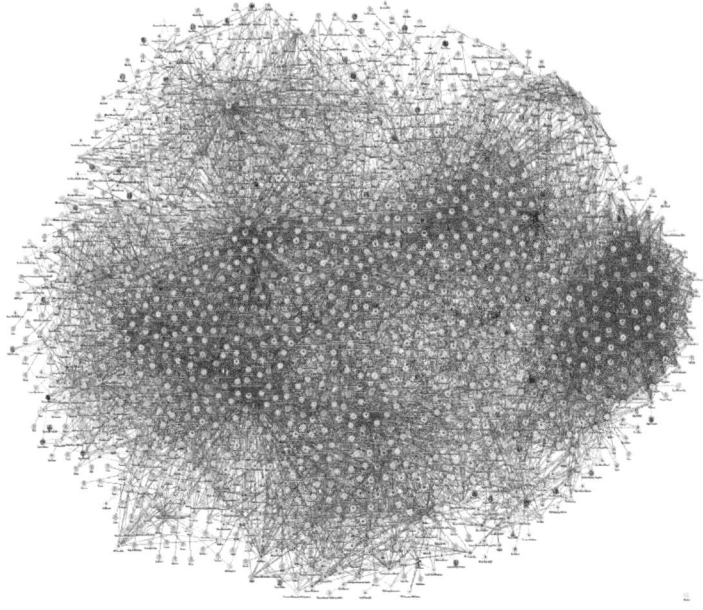

Fig. 3. Force-Directed layout applied to the model [12].

on reusing elements across diagrams, but they typically lack querying and reporting functionality. Finally, diagramming tools do not support querying or reporting.

Comparison Summary. Find a summary of the comparison in Table 2. Note that this is a generalized comparison. It could be the case that specific tools of a type perform better or worse on those characteristics.

Table 2. Comparison different types of EA Tools [12].

Characteristic	Diagramming tools	Modelling tools	EA Tools
Learning curve	Low	Low-Medium	Medium-High
Shape Libraries	Large	Large	Medium + custom
Re-use	None/Low	Low	High
Layout Area	Unlimited	Unlimited	Unlimited
Layout Manual corrections	High	Low	Low-None
Ability to customize Layout	High	High	Low
Centralized Repository	No	No	Yes
Data/File Scattering	Low-High	Low-High	None
Query engine	No	No/Limited	Yes
Reporting engine	No	No/limited	Yes

6 What Type of EA Tool Should Be Used?

In what follows we will refer as Office suites as those that include word processing, presentation tools (i.e. Microsoft Office, OpenOffice) but it can also be considered web-based wiki products like Confluence and similar products.

6.1 EA Maturity and Budget-Based Decision

Based on our past experience, diagramming and modelling tools are usually cheaper than EAM tools, at least to start with a small set of users. However, it is out of the scope of this paper to include any mention to products' pricing. If the reader is interested, it is advisable to conduct their own evaluation and seek information or proposals independently.

When the EA maturity in the company is low, starting with a simple diagramming tool should suffice plus (or just) an office suite already available in the company should be sufficient. In such case, the aim is to gain knowledge and confidence, and being able to prove EA can provide tangible value. This situation is usually associated with an initial low budget or none at all.

On the other hand, when there is a remarkable EA maturity (i.e. with TOGAF certified professionals and several years of experience) it should be easier to prove value and get some budget, then see next subsection. In contrast, if there is an structural lack of budget or similar limitation, considering cheap or free diagramming and modelling tools that supports ArchiMate plus the office suite could make the trick.

6.2 When to Use Each Type of EA Tool: Generic Strategy

This section, assumes sufficient level of EA maturity and no major budget restrictions.

In what follows, we will go over high-level guidelines for when to use each type of EA tool, assuming budget is not a main stopper. Indeed, it is common that EA teams have more than one EA tool.

In general, use *diagramming tools* for: (i) Summarized architecture diagrams or artifacts for executive presentations. (ii) Work in progress, not finalized architecture diagrams or artifacts. (iii) Any artifact created and maintained by a single person with no expectation of future maintenance or reuse of elements.

Regarding *modelling tools*, use them for: (i) Potentially, the same as diagramming tools. (ii) Low-level or extremely detailed architectures that quickly become obsolete where you need to reuse components. Consider a UML design for software development; the next day, it may become obsolete as new requirements are added. However, you must also define the low level architecture and reuse elements on different artifacts. (iii) Any artifact created and maintained by a small group of people working together in the hope of reusing some components in the near future.

Finally, use *EA Management tools* for: (i) High-level architectures or artifacts that do not change frequently. The challenge is detecting when changes occur. (ii) Any artifact created and maintained by a global owner or team that is meant to be kept up to date (low frequency of change is expected). (iii) Any artifact that is expected to be fed with information from several stakeholders using an structured and understandable approach (i.e. an online survey or a user friendly interface). (iv) There is an intention to run queries and facilitate the creation of reports and visualizations based on the data hold in the tool.

6.3 EA Tools for the Different Artifacts

When it comes to artifacts such as principles, policies, IT reference models, EA GAPs, they are typically documented in written form. To create these documents, you can utilize office suites. For diagrams and visual representations that may appear in such documents, it is recommended to use dedicated diagramming/modelling tool, and then copy the resulting diagram into the office suite (i.e. as an image) as usually there is no intention to re-use it in the future. Note that for some artifacts like principles and policies there are often two main versions: (i) a summarized version in a 1 pager or slide, (ii) and an extended one with a proper detailed explanation of each principle or policy.

Similarly for Solutions options Assessments, High-Level and low-Level designs, office suites plus diagramming/modelling tools can be used. In the specific context of low-level designs, it may be necessary to employ UML modelling, cloud infrastructure diagrams, etc. Documentation of a business process in BPMN might be needed also to understand current and future state of the process. It is important to note that future reusability is unlikely since these designs are likely to evolve while the implementation progresses. Hence, many times the first version of a Low-Level Design is documented but it is up to the teams to keep it up to date. For high-level designs many times it is presented as a partial application landscape that can be documented in a EAM tool only when the implementation is completed (see next subsection). Solution option assessments convey the information to compare several solutions for a particular business problem, and it usually contains a high-level architecture for each solution option.

When it comes to Architecture and IT roadmaps, given their continuous evolution and reliance on assumptions, they can be crafted using various tools. For high-level representations, office suites can be suitable. Specific project management tools or diagramming/modelling tools are also viable options specially when a lot of details needs to be recorded. However, if there is a firm commitment to the agreed-upon roadmaps, though this is uncommon due to frequent changes in business priorities, they can potentially be transitioned to Enterprise Architecture Management (EAM) tools.

When dealing with Data Models, high-level data architecture models that encapsulate the core concepts (customer, product, etc.) can be stored within an Enterprise Architecture Management (EAM) tool. On the other hand, for detailed database or similar low-level modelling, diagramming and modelling tools are more suitable.

When it comes to managing inventories of Applications and Assets, the preferred approach is to utilize Enterprise Architecture Management (EAM) tools whenever possible. This is especially beneficial as long as the data related to these assets does not changes frequently (i.e. refreshes every 4 or 6 months are sufficient). For example, this is the case for applications inventories. This facilitates future queries and visualizations over the data, and the collaboration of external teams to maintain the data up to date.

See next section for the Application Landscape artifacts.

6.4 EA Tools for the Application Landscape Management Artifacts

We moved the discussion about this particular artifact in a separated subsection given its relevance. It is one of the most commonly used artifacts, and many stakeholders step up to create them including the business stakeholders.

Assume you are starting a new project and you need to document the high-level architecture in the form of a partial application landscape. Initially, use a diagramming or modelling tool to create a partial application landscape. Many details are unknown, and you will need to iterate until you reach a stable version. Once you have a good understanding of the applications and integrations involved, document them in your Enterprise Architecture Management Tool. To avoid rework, you may want to wait until the implementation is advanced before moving the information to the EA Management Tool, especially the information regarding integrations as they may change during such phase. After the data has been loaded into the EA Management Tool, you can update or add new visualizations or reports that may be of interest. Returning to the design or implementation phases, low level designs may be created using diagramming or modelling tools which are usually not transferred to EA Management Tools.

Recent studies[2] suggest that on average, (global) organizations are using around 1000 individual applications. This can represent a large number of nodes on a graph representation. If many interconnections (arcs) are also documented which link many applications (nodes), it can make low or difficult to represent some visualizations. This is a known issue of EA Management Tools.

As a result, it is advised to create visualizations of partial landscapes based on domains (i.e. Marketing apps, Order to cash apps, etc.). In any case, showing the entire full application landscape of the company would be overwhelming for the audience and would make little sense.

7 Generative AI in EA Tools

The public release of *ChatGPT* [3] in November 2022 by OpenAI marked a relevant transformation in the way companies take advantage of Generative Artificial Intelligence (AI) technologies. One notable application of this innovation is the Text-to-Code feature in traditional software development. In essence, software developers can draft a few specifications in natural language and let ChatGPT to generate the code. Developers can also incorporate existing code and seek assistance from ChatGPT in identifying bugs or issues. Similarly, recently several Low-Code application development tools empower developers to write in natural language the specifications and directly produce the database and user interface elements for the Low-Code applications.

In a similar way, several diagramming and Enterprise Architecture (EA) tools are or will be introducing analogous capabilities, where users can provide a textual description

---
[2] https://www.mulesoft.com/press-center/feb-2022-connectivity-benchmark-report.

of a diagram or visualization, and the tool automatically generates a draft version. It is worth noting that these functionalities will be essentially available through Software as a Service (SaaS) products but are unlikely to be integrated into desktop installed software.

8 Conclusions

Enterprise Architecture (EA) is a discipline for aligning a company's business and information technology strategies. EA includes the creation and maintenance of essential artifacts, including documents and architectural diagrams, that help to convey tangible value to stakeholders.

First, we have revisited the evolution of Enterprise Architecture, the challenges in demonstrating its value [7,9], and how EA Tools have evolved during the time to partially address this. Enterprise architecture has evolved significantly over the past two decades, moving away from a traditional IT Centric approach to a more collaborative approach with business stakeholders. Modern EA Tools are developed as Software as a Service (SaaS) solutions, incorporating simplified models inspired by the TOGAF framework, aimed at enhancing comprehension for business stakeholders. Newer EA tools provide a unified data repository or do not rely on files located in local folders, preventing data fragmentation (data scattered in many places), facilitate user contributions through user-friendly interfaces or surveys, and in general have an enhanced user experience.

Then, we have examined several types of artifacts commonly created and maintained by EA teams and the various types of tools used by Enterprise Architects and related functions. The tools have been compared, and it has been stated when each makes more sense to use. Additionally, a recommendation on when to use each type of Tool has been provided for the several artifacts. In general, we would recommend using diagramming or modelling tools to quickly sketch diagrams that are unlikely to be maintained over time. Instead, use EA Management Tools to document high-level information that does not change frequently and is expected to be accessible in a centralized location by any stakeholder in the company in the form of various reports or visualizations of their interest. Finally, for each of type of EA artifact several strategies have been presented to decide when usually makes more sense to use each type of EA Tool.

9 Future Work

In this paper, we examined various Enterprise Architecture Tools within the context of several typical EA artifacts. We have also observed the enhanced emphasis on collaboration with Enterprise Architects and business stakeholders in some of the most recent EA tools making them more accessible for visualization and providing diverse approaches for collecting input from all kind of stakeholders.

As future work, we plan to investigate deeper into the ongoing development and transformative potential of Generative AI in the area of Enterprise Architecture Tools. We aim to explore how this evolution could potentially benefit the EA discipline and how it may reshape the interactions between Enterprise Architects, non IT stakeholders, and the EA tools.

References

1. Iso/iec 19501:2005 information technology - open distributed processing - unified modeling language (uml) (international organization for standarization) (2005)
2. Ardoq: Ardoq. In: Ardoq Software as a Service (2022). https://www.ardoq.com/
3. Brown, T.B., et al.: Language models are few-shot learners. In: Larochelle, H., Ranzato, M., Hadsell, R., Balcan, M., Lin, H. (eds.) Advances in Neural Information Processing Systems 33: Annual Conference on Neural Information Processing Systems 2020, NeurIPS 2020, 6–12 December, 2020, virtual (2020). https://proceedings.neurips.cc/paper/2020/hash/1457c0d6bfcb4967418bfb8ac142f64a-Abstract.html
4. Buschle, M., Holm, H., Sommestad, T., Ekstedt, M., Shahzad, K.: A tool for automatic enterprise architecture modeling. In: Nurcan, S. (ed.) CAiSE Forum 2011. LNBIP, vol. 107, pp. 1–15. Springer, Heidelberg (2012). https://doi.org/10.1007/978-3-642-29749-6_1
5. Dumas, M., Rosa, M.L., Mendling, J., Reijers, H.A.: Fundamentals of Business Process Management. 2nd edn. Springer (2018). https://doi.org/10.1007/978-3-662-56509-4
6. Ebneter, D., Grivas, S.G., Kumar, T.U., Wache, H.: Enterprise architecture frameworks for enabling cloud computing. In: IEEE International Conference on Cloud Computing, CLOUD 2010, Miami, FL, USA, 5–10 July, 2010, pp. 542–543. IEEE Computer Society (2010). https://doi.org/10.1109/CLOUD.2010.47
7. Frampton, K., Shanks, G.G., Tamm, T., Kurnia, S., Milton, S.K.: Enterprise architecture service provision: Pathways to value. In: Becker, J., vom Brocke, J., de Marco, M. (eds.) 23rd European Conference on Information Systems, ECIS 2015, Münster, Germany, 26–29 May, 2015 (2015). http://aisel.aisnet.org/ecis2015_rip/62
8. Fruchterman, T.M.J., Reingold, E.M.: Graph drawing by force-directed placement. Softw. Pract. Exp. **21**(11), 1129–1164 (1991). https://doi.org/10.1002/spe.4380211102
9. Gong, Y., Janssen, M.: The value of and myths about enterprise architecture. Int. J. Inf. Manag. **46**, 1–9 (2019). https://doi.org/10.1016/j.ijinfomgt.2018.11.006
10. Group, O.M.: Omg bpmn 2.0.2 (2014). https://www.omg.org/spec/BPMN/2.0.2/PDF/
11. Haki, M.K., Legner, C., Ahlemann, F.: Beyond EA frameworks: towards an understanding of the adoption of enterprise architecture management. In: 20th European Conference on Information Systems, ECIS 2012, Barcelona, Spain, 10–13 June, 2012, p. 241 (2012). http://aisel.aisnet.org/ecis2012/241
12. Heras, F.: A comparison of enterprise architecture tools. In: Hammoudi, S., Wijnhoven, F., van Sinderen, M. (eds.) Proceedings of the 20th International Conference on Smart Business Technologies, ICSBT 2023, Rome, Italy, 11–13 July, 2023, pp. 186–192. SCITEPRESS (2023). https://doi.org/10.5220/0012121500003552
13. Kleehaus, M., Hauder, M., Uludag, Ö., Matthes, F., Villasana, N.C.: IT landscape discovery via runtime instrumentation for automating enterprise architecture model maintenance. In: 25th Americas Conference on Information Systems, AMCIS 2019, Cancún, Mexico, August 15-17, 2019. Association for Information Systems (2019) https://aisel.aisnet.org/amcis2019/org_transformation_is/org_transformation_is/4
14. Korhonen, J.J., Halen, M.: Enterprise architecture for digital transformation. In: Loucopoulos, P., Manolopoulos, Y., Pastor, O., Theodoulidis, B., Zdravkovic, J. (eds.) 19th IEEE Conference on Business Informatics, CBI 2017, Thessaloniki, Greece, July 24-27, 2017, Volume 1: Conference Papers, pp. 349–358. IEEE Computer Society (2017). https://doi.org/10.1109/CBI.2017.45

15. Kotusev, S.: The history of enterprise architecture: an evidence-based review. J. Enterprise Archit. **12**, 29–37 (2016)
16. Kotusev, S., Kurnia, S., Dilnutt, R.: Enterprise architecture artifacts as boundary objects: an empirical analysis. Inf. Softw. Technol. **155**, 107108 (2023). https://doi.org/10.1016/J.INFSOF.2022.107108
17. Kurnia, S., Kotusev, S., Shanks, G.G., Dilnutt, R., Taylor, P., Milton, S.K.: Enterprise architecture practice under a magnifying glass: linking artifacts, activities, benefits, and blockers. Commun. Assoc. Inf. Syst. **49**, 34 (2021). https://doi.org/10.17705/1cais.04936
18. LeanIX: Leanix enterprise architecture management. In: LeanIX Software as a Service (2022). https://www.leanix.net/en/products/enterprise-architecture-management
19. Lucid: Lucidchart. In: LucidChart Software as a Service (2022). https://www.lucidchart.com/
20. Martin, R., Robertson, E.: A comparison of frameworks for enterprise architecture modeling. In: Song, I.-Y., Liddle, S.W., Ling, T.-W., Scheuermann, P. (eds.) ER 2003. LNCS, vol. 2813, pp. 562–564. Springer, Heidelberg (2003). https://doi.org/10.1007/978-3-540-39648-2_43
21. Neubert, C., Buckl, S., Schweda, C.M., Matthes, F.: Lightweight approach for enterprise architecture modeling and documentation. In: Soffer, P., Proper, E. (eds.) Proceedings of the CAiSE Forum 2010, Hammamet, Tunisia, 9–11 June, 2010. CEUR Workshop Proceedings, vol. 592. CEUR-WS.org (2010). https://ceur-ws.org/Vol-592/PaperDemo13.pdf
22. Sommestad, T., Ekstedt, M., Johnson, P.: A probabilistic relational model for security risk analysis. Comput. Secur. **29**(6), 659–679 (2010). https://doi.org/10.1016/j.cose.2010.02.002
23. Systems, S.: Sparx systems enterprise architect. In: Sparx Systems Enterprise Architect version 16 (2022). https://sparxsystems.com/
24. Tamm, T., Seddon, P.B., Shanks, G.G.: How enterprise architecture leads to organisational benefits. Int. J. Inf. Manag. **67**, 102554 (2022). https://doi.org/10.1016/j.ijinfomgt.2022.102554
25. TOGAF: The togaf® standard, 10th edition. In: The Open Group Architecture Framework Version 10 (2022). https://www.opengroup.org/togaf
26. Tzitzikas, Y., Hainaut, J.-L.: How to tame a very large ER diagram (using link analysis and force-directed drawing algorithms). In: Delcambre, L., Kop, C., Mayr, H.C., Mylopoulos, J., Pastor, O. (eds.) ER 2005. LNCS, vol. 3716, pp. 144–159. Springer, Heidelberg (2005). https://doi.org/10.1007/11568322_10
27. Zachman, J.A.: A framework for information systems architecture. IBM Syst. J. **26**(3), 276–292 (1987). https://doi.org/10.1147/sj.263.0276
28. Zhi, Q., Zhou, Z.: Empirically modeling enterprise architecture using archimate. Comput. Syst. Sci. Eng. **40**(1), 357–374 (2022). https://doi.org/10.32604/csse.2022.018759
29. Zimmermann, A., Schmidt, R., Sandkuhl, K., Jugel, D., Bogner, J., Möhring, M.: Evolution of enterprise architecture for digital transformation. In: 22nd IEEE International Enterprise Distributed Object Computing Workshop, EDOC Workshops 2018, Stockholm, Sweden, 16–19 October, 2018, pp. 87–96. IEEE Computer Society (2018). https://doi.org/10.1109/EDOCW.2018.00023

Real-Time Context Monitoring and Analysis for Detecting Process Adaptation Needs

Jamila Oukharijane[1,4](✉), Mohamed Amine Chaâbane[1], Imen Ben Said[2], Eric Andonoff[3], and Rafik Bouaziz[1]

[1] MIRACL Laboratory, University of Sfax, Sfax, Tunisia
[2] Digital Research Center of Sfax, Technopark of Sfax, PO Box 275, 3021 Sfax, Tunisia
[3] IRIT, Toulouse 1-Capitole University, 2 rue du Doyen Gabriel Marty, 31042 Toulouse Cedex, France
[4] Faculty of Engineering, Free University of Bozen-Bolzano, Piazza Domenicani 3, 39100 Bolzano, Italy
jamila.oukharijane@gmail.com

Abstract. The increasingly dynamic and changing environment in which business processes are evolving requires companies to adapt them frequently. Thus, we deal in this paper with an adaptation engine ensuring the adaptation need detection of running processes, and more precisely of its first two components: the Monitor (M) and Analyze (A) components. This adaptation engine implements the MAPE-K loop and uses a contextual approach for the detection of the adaptation needs. It is based on a model that enables a complete representation of the process operating environment (OE) using the context notion. More precisely, this paper presents the architecture of the MAPE-K-based adaptation engine and introduces the BPMN4Context meta-model, which supports the modeling of the operating environment using the context along with the model of all processes and their use conditions. In addition, the paper introduces the recommended context-based approach that advocates (i) a filtering activity to select only significant context changes in the monitored data, considered as low-level context parameters, (ii) a reasoning activity to deduce high-level context parameters from filtered low-level ones, enhancing the current situation of running processes and (iii) the examining of the current situation before its analysis in order to resolve problems related to the used units and synonym values. Our approach is implemented as a system that instantiates the M and A components of MAPE-K loop. The feasibility and applicability of this approach is demonstrated by a case study from the crisis domain, a set of criteria and two performance tests.

Keywords: Context · Real-time monitoring · Situation reasoning · Situation filtering · Adaptation need detection · Context analysis

1 Introduction

To remain competitive, companies have to immediately take into account the changes occurring in their environment and adapt their business processes accordingly. Thus, their capability to rapidly and efficiently adapt their running processes to changes is an essential requirement for them. Currently, Business Process Management Systems (BPMS) implementing processes mainly support only manual adaptation: the process designer has to identify which changes in the OE require an adaptation and to resolve them by defining the required adaptation operations and carrying them out [1]. However, the manual process adaptation is a costly, time-consuming and error-prone task [2]; it requires the presence of a business expert who must possess knowledge of the environment in which supervised processes operate to identify each adaptation need and resolve it. Consequently, self-adaptation is seen as an effective solution to deal with the complexity of process adaptation with minimum human intervention [3].

Business processes self-adaptation can be ensured by way of autonomic adaptation and context-awareness. On the one hand, autonomic adaptation of running processes is usually achieved using a MAPE-K loop [4], which is an efficient solution for self-adaptation of systems in autonomic computing. This loop is conceived as a sequence of the four following steps, *Monitor* (M), *Analyze* (A), *Plan* (P) and *Execute* (E), using a *Knowledge* base (K). The latter allows managing the data of the considered system and of its OE, along with other relevant data shared by the four components implementing these four steps. The M component collects data about this system and its OE from sensors, aggregates them into symptoms, and stores them in the K base. The A component analyzes these symptoms to detect if an adaptation is required. If so, it triggers the P component, which defines the adaptation operations needed to adapt the behavior of the considered system. These operations are then carried out and transferred by the E component through effectors towards this system. As this paper deals with the adaptation need detection issue, it focuses on the M and A components.

On the other hand, self-adaptive systems must have the capability of self-adjusting to variations of their OE, often considered as their context. This latter is used to detect process adaptation needs in order to address process self-adaptation. In the BPM area, the notion of context is defined in Rosemann's taxonomy [5] as *"the minimum of variables containing all relevant information that impacts the design and the execution of a process"*. [5] outlined that four relevant types of context must be considered: (i) an *immediate context*, which covers information on the behavioral, informational and organizational dimensions of processes, which are three important dimensions to be considered when modeling processes, (ii) an *internal context*, which covers information about the internal environment of an organization that impacts the processes, (iii) an *external context*, which covers information about the external stakeholders of an organization, and finally, (iv) an *environmental context*, which covers information about external factors.

If several literature contributions [6–10] addressed the adaptation need detection issue, their recommended solutions have drawbacks. Firstly, they do not address the modeling of the OE in a comprehensive way as they do not consider all context types defined in [5]. Second, their models that support the representation of the OE are rather simplistic or even poor, as only low-level context parameters are supported to model it as a context. They do not contain high-level context parameters inferred by a reasoning component in order to deduce new information that enhances the current situation knowledge.

To overcome these weaknesses, we recommend an adaptation engine supporting a context-based approach to address the adaptation need detection issue. This engine has the four following features:

– First, it aims to provide a powerful monitoring of the OE of running processes, able to capture relevant context changes and enhance context parameters. Therefore, it allows better analysis of changes to identify whether or not process adaptations are required.
– Second, it recommends the context notion to represent the OE of processes, i.e., the current situation in which running processes operate, using context parameters belonging to any type of context parameter types defined in Rosemann's taxonomy.
– Third, it recommends the context changes filtering in order to only analyze significant changes.
– Finally, it recommends the reasoning on context parameters, which contributes to enhance the current situation by high-level context parameters, and thus the improvement of the decision-making for process adaptation.

This paper is an extended version of our paper published in the International Conference on Smart Business Technologies (ICSBT, 2023) [15]. It extends it (1) by revisiting and enhancing the context-based approach highlighting the detection of process adaptation needs and (2) by adding (i) a depth literature review which evaluate related works with a set of criteria, (ii) implementation details to introduce the developed system, and (iii) a qualitative evaluation of the proposed contributions.

Accordingly, the remainder of the paper is organized as follows. Section 2 provides the state-of-the-art on self-adaptation of processes, focusing mainly on adaptation need detection. Section 3 gives an overview of the recommended adaptation engine for self-adaptation of BPMN processes. Section 4 introduces the BPMN4Context we propose for the modeling of knowledge required by the adaptation need detection. Section 5 discusses in detail the context-based approach proposed for process adaptation need detection. Section 6 reports on the implementation of the recommended approach as a system that instantiates the M and A components of MAPE-K loop. Section 7 demonstrates the feasibility of our approach and its support system using qualitative and quantitative evaluations. Finally, Sect. 8 summarizes the paper contributions and gives some directions for future research.

2 Related Work

In the literature, there are several works addressing the detection of adaptation needs of processes and eventually proposing solutions to resolve them at runtime (*e.g..*, [3,6–11]). Due to the space limitation, this section considers only the contributions addressing this issue and discussing how to use the MAPE-K loop for the detection of adaptation needs.

We start with the contribution described in [7]. Its authors introduced an adaptation engine that implements the MAPE-K loop to self-adapt processes, with the *Monitor*, *Analyze*, *Plan* and *Execute* components. The *Monitor* component periodically pulls the contextual information about the instrumented system and transfers it to the *Analyze* component. The latter checks all the variation points and evaluates the received values according to the modeled context in each variant in order to detect the adaptation needs and informs the *Plan* component about detected adaptation needs.

Another interesting contribution is proposed in [8]. It introduced an agent-based adaptation engine for the self-adaptation of processes at run-time. This adaptation engine is also based on the MAPE-K loop where (i) the intelligent agents, in this case the *Monitor*, the *Adapter* and the *Executor*, implement the different steps of this loop, and (ii) the knowledge repository encompasses the knowledge shared among agents. When the *Monitor* agent, which continuously acquires and evaluates the current state of each process and its context, determines a symptom that needs to be analyzed (*e.g..*, indicates a business rule violation), it triggers the *Adapter* agent. The latter in turn triggers its first sub-agent, the *Analyzer*, which implements an adaptation need detection driven by goal and business rule analysis. Then, the *Planner* sub-agent implements the definition of adaptation operations required to resolve the identified needs. As for the third sub-agent, the *Simulator*, it verifies if there are some inconsistencies after applying the identified adaptation operations. If so, this new situation goes to the Analyzer.

For their part, Ayoub and Elgammal introduced, in [9], a framework for monitoring and improving social business processes (*i.e.*, processes that integrate Web 2.0 technologies such as Facebook and Twitter). This framework is presented as an instantiation of the MAPE-K loop for social data monitoring where the *Monitor* component collects the customers' social data (*e.g..*, tweets), which will be modeled in a raw format then stored in the knowledge database, precisely in social logs. Then, when enough raw social data are available in the social logs, the *Analyze* component pulls and filters them by keeping only social data representing the customers' problems. Afterwards, it moves to a social data analysis using data mining and machine learning techniques to discover the need for adaptation. If an adaptation need is detected, the *Plan* component is triggered.

Finally, Seiger *et al.* suggested, in [10], a self-adaptation of processes based on their goals, by defining a framework enabling process self-adaption in Cyber-Physical Systems (CPS). This framework is based on the MAPE-K loop, that has to be initialized with the goal and objectives of the running task, to check any inconsistency between the physical and the assumed cyber world. Once the context elements are collected in the *Monitor* step from the physical world related to the task goals, the framework analyzes them in order to check for the CPS consistency after the task execution with respect to the task goals. In case an inconsistency is detected, *i.e.*, a task goal is not satisfied, the task is adapted by replacing the resource involved in the task execution with another.

Table 1 shows a comparison of previous research studies about the detection of adaptation need, which is the focus of this paper, based on the following related criteria:

- *Observed Context Parameters*: They indicate which context types of the taxonomy defined by [5] are considered in the examined work, and thus which context parameter types serve as a support for the detection of the adaptation need,
- *Current situation modeling*: It indicates which modeling technique is used for the modeling of the acquired situation of the OE,
- *Current Situation Level*: It indicates the granularity level of the acquired context parameters,
- *Analysis Strategy*: It indicates which analysis strategy is used by the *Analyze* component for the adaptation decision making,
- *Current Situation Translation*: It checks whether the examined contribution implements or not the translation of the current situation in order to resolve problems related to the used units and to the synonymous values of the context parameters.

Table 1. Evaluation of the related research studies.

Works Criteria	Oliveira et al., [7]	Ferro and Rubira, [8]	Ayoub and Elgammal, [9]	Seiger et al., [10]
Observed context parameters	Not indicated	Internal	External	Internal
Current situation modeling	Model-based	Ontology-based	Model-based	Model-based
Current situation level	Low-level	Low-level	Low-level	Low-level
Analysis strategy	Scenario-based analysis	Condition-based analysis	Predictive analysis	Condition-based analysis
Current situation translation	Not implemented	Not implemented	Not implemented	Not implemented

The first and main observation we can make from Table 1 is based on the observed context parameter criteria: no one of the examined contributions covers the Rosemann's taxonomy [5]. For [8] and [10], the modeled context parameters refer to the internal context of processes since only the variables involved in sub-process or task goals and in business rules are modeled. In both contributions, the decision-making for adaptation is based on the comparison of the values that context parameters have in the OE to the values describing the goals of the running sub-process or task. Thus, they recommend the condition-based strategy for context analysis. As for [7], only the process variables involved in the variation points are modeled, without knowing which context type the context parameters refer to. In this contribution, the decision-making process for adaptation is based on the comparison of the values that the context parameters have in the OE and the values of these parameters in the variation points for each possible situation of the OE. Thus, it recommends a scenario-based strategy for the context analysis. For their part, in [9] the modeled context parameters refer to the external context of processes since only the variables related to social data posted by customers in social media are defined. In this contribution, the decision-making process for adaptation is based on social data analysis using data mining and machine learning techniques; so the predictive analysis strategy is recommended.

As for the *current situation modeling*, the notion of context serves as a support for the OE modeling. In the examined contributions, the used modeling technique is either ontology-based, as in [8], or model-based, as in [7,9,10]. However, none of the examined contributions, including that advocating an ontology-based approach, implements a reasoning technique. This means that the current situation level only supports low-level context parameters.

Finally, regarding the *current situation translation*, none of the examined contributions detects and resolves situation problems related to the used units and to the synonymous values.

To overcome the weaknesses of the examined contributions, we recommend a self-diagnosis approach that considers the interesting features of the examined adaptation contributions, namely, the use of the context-based model to define the current situation context of each running process. But our approach differs from them in the following respects. First, it advocates considering the Rosemann's taxonomy for a comprehensive modeling of process contexts, where the context parameters observed from the immediate, internal, external and environmental contexts of processes may be represented. Second, it supports real-time context changes monitoring and filtering in order to only analyze significant changes. Finally, it recommends the reasoning on context parameters in order to infer new knowledge.

3 An Overview of Our Adaptation Engine

Figure 1 introduces the architecture of the adaptation engine we proposed in [3] for processes self-adaptation. In accordance with the purpose of this paper, this section only gives a global description of the different components of this engine intended for process monitoring and adaptation. The next sections focus only on presenting the details of the *Monitor* (M) and the *Analyze* (A) components, which are the components involved in the detection of adaptation needs, and the processed *knowledge* (K).

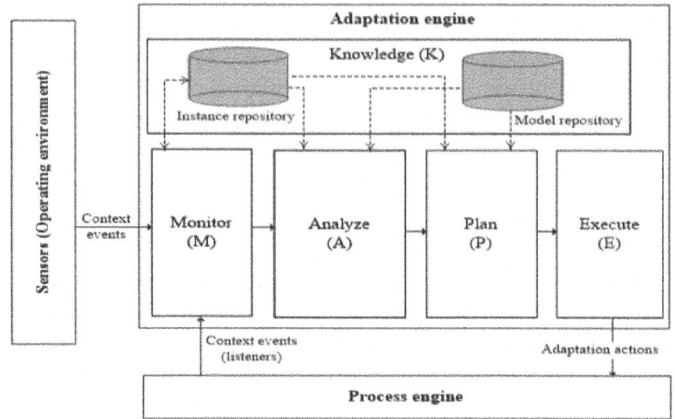

Fig. 1. Architecture of the adaptation engine.

Regarding Knowledge base (K), it is composed of two repositories: the *Model repository* and the *Instance repository*. The former stores processes along with their use conditions involving context parameters, while the latter gives an accurate picture of the state of each running process and its OE, through the data captured from both the process engine listeners and the OE sensors. Both repositories are modeled according to the BPMN4Context meta-model, which will be presented in Sect. 4.

The *Monitor* component aims at getting an accurate picture of the running processes' OE. In order to monitor a process, it subscribes/connects to the sensors of the OE and to the listeners of the process engine, and collects the values of the corresponding low-level context parameters. The *Monitor* is also responsible for filtering, aggregating and interpreting high level context parameter values according to the aggregation functions and deduction rules. As for the *Analyze* component, it is responsible for the detection of adaptation needs by comparing the use condition of the considered process described in the *Model repository* to the context featuring the current situation described in the *Instance repository*. Thus, the detection of the adaptation needs is based on context comparison. If a need for adaptation is detected by the *Analyze* component, the *Plan* component is triggered to define the set of operations to be carried out using the hybrid approach recommended in [11]. The *Execute* component is then triggered to map the adaptation operations according to the target process engine, and to invoke this latter to execute the mapped adaptation operations.

4 Knowledge for Adaptation Need Detection

The Knowledge base (K) handled and shared by MAPE components is composed of the *Model repository* and the *Instance repository*. K is modeled as instances of an appropriate meta-model, the BPMN4Context meta-model. So, in this section we start by introducing this meta-model for modeling knowledge required by the adaptation need detection. Then, we illustrate the modeling of this knowledge using a case study related to the process of flood crisis management.

4.1 The BPMN4Context Meta-Model

Our approach recommends to model knowledge required by the adaptation need detection using the two levels of BPMN4Context meta-model recommended in [11]. An excerpt of the UML class diagram of BPMN4Context is given in Fig. 2. This figure adopts the following policies: blue background for concepts related to private processes, grey background for concepts related to the definition of the use conditions of processes, yellow background for concepts corresponding to process executions, and finally green background for concepts related to current situation modeling of running process. In this figure, we particularly focus on two abstraction levels for the modeling of the context parameters: (i) the *model level*, in which we describe the use conditions of processes at design-time, and (ii) the *instance level*, in which we describe the current situation of running processes at run-time. These levels declare the structures of the knowledge base as described below.

Model Level. This level (*cf.* left side of Fig. 2) of BPMN4Context meta-model concerns the concepts involved in the definition of processes, sub-processes and tasks, with their use conditions at design-time. This meta-model introduces new classes to define these conditions of use and the involved context parameters. A use condition may be atomic or composite. Therefore, the class of the *Use condition* is specialized in two sub-classes: *Atomic use condition* and *Composite use condition*. An atomic use condition refers to the *context parameter* involved in this condition and defines the associated *operator*, *value* and *unit* of measurement. A composite use condition is an aggregation of several use conditions connected together by logical operators (and, or). It should be noted that the use condition of a process (or sub-process) is the combination of the use conditions of activities (which are tasks or sub-processes) that make up this process (or sub-process).

Instance Level. This level (*cf.* right side of Fig. 2) of BPMN4Context meta-model enables to model the OE of running processes. It deals with the concepts involved in the definition of running processes and their corresponding current situations. Each occurrence of *Running process* is related to exactly one occurrence of *Process*, but an occurrence of *Process* can be related to several occurrences of *Running process*. An occurrence of *Running process* is composed of a

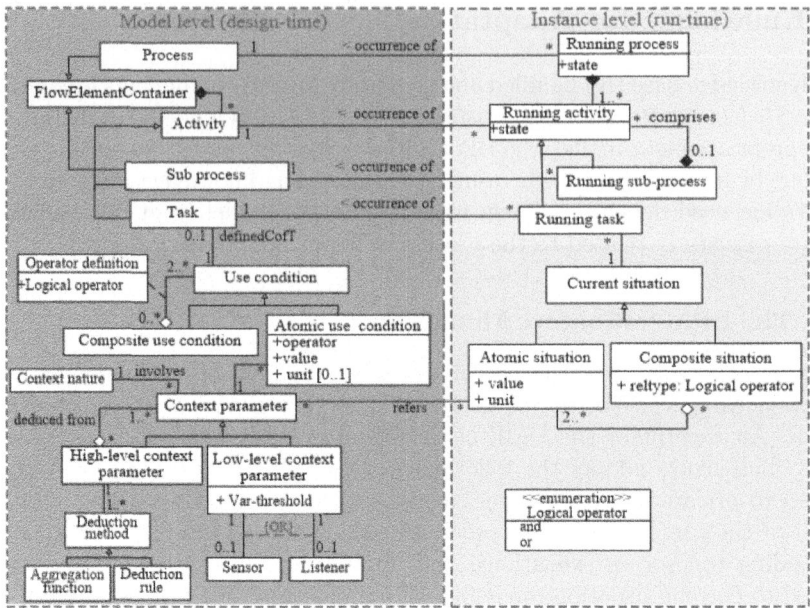

Fig. 2. BPMN4Context meta-model as a UML class diagram [11].

set of occurrences of *Running activity*. An occurrence of *Running activity* can be an occurrence of *Running sub-process* or of *Running task*. Moreover, current situations of running tasks are modeled as instances of the class *Current situation*, which may be either atomic or composite. A *Composite situation* is a set of atomic situations, while an *Atomic situation* is defined as a triplet: a *context parameter*, current *value* of this parameter and the used *unit* for measuring this value. A *Context parameter* can be a *Low-level context parameter* or a *High-level context parameter*. According to Rosemann's taxonomy, a context parameter has an occurrence of *Context Nature*, which can be immediate, internal, external or environmental. As for *value*, it specifies (i) the captured value by a sensor, represented as an occurrence of *Sensor* class, or by a process engine listener, represented as an occurrence of *Listener* class, for a low-level context parameter, or (ii) the value deduced by the *Monitor* component using a *Deduction method*, which can be an *Aggregation function* or *Deduction rule* from other(s) context parameter(s) value(s) for a high-level context parameter. The update of such a value is executed only if the difference between the obtained value from the concerned sensor or listener and the value stored in the *Model repository* is higher than the *variation threshold* (Var-threshold) of the low-level context parameter.

Note that the current situation of a running process or sub-process is the union of the current situations of its running activities, *i.e.*, running tasks and running sub-processes.

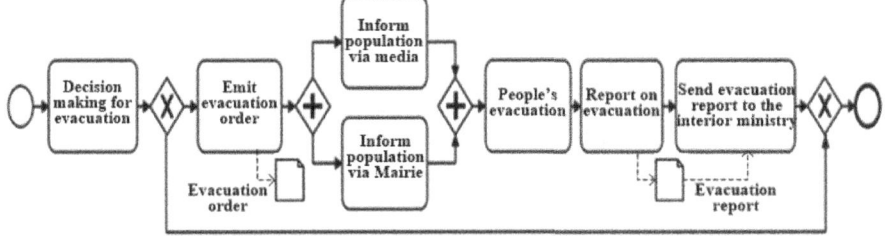

Fig. 3. Flood management process model [15].

4.2 Knowledge Modeling for Flood Management Process

This sub-section presents a real case study related to the process of flood crisis management of the major French river, the Loire, on the city of Orléans. As shown in Fig. 3, this process is triggered in urbanized impacted area when the water level of the river Loire rises above 3 m. In response to this event, the crisis cell decides whether or not to evacuate people from the flooded zones by assessing the flooding situation. In case an evacuation is needed, the Prefect emits an evacuation order, then the COD, which is the operational committee set up within the crisis cell and the town hall inform the media and the population about the flood. After that the gendarmes proceed to the evacuation of people from the flooded zones. Finally, the crisis cell reports on the evacuation, and the Prefect sends the report to the interior ministry. Like any other process, the flood management process might be subject to different OE variations, such as water level, water flow rate and precipitation amount, that could interrupt its functioning. In order to supervise this environment, we refer to the following context parameters among others:

- **Water level**, which indicates the level of water rising in the Loire. In the Orléans city, this parameter refers to the average water levels recorded at the following two stations: the Pont Royal station and the Quai du Roi station.
- **Water velocity**, which indicates the speed of the water in the Loire in the different source points of water to the Loire. This parameter refers to the average water velocities recorded at Pont Royal and Quai du Roi stations.
- **Impacted area**, which features the size of the population potentially impacted.
- **Road state**, which can be *not flooded, flooded and derivable* or *flooded and blocked*. When the roads are not flooded, people evacuate themselves. On the other hand, when the roads are flooded but still derivable, the evacuation method is carried out by land, which means that the evacuation task is carried out using specific vehicles with the help of gendarmes. However, when the roads are blocked because they are highly flooded, people's evacuation must be carried out by firefighters with zodiacs or helicopters in the most extreme cases.

– **Risk level**, which can be *low, moderate* or *high*. Indeed, the risk level of flooded zones is deduced from the following context parameters: *water level* and *water velocity*. Thus, when the water level is below of 2 m and the water velocity is below of 2,500 m^3/s, thus the risk level is "low", whereas when the water level is more or equal to 2 m and a water velocity is below of 2,500 m^3/s, so the risk level is "moderate". While, when the water level is higher than 3 m and water velocity is more than 2500 m^3/s, thus the risk level is "high".

On the basis of the previous context description, the parameters *Impacted area, Water level of a station, Water velocity of a station* and *Road state* represent the low-level context that must be measured by sensors and process engine listeners. For each of these parameters, of the numeric type, a threshold value was defined (*cf.* Table 2) in order to verify if the received change is significant or not. We note that these context parameters can be measured at different station points; for example, for the Orléans city the water level is measured at both the Pont Royal and the Quai du Roi stations. As for the high-level context parameters, such as the Water level, Water velocity, Risk level, Personnel's role and Type of equipment, they are deduced from the low-level ones according to the aggregations functions and deduction rules defined by domain experts. Some rules are given in Table 3, as an example.

Table 2. Variation threshold of low-level parameters [15].

Context parameter	Threshold value
Water level of a station	0.5 m
Water velocity of a station	150 m^3/s

Table 3. An expect of the deduction rules [15].

N	Deduction rule
R1	If water level < 2 m and Water velocity < 2500 m^3/s then Risk level = "low"
R2	If Water level ≥ 2 m and Water velocity < 2500 m^3/s then Risk level = "moderate"
R3	If Water level > 3 m and Water velocity ≥ 2500 m^3/s then Risk level = "high"
R4	If Road state = "Not flooded" Then Type of equipment = "Vehicle"
R5	If Road state = "Flooded and derivable" Then Personnel role = "Gendarme" and Type of equipment = "Vehicle"
R6	If Road state = "Flooded and blocked" Then Personnel role = "Firefighter" and Type of equipment = "Zodiac"

It is to highlight that, according to cell crisis, the flood management process defined in Fig. 3 is to use in the following context (*i.e.*, use condition): Impacted area is urbanized, Water level is more than 3 m, Water velocity is below of 2500 m^3/s, road state is flooded and derivable, Type of equipment is vehicle, personnel role of evacuation is gendarme and Risk level is moderate.

5 The Context-Based Approach for the Process Adaptation Need Detection

5.1 General Description of the Recommended Approach

Our approach addresses the adaptation need detection aiming at analyzing changes occurring in the OE to identify whether or not process adaptations are required. It helps implement efficient *Monitor* and *Analyze* components of the *MAPE-K* loop. This approach is based on (i) the real-time capture of context parameter values using sensors, (ii) the use of the context notion to represent both the OE of process models (the current situation in which running processes operate) and the use condition of each process model, and (iii) a reasoning mechanism to infer high-level context parameters from low-level ones. Therefore, the notion of context is crucial because it serves as a basis for identifying adaptation needs. Indeed, identifying adaptation needs for a running process boils down to comparing its two contexts (*i.e.*, its current situation and its use condition). The process driving this approach is shown in Fig. 4 as a BPMN collaboration diagram.

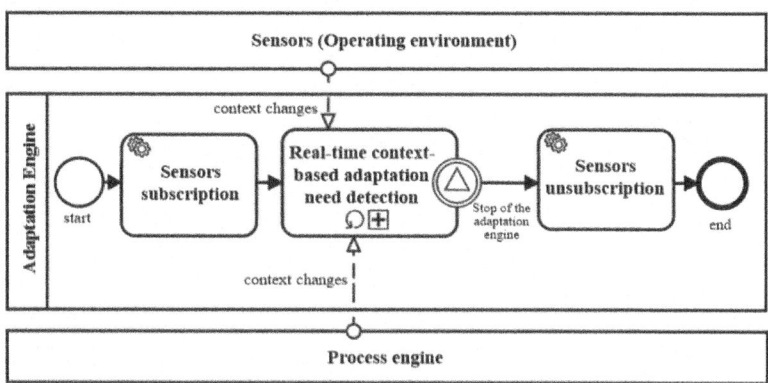

Fig. 4. Context-based approach as a BPMN collaboration diagram.

This process includes the following sub-processes:

- The ***Sensors subscription***: It includes operations required to configure the *adaptation engine* so that the OE can be observed using the push mode. More precisely, this activity (i) identifies which sensors can be used to observe the OE of the supervised process according to the defined context parameters in the *Model repository* and (ii) subscribes to each identified sensor.

- The ***Real-time context-based adaptation need detection***: It refers to the activities triggered by both the *Monitor* and *Analyze* components during the execution of one or more processes. The role of this sub-process consists in receiving and processing the data sent from the sensors or the process engine listeners, and analyzing them to detect if an adaptation of a process instance is needed, accordingly.
- The ***Sensors un-subscription***: It is triggered when the adaptation engine is stopped. In this case, the *Monitor* component stops monitoring the OE of the supervised processes and no longer follows the context changes of their sensors or listeners. The sub-process, *Real-time context-based adaptation need detection* requires more details, which are given in the following sub-section.

5.2 How Does the Real-Time Context-Based Adaptation Need Detection Sub-process Work

Figure 5 illustrates the behavior of the Real-time context-based adaptation need detection sub-process modeled as a BPMN diagram.

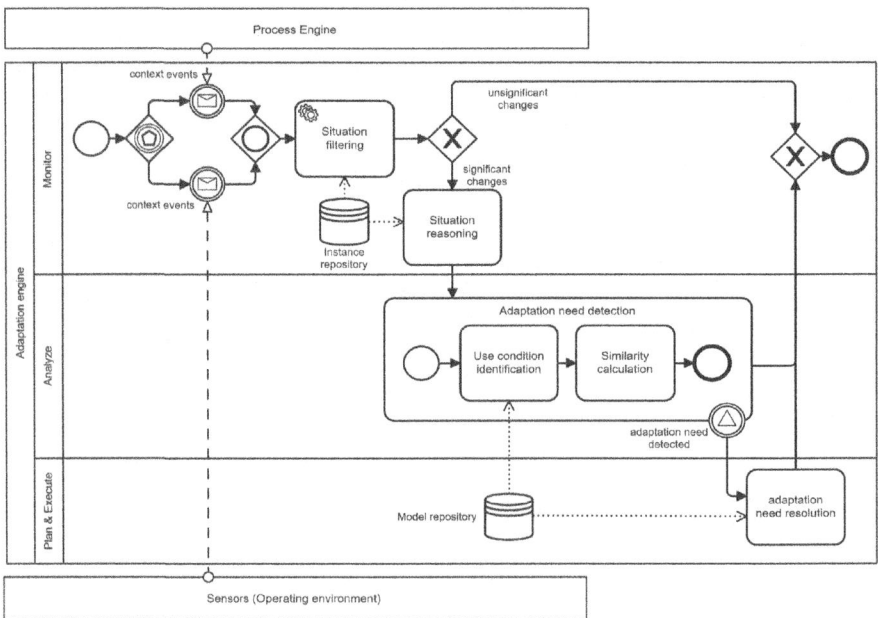

Fig. 5. Real-time context-based adaptation need detection sub-process as a BPMN diagram.

As shown in this diagram, process engine listeners and sensors simultaneously observe the execution of the running processes and their OE, and push to the *adaptation engine* the events indicating changes occurring on the context parameters. But as indicated in [12], the received data from sensors, without any further interpretation, can be meaningless, trivial, vulnerable, or uncertain due to small changes. To overcome this problem, our *adaptation engine* first executes a situation filtering activity to ensure that the reasoning activity will process only the significant data changes. This *Situation filtering* activity filters the received data and keeps only the significant changes of context parameters values. To do so, this activity compares the absolute value of the difference between the received value of each low-level context parameter and the last stored value in the *Model repository* to a certain variation threshold (*var-threshold*) stored also in the *Model repository*. So, it verifies if the received change of each context parameter value is significant (*i.e.*, the absolute value of the difference is higher than the variation threshold) or insignificant. In case all the received context changes are insignificant, the *Adaptation engine* does not trigger the situation reasoning, nor the adaptation need identification. Consequently, both the reasoning and analysis times are reduced, only by processing and analyzing the significant context changes. Otherwise (*i.e.*, when there is one or more significant context changes are received), both activities *"Situation reasoning"* and *"Adaptation need identification"* are triggered for enhancing the situation awareness by high-level context parameters values and detecting the need for process adaptation, respectively. More precisely, the first activity includes the following both internal operations to deduce the high-level context parameters from filtered low-level ones:

- The first operation, *Situation aggregation*, uses aggregation functions (*i.e.*, average, count, max, sum, etc.) of (low-level/high-level) context parameters to deduce high-level context parameters. For instance, the value of the high-level context parameter *precipitation amount* is the aggregation *sum* of the precipitation measurements acquired by the precipitation sensors located at different sources points of a river.
- The second operation, *Situation deduction*, executes the rules that ensure deducing new high-level context parameters using low-level/high-level context parameters. Let us remember that the deduction rules are defined by domain experts in the *Model repository*. The aim of this operation is to deduce a set of high-level context parameters enhancing the current situation awareness of running processes, consequently helping the process adaptation.

After executing these operations, the **Adaptation needs identification** activity is triggered to identify the possible adaptation needs of the considered process instance. This activity is modeled as sub-process in the BPMN diagram, which includes the following atomic activities: *"Use condition identification"* and *"Similarity calculation"*. The **Use condition identification** activity allows obtaining the use condition corresponding to the considered process P; it generates an appropriate query to access the *Model repository* implementing the *Model part of the BPMN4Context meta-model* and retrieve the use condition C of P. Then, the second activity, Similarity calculation, calculates the similarity between the identified use condition C and the enhanced current situation awareness S of P. The algorithm called *Sim*, shown below, implements the similarity calculation. It receives both C and S of the process P as input, and returns a similarity percentage "sim_p" of P. It calculates the similarity value "sim" of P as the number of its atomic use conditions verified by the values of the context parameters of the current situation. It compares the value of each context parameter in the current situation "PC_{CS}" to the value of the context parameter specified in the atomic use condition "PC_{UC}". Note that this comparison may require a conversion of PC_{CS} or its replacement with the appropriate synonym when PC_{UC} is expressed with a different unit of measure or a synonym of PC_{CS}, respectively. If an atomic use condition is verified, then sim is incremented by 1. Finally, the algorithm returns the similarity percentage sim_p of the atomic usage conditions. sim_p is equal to the number of the verified atomic usage conditions of P divided by its total number of atomic usage conditions. This algorithm uses the following functions:

- **convertUnit (vs, us, uc):** it converts the context parameter value vs if necessary from the unit of measurement us defined in the atomic situation to the unit of measurement uc defined in the atomic use condition. For example, the current value of the context parameter temperature is measured using the *Fahrenheit unit* (*e.g.*, 77°F), whereas the unit of *temperature* is defined in *degrees Celsius* in the atomic use condition. Then, the current value of the context parameter *temperature* is converted into degrees Celsius (*e.g..*, 23°C) by this function.
- **synonyms (v):** it resolves the possible synonymy problem when the value v of a context parameter is expressed by a synonym of that defined in the atomic use condition, using a dictionary of equivalent representations. For instance, the value of the context parameter *resource availability* can be 0 or 1 in the current situation, whereas the defined value of *resource availability* in the atomic use condition is rather "available" or "unavailable".
- **checkCondition** (v_s, op_c, v_c): It returns *true* if the value vs of the context parameter involved in the atomic situation is verified in the use condition; otherwise, it returns *false*. More precisely, it compares the current value vs of the context parameter to the defined value v_c in the atomic use condition using the operator op_c.
- **card (cs):** It returns the number of atomic situations involved in the current situation *cs*.

It should be noted that *Algorithm Sim* returns 1 as similarity value when all atomic situations featuring the current situation verify the use condition of the considered process. This means that the current situation of the considered process exactly matches the use condition of this process. But when this algorithm returns a similarity value < 1, a need for process adaptation is identified. In this case, a signal event (*need process instance adaptation* event) is triggered for defining the operations required to address this need using the hybrid approach recommended in [11].

Algorithm 1 Similarity calculation: Sim.

Require: S: Current situation, C: Use condition
Local
$sim \leftarrow 0$: real, ps: Atomic situation, c: Atomic use condition
begin function
for each c in C **do**
   if isCompositeCond (c) **then**
      SimilarityCalculation (S, c)
   else
      for each s in S **do**
         if (c.getContextPar () = s.getContextPar ()) **then**
            if $(s.getUnit() \neq c.getUnit())$ **then**
               $vs \leftarrow$ convertUnit (s.getValue (), s.getUnit (), c.getUnit ())
            end if
            if checkCondition (vs, c.getOperator (), Synonyms (c.getValue ()))
then
               $sim \leftarrow sim + 1$
            end if
         end if
      end for
   end if
end for
Return $sim/card(S)$
end function

6 Proof-Of-Concept Prototype

This section presents a proof-of-concept in order to evaluate the feasibility of the proposed context-based approach for the detection of the adaptation need. First, we give an overview of the proposed system, entitled Contextual Adaptation Need Detection System (ContAdaptNDS), implementing our contributions. Then, we illustrate the simulation of its functionalities through an example illustrating the adaptation need detection of the flood management process.

6.1 ContAdaptNDS Overview

ContAdaptNDS (Contextual Adaptation Need Detection System) is the system we developed to implement our context-based approach described in Sect. 5. It includes the *Monitor* and *Analyze* components of the adaptation engine. Figure 6 shows in detail the structure of this prototype and its interactions with other components (displayed as rectangles) and two repositories (displayed as cylinders) *Model repository* and *Instance repository*.

First, we used the jBPM[1] process engine to execute the modeled processes. We chose this engine because it is an open source engine that implements the

---
[1] https://www.jboss.org/jbpm/.

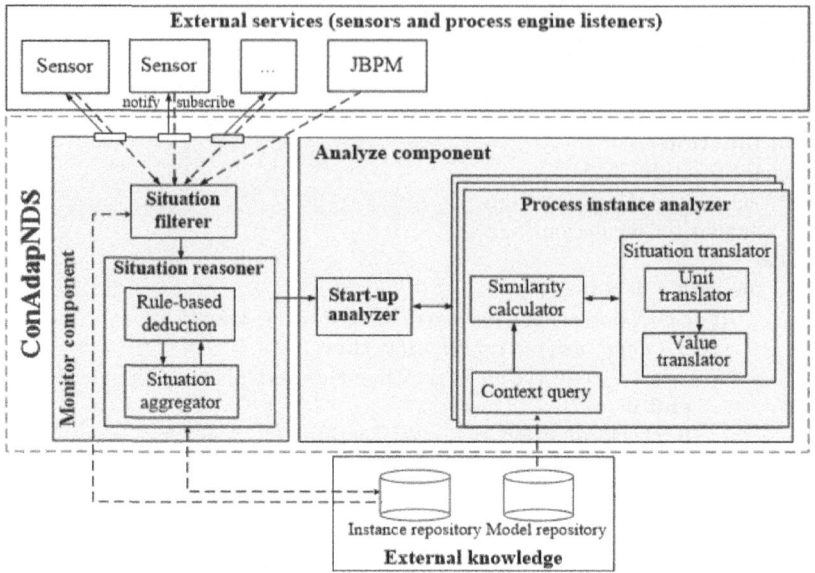

Fig. 6. Overview of ContAdaptNDS and its interactions.

standard BPMN 2.0 and provides methods for registering the listeners of process-related events, like starting or completing a process, starting or completing a task, changing a process variable, user's logout, etc.

Moreover, the *Monitor* component and the sensors and listeners, as well as their relationships, are implemented using the observer design pattern [14]. As shown in Fig. 7, the *Monitor* component plays the observer role, while the subject role is played by the sensors and listeners. Moreover, the *Monitor* component implements the *Observer* interface. However, each listener or sensor is implemented as a Java class that (i) implements the *Subject* interface, (ii) gets reading the current value of a monitored context parameter using the get *Reading* function, either from the physical entity of a physical sensor or the target system of a logical sensor, or from the process engine, and (iii) notifies the *Monitor* component using the *Notify Observers* function. The latter triggers the *Update* function that implements the context monitoring approach described in Sect. 5. In addition, the *Monitor* component calls the *Subscribe* and *Unsubscribe* functions of the Sensor/Listener classes to subscribe to or unsubscribe from the sensors or listeners in the start or the end, respectively, of each monitor execution session.

The *Monitor* component includes two sub-components:

1. **Situation filterer**, which implements the *Situation filtering* activity described in Sect. 5.2. It receives low level context parameters values from various sources, from sensors and listeners, and filters them to keep only significant context changes.

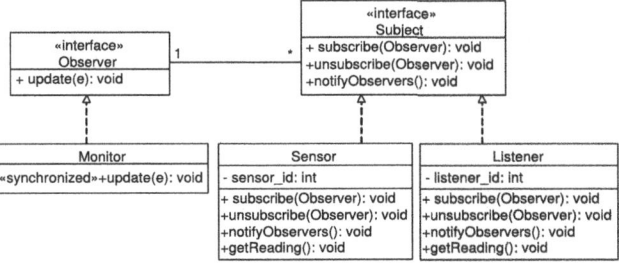

Fig. 7. Overview of the *Monitor* component and its interactions.

2. **Situation reasoner**, which implements the *Situation reasoning* activity described in Sect. 5.2. It in turn includes the following sub-components ensuring the two operations of the *Situation reasoning* activity:
    – **Situation aggregator**, which implements the *Situation aggregation* operation to transform low-level context parameters values using aggregation functions stored in the *Model repository*.
    – **Rule-based deduction**, which implements the *Situation deduction* operation. It uses the open source rule engine JBoss Drools to specify the deduction rules with the Drools Rule Language (DRL), and to infer high-level context parameters that describe the current situation of the OE.

As for the *Analyze* component of the adaptation engine, it implements in Java the adaptation need detection sub-process described in Sect. 5. It is triggered when the current situation of running processes changes and acts through the following sub-components:

1. **Start-up Analyzer.** It creates a *Process instance analyzer* for each process instance when its current situation is changed, and destroy it when the adaptation decision of this instance is completed.
2. **Process instance analyzer**: its responsibility is to detect any adaptation need of the concerned process. This analyzer consists of the following sub-components:
    – **Context Query.** This sub-component implements the *Use condition identification* activity described in Sect. 5. It is used when a *Process instance analyzer* wants to retrieve the use condition of the supervised running process.
    – **Similarity Calculator.** This sub-component implements *Algorithm Sim*, described in Sect. 5. It receives as input the current situation and the use condition of the supervised running process. Then it calls the *Situation translator* sub-component to translate the current situation by converting context parameters values of the current situation, according to the defined units and the representation in the use condition. Finally, it calculates the similarity between the received use condition and the translated current situation.

– **Situation Translator.** This sub-component consists of two modules: *Unit translator* and *Value translator*. The *Unit translator* implements the *Unit translator* function of the similarity calculation *Algorithm Sim*. It is responsible of translating the received values expressed with the units cu_cs used to describe the current situation, acquired by the *Monitor* component, into values expressed with the units cu_uc defined in the *Use Condition* class of the supervised running processes, when u_cs differs from cu_uc. In fact, once this module is deployed, it deploys several unit convertors, each of which is in charge of transforming a context parameter value from the measurement unit cu_cs of the current situation into the desired unit cu_uc. As for the *Value translator* module, it implements the *Synonyms* function of *Algorithm Sim*. This module uses the dictionary of possible equivalent representations to translate the original value v_{cs} acquired by the *Monitor* component into its equivalent value cv_{uc} defined in the *Use Condition* class when cv_{cs} is not the same as cv_{uc}, but is a synonym of cv_{uc}.

In addition to the components listed above, we have also implemented two user interfaces (*cf.* Fig. 8). The first one (*cf.* Fig. 8(a)) enables an administrator to observe all process instances and their adaptation needs. It includes two parts: *part* (1) displays a list of all supervised process instances and their states (equal to running, completed, suspended or needing adaptation), while *part* (2) contains a button titled "Fix adaptation need", which allows displaying the defined adaptation operations by the *Plan* component for resolving the adaptation need of the selected process instance.

As for the second user interface (cf. Fig. 8(b)), it is shown when the administrator clicks on the button for displaying more information about the identified adaptation need of the corresponding process. This user interface allows an administrator to observe both the (1) **current situation** produced by the *Monitor* component and stored in the *Instance repository*, (2) the **use condition** stored in the *Model repository* of the selected task instance, and (3) a short **description of the identified adaptation need** specifying the list of context parameters whose conditions are not verified.

6.2 ContAdaptNDS Simulation

In this sub-section, we illustrate the simulation of our system for the detection of the adaptation need. In order to demonstrate this, we suppose that the flood management process (*cf.,* Fig. 3) is running for Orléans city affected by Loire's floods. For this illustration, we refer to the following changes from the OE that need adaptation: *Water level of Pont Royal station = 3m* and *Water level of Quai du Roi station = 4 m* and *Water velocity of Pont Royal station = 3100 m^3/s* and *Water velocity of Quai du Roi station = 3300 m^3/s* and *Impacted area = "Urbanized"* and *Road state = "Flooded and derivable"*.

Once ContAdaptNDS, precisely the *Monitor* component receives these changes, it starts its *Situation filterer* sub-component to filter and keep only

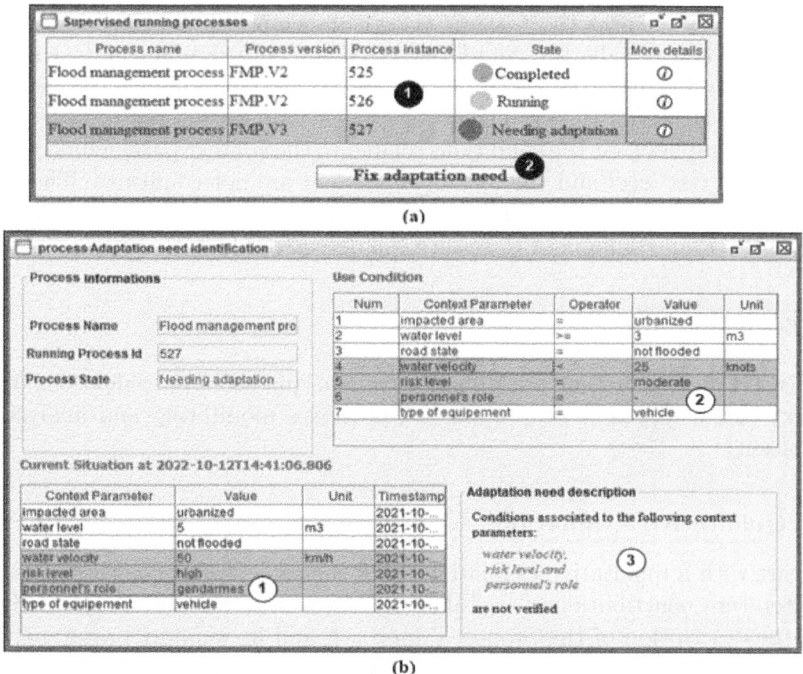

Fig. 8. A screenshot of both user interfaces showing the result of ContAdaptNDS for the detection of adaptation needs.

the significant changes. Then, it triggers the *Situation reasoner* sub-component to enhance the current situation awareness thanks to its both sub-components: *Rule-based deduction* and *Situation aggregator*. The *Rule-based deduction* sub-component enhances the situation awareness thanks to aggregation functions (average) and deduces the values of the water level and velocity of the Loire from the measured values at both Pont Royal and Quai du Roi stations. These functions led respectively to the addition of the following average values: "3.5 m" and "3200 m^3/s" for the two high-level context parameters "Water level" and "Water velocity" describing the average water level and velocity of the Loire. After that, the *Situation aggregator* sub-component enhances the situation awareness thanks to the deduction rules R3 and R5 defined in Table 2. Once the deduction is made, (i) the current situation awareness will be enhanced by new high-level context parameters *"risk level"*, *"Personnel role"* and *"Type of equipment"* having respectively "high", "Gendarme" and "vehicles" values, and (ii) the *Analyze* component is triggered to analyze all the significant situation changes. Once the *Analyze* component is started, it creates an *Process Instance Analyzer* for the current running processes through the *Start-up analyzer*. Let us remember that a *Process Instance Analyzer* is responsible for identifying any adaptation need for the considered process. In our example, there is one *Analyzer* for running flood management process in the Orléans city. This *analyzer* acts as follows. First, it asks the *Context query* sub-component to retrieve their use condition. Then it calls the *Similarity calculator* sub-component to calculate the similarity between the retrieved use condition and the enhanced situation awareness using Algorithm 1. The latter gives a similarity in the result equal to 0.67, which implies that the conditions related to the context parameters of *water velocity*, the *risk level* and the *type of equipment* are not confirmed. Therefore, the running process needs adaptation. Finally, the *analyzer* of running process triggers the *Plan* component to resolve the detected adaptation need.

7 Evaluations

In this section, we present both qualitative and quantitative evaluations of the context based approach we propose for processes monitoring and analysis by simulations.

7.1 Qualitative Evaluation

We start with a qualitative evaluation using the same criteria as those used for the literature contributions (*cf.* Table 1). Values of these criteria are deduced from the description of the proposed approach and its support prototype. The results of this qualitative evaluation are shown in Table 4.

Table 4. Qualitative evaluation of our contribution.

Criteria	Our approach
Observed context	All context types of Rosemann taxonomy are supported.
Current situation acquisition	*Push* mode: using this mode, sensors keep running simultaneously and notify the *Monitor* component of any change occurred to their data.
Current situation modeling	*Model-based technique*: the context situations are modeled according to the BPMN4Context Meta-Model
Current situation filtering	Yes: it is implemented by the *Situation filterer* sub-component.
Current situation level	*Low-level* parameters are captured by sensors and process engine listeners. *High-level* parameters are deduced by the *Situation reasoner* sub-component using aggregation functions and deduction rules.
Analysis strategy	Condition-based analysis by comparing the context situation to the use condition of the considered process.
Current situation translation	Yes: it is implemented by the *Situation translator* sub-component.

As seen in this table, most of the proposed criteria are considered by our context-based approach. The strengths of this approach are as follows. First, considering the *push* mode for context situation acquisition from sensors ensures a continuous and real-time context monitoring. Second, supporting reasoning on context parameter enhances the current situation awareness by high-level context parameters, which contributes to improve the decision making for process adaptation. Third, filtering the received context changes reduces the number of write operations on the *Instance repository* and the reasoning time, by processing only the significant context changes. Finally, translating the acquired situation enhances the decision making for process adaptation. However, our approach have a weakness; it does not support the predictive analysis for the detection of adaptation need.

7.2 Quantitative Evaluation

In this sub-section, we also evaluate by simulations our contributions for the context monitoring and the analysis functionalities. To this end, we perform two performance tests.

In the first test, we evaluate the reasoning execution times consumed by the adaptation engine using or not the *Situation Filterer* sub-component to verify that the use of this sub-component really reduces the reasoning time, and thus enhances the performance of adaptation engine.

Whereas, the second test evaluates the impact of the reasoning on context parameters to improve the outcome of the analyzer (*i.e.*, adaptation need, no adaptation need) using precision, recall, f-measure and error rate metrics.

First Performance Test. Our aim in this sub-section is to report on an evaluation that measures the advantages of using *Situation Filterer* sub-component to enhance the performance of context monitoring. To conduct this evaluation, we vary the number of sensors/listeners from 50 to 200, and we realize two experiments:

– First experiment (without filtering the received context changes from sensors/listeners): in this experiment, all the received context changes are interpreted in order to enrich the current situation awareness with high-level context parameters.
– Second experiment (with filtering the received context changes from sensors/listeners): in this experiment, the adaptation engine uses variation thresholds of low-level context parameters in order to filter the received changes by eliminating all the insignificant ones. Therefore, only notable changes are interpreted for inferring high-level context parameters values.

Fig. 9 illustrates the benefits of an upstream situation filtering on the reduction of the reasoning execution times consumed by the *Situation Reasoner* sub-component, respectively.

In the first experiment (without using an upstream situation filtering), we let the adaptation engine interprets all the received changes from sensors and listeners without filtering them. The results of this experiment are displayed by

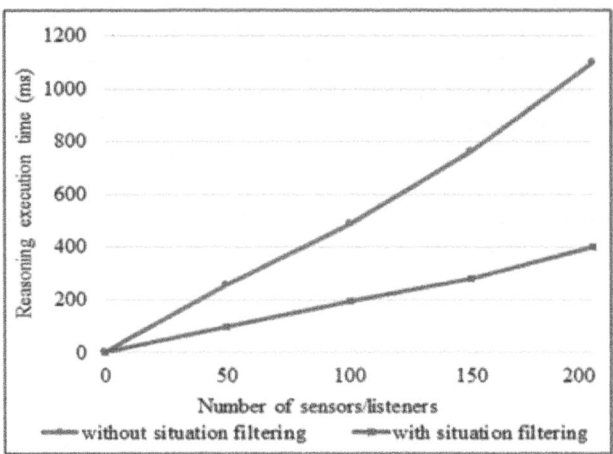

Fig. 9. Comparison of the reasoning execution times with and without performing an upstream situation filtering [15]

the red charts which confirm that the reasoning execution times grow exponentially with the number of sensors and listeners. For the case of 200 sensors and listeners for example, the time taken by the *Situation Reasoner* sub-component is about 1096.8 ms (*cf.* Fig. 9, red chart).

In the second experiment (with using an upstream situation filtering), we let the adaptation engine filters all the received changes of context parameters values by using the variation threshold (Var-threshold) of each context parameter and keeps only the significant ones. Figure 9 illustrates that the reasoning execution times are remarkably reduced, since a context parameter value is updated only if the difference between the received value and the stored value in the *Model repository* is higher than its variation threshold. In the case of 200 sensors and listeners, the reasoning execution time is decreased from more than 1096.8 ms (cf. Fig. 9, red chart) to about 400.3 ms (cf. Fig. 9, blue chart) by performing a situation filtering upstream of the situation reasoning, for example. Indeed, here when the number sensors/listeners, sending changes to the adaptation engine, is increased, the monitoring performance is not seriously affected; this is the contribution of the *Situation filterer* sub-component that eliminates all insignificant context changes.

Second Performance Test. Here, we evaluate the effectiveness of our approach for the detection of the adaptation needs by reporting on an assessment that measures the advantages of implementing the *Situation reasoner* sub-component to enhance the current situation awareness, and thus increase the accuracy adaptation engine of the adaptation needs. In this evaluation, we use different possible scenarios for the detection of the adaptation needs. For each of these scenarios, we compared the provided results with our adaptation engine in which the *Situation reasoner* sub-component is implemented against the results provided without implementing this sub-component. These scenarios, five in number, are as follows:

- SC1 (reasoning is not needed:) detecting adaptation needs considering (i) a use condition that contains only low-level context parameters and (ii) a sensed situation containing all the low-level context parameters of the considered use condition.
- SC2 (unit translation is needed): detecting adaptation needs considering (i) a use condition that contains only low-level context parameters and (ii) a sensed situation containing low-level context parameter values expressed with units different from those specified in the considered use condition.
- SC3 (value translation is needed:) detecting adaptation needs considering (i) a use condition that contains only low-level context parameters and (ii) a sensed situation containing low-level context parameters values which are synonyms of those of the considered use condition.
- SC4 (high-level context parameter deduction is needed): detecting adaptation needs considering (i) a use condition that contains both low and high-level context parameters and (ii) a sensed situation that contains all low-level context parameters of the defined use condition of the supervised task.
- SC5 (all the reasoning types are needed:) detecting adaptation needs considering (i) a use condition that contains both low and high-level context parameters and (ii) a sensed situation containing low-level context parameter values expressed with units different from those specified in the considered use condition and others which are synonyms of those of this use condition.

To evaluate the effectiveness of our context-based approach for the detection of the adaptation needs, we have considered several changes related to the current situation of the flood management environment. For each of these scenarios, we have classified the outcome of adaptation engine using a confusion matrix. In this matrix, each column represents the outcome of the implemented adaptation engine (adaptation need, no adaptation need), where each row represents the real outcome. Then, we have measured the following metrics: (1) **Precision** defines how many adaptation needs are correctly identified among all the identified adaptation needs, (2) **Recall** defines how many adaptation needs are correctly identified among all the adaptation ones (correctly identified and not identified), (3) **F-measure** refers to the balanced mean between the precision and recall metrics, and (4) **Error rate** is calculated as the number of all incorrect cases divided by the total number of test cases. The best error rate is 0, whereas the worst is 1.

Table 5 summarizes the results obtained using these metrics for the two adaptation need detection approaches that respectively implement or not the situation reasoning.

Let us comment some of these results. For the first scenario (SC1) and as indicated in Table 5, the precision and recall metrics are both equal to 1 for both approaches as the both versions of adaptation engine (with and without implementing the *Situation reasoner* sub-component) outcomes match exactly

Table 5. Evaluation outcomes of the two context-based approaches for the detection of the adaptation needs [15].

Scenarios	Results without considering situation reasoning				Results with considering situation reasoning			
	Precision	Recall	F-measure	Error	Precision	Recall	F-measure	Error
SC1	1	1	1	0	1	1	1	0
SC2	0.25	0.4	0.3	0.82	1	1	1	0
SC3	0.33	1	0.5	0.67	0.75	1	0.85	0.14
SC4	1	0.29	0.45	0.5	1	1	1	0
SC5	0	0	0	1	0.8	0.85	0.82	0.29

the real outcomes for all scenario test cases. This is due to the fact that each context parameter exists in both the use condition and the current situation with the same unit and representation.

Regarding the result of SC2, detecting the adaptation needs with a translated situation, thanks to the *Unit translator*, is more efficient than detecting the adaptation needs without translating the situation received from sensors. Indeed, the *Unit translator* function takes care of translating the units of the received situation from sensors to the units defined in the use condition. Thus, the precision, recall and f-measure metrics for adaptation engine implementing this function are all equal to 1, and the error rate metric is equal to 0. While for the detection of the adaptation needs considering the situation received from sensors without unit translation, the precision metric is equal to 0.25 and the recall is equal to 0.4. This means that (i) a set of incorrect adaptation needs are identified for some scenario test cases and (ii) a set of adaptation needs that must be detected are not identified for some other cases. As a consequence, the values of the f-measure and error rate metrics are equal to 0.3 and 0.82, respectively.

As for the result of SC3, detecting the adaptation needs considering an enhanced situation awareness, thanks to the *Value translator*, gives very acceptable results, where the values of the precision and recall are on average equal to 0.75 and 1, respectively. On the other hand, detecting the adaptation needs considering only the situation received from sensors (without enhancement) sends back the values of 0.33 for the precision and 1 for the recall. As the recall metrics are equal to 1 for both used detections of the adaptation needs, it turns out that all adaptation needs that should have been detected are identified in the different simulated test cases of SC3. As a consequence, the values of the f-measure and error rate metrics are equal to (i) 0.85 and 0.14, respectively, where the situation reasoning is considered and (ii) 0.5 and 0.67, respectively, where the situation reasoning is not considered.

For the result of SC4, detecting the adaptation needs considering an enhanced situation awareness with high-level context parameters, thanks to the *Situation reasoner*, returns values equal to 1 for the precision and recall metrics. On the other side, detecting the adaptation needs considering a situation without enhancement returns values equal to 1 and 0.29, respectively, for the precision and recall metrics. It should be noted that the precision metrics are always equal to 1, since all adaptation needs are correctly identified in the different simulated test cases of SC4, because they are detected on the basis of only the low-level context parameter values. However, the values of the f-measure and error rate metrics considering the situation reasoning is better than the values of these metrics without considering the situation reasoning. These results highlight the importance of the *Situation reasoner* sub-component.

Finally, regarding the result of SC5, detecting the adaptation needs considering an enhanced situation awareness is more efficient than detecting the adaptation needs without implementing the situation reasoning and translating. Indeed, the situation reasoning activity (i) detects and resolves situation problems related to the used units and to the synonymous values, and (ii) enriches the current situation awareness with high-level context parameter values. Thus the error rate of the adaptation need detection is considerably reduced (from 1 to 0.29).

8 Conclusion

The complexity of processes, the dynamism of the environments in which they operate, and the need for process adaptation to context changes are growing rapidly. To avoid manual process adaptations, which are costly, time consuming and error prone tasks, we recommends an adaptation engine. The latter has the following features: (i) it is designed separately from any process engine, (ii) it is based on the MAPE-K approach from autonomic computing, and (iii) it is context-based for both the modeling of the OE of running processes and the use conditions of these processes. This paper, which deals only with the *Monitor* and *Analyze* components of our adaptation engine, recommends an approach for real-time adaptation need detection. Its contributions are as follows:

- It is context-based, which has enabled it to improve the detection of the adaptation needs. The context is represented by parameters from any type of contexts defined in Rosemann's taxonomy.
- It recommends (i) the use of *sensors* and the *push* mode to support a real-time monitoring of the OE of processes, (ii) the context changes filtering in order to only analyze significant changes, and (iii) the reasoning on context parameters to enhance the current situation.
- It ensures the translation of the context parameters values related to units and synonyms before analyzing. This translation makes it possible to avoid divergences of representation of these values in the current situation and in the use conditions, and thus to improve decision-making for process adaptations.
- It is tool-based; ContAdaptNDS ensures a self-context monitoring and analysis of running processes for the detection of adaptation needs according to its principles.

The advantages of our approach are as follows (i) the two levels of BPMN4Context meta-model allow well modeling the knowledge required for the adaptation need detections, (ii) the use of *sensors* and the *push* mode allow supporting a real-time monitoring of the OE of processes, (iii) the context changes filtering makes it possible to only analyze significant changes and (iv) the reasoning on context parameters enhances the current situation awareness.

However, our approach can be improved. As future work, we plan to incorporate ontology to better capture the semantics of the current situation of running processes and take advantage of semantic aspects. In addition, we plan to study how to structure and exploit historical data and how to conduct predictive analysis of the current situation of the OE in order to predict the future adaptation needs before they arise. Moreover, we have to evaluate the usability of our contributions.

References

1. Rinderle, S., Reichert, M., Dadam, P.: Correctness criteria for dynamic changes in workflow systems-a survey. Data Knowl. Eng. **50**(1), 9–34 (2004)
2. Masoumi, A., Marrella, A., Soutchanski, M.: Towards a planning-based approach to the automated design of chemical processes. In: International Conference of the Italian Association for Artificial Intelligence, pp. 61–70. Trento, Italy (2013)
3. Oukharijane, J., Ben Said, I., Chaâbane, M.A., Andonoff, E., Bouaziz, R.: Towards a new adaptation engine for self-adaptation of BPMN processes instances. In: International Conference on Evaluation of Novel Approaches to Software Engineering, pp. 218–225. Heraklion, Crete, Greece (2019)
4. IBM: An Architectural Blueprint for Autonomic Computing, p. 31. IBM White Paper, Citeseer (2006)
5. Rosemann, M., Recker, J., Flender, C.: Contextualisation of business processes. Int. J. Bus. Process Integr. Manage. Inderscience Publishers **3**(1), 47–60 (2008)
6. Ayora, C., Torres, V., Pelechano, V., Alférez, G.H.: Applying CVL to business process variability management. In: VARiability for You Workshop: Variability Modeling Made Useful for Everyone, pp. 26–31. ACM, Innsbruck, Austria (2012)
7. Oliveira, K.M.A.: MABUP: multi-level autonomic business process", Ph.D. thesis, Universidade Federal de Pernambuco (2015)
8. Ferro, S., Rubira, C.: An architecture for dynamic self-adaptation in workflows. In: International Conference on Software Engineering Research and Practice (SERP), pp. 35–41 (2015)
9. Ayoub, A., Elgammal, A.: Utilizing Twitter data for identifying and resolving runtime business process disruptions. In: OTM Confederated International Conferences, On the Move to Meaningful Internet Systems, pp. 189–206 (2018)
10. Seiger, R., Huber, S., Heisig, P., Assmann, U.: Enabling self-adaptive workflows for cyber-physical systems. Softw. Syst. Model. **18**(2), 1117–1134 (2019)
11. Oukharijane, J., Chaâbane, M.A., Ben Said, I., Andonoff, E., Bouaziz, R.: Self-adaptive business processes: a hybrid approach for the resolution of adaptation needs. Innovations Syst. Softw. Eng. 1–23 (2021). https://doi.org/10.1007/s11334-021-00417-3
12. Da, K., Dalmau, M., Roose, P.: A survey of adaptation systems. Int. J. Internet Distrib. Comput. Syst. **2**(1), 1–18 (2011)
13. Ye, J., Coyle, L., Dobson, S., Nixon, P.: Using situation lattices to model and reason about context. In: International Workshop on Modeling and Reasoning in Context. Denmark, pp. 1–12 (2007)

14. Gamma, E., Helm, R., Johnson, R., Vlissides, J.: Design patterns: abstraction and reuse of object-oriented design. In: Nierstrasz, O.M. (ed.) ECOOP 1993. LNCS, vol. 707, pp. 406–431. Springer, Heidelberg (1993). https://doi.org/10.1007/3-540-47910-4_21
15. Oukharijane, J., Ben Said, I., Chaâbane, M.A., Andonoff, E., Bouaziz, R.: A context-based approach for real-time adaptation need detection. In: 20th International Conference on Smart Business Technologies, pp. 114–125. Italy, Rome (2023)

Indoor and Outdoor Navigation for Personalised Shopping: Assisted Path to Desired Products

Mehmed Cihan Sakman[1], Oliver Cvetkovski[1], Panagiotis Gkikopoulos[1], Francesco Martella[2], Massimo Villari[2], and Josef Spillner[1(✉)]

[1] School of Engineering, Zurich University of Applied Sciences, Technikumstrasse 9, Winterthur, Switzerland
{sakmameh,cvetkoli}@students.zhaw.ch,
{pang,josef.spillner}@zhaw.ch
[2] MIFT Department, University of Messina, Messina, Italy
{fmartella,mvillari}@unime.it

Abstract. Purchasing products in the real world has seen increasing levels of digital support. In this article, we describe the combination of multiple research results leading to the first end-to-end *smart shopping* process. It involves first finding a set of suitable shops for a product or set of products through *physical web search*, and then navigating inside each shop through *indoor navigation*. The necessary technologies around multimodal input of desired products, signalling and navigation, as well as notification are described in detail with concrete technologies. This permits the assessment of cost in addition to the feasibility of implementation.

Keywords: Smart shopping · Product search · Real-time location services

1 Introduction

Smart shopping subsumes all retail processes from the perspective of either the customer or the store owner that are supported by digitalisation, including in the real world through appropriate sensing and signalling. From the consumer perspective, digital companions shift those processes from offer-oriented to needs-oriented ones, taking the personal preferences into account. A particular goal of smart shopping research is to match the efficiency and convenience of e-commerce shopping on the web, while bringing additional advantages such as privacy, fulfilment speed and strengthening regional and sustainable retail structures. Solution approaches need to take the whole journey into account: Finding appropriate stores, navigating to them, and finding the right products within those stores.

Technology is a key driver behind capturing personal preferences, expressing recommendations, giving guidance and other contributors to that experience. Outdoors, this involves capturing the shopping needs through multimodal user interfaces such as voice (VUI), precise navigation through global satellite networks (GNSS); and routing through maps and transportation planning, push notifications from nearby places through beacons [1]. Indoors, it involves access points, mobile devices, smart shelves and dispensers, electronic shelf labels (ESL) and point of sales (POS) stations, cameras and other sensors; and industry-specific software such as Enterprise Resource Planning (ERP) for dynamic stock management, label designers, rule engines and campaign dashboards [21]. Apart from being technologically sophisticated, the technology needs to be robust, affordable and accepted by customers [18, 23].

Mapping the web-based convenience from e-commerce to the real world, given the technologies mentioned before, the *physical web* is a term that refers to customer activities in the physical world in analogy to what is common on the world wide web: browsing, searching and navigating, socially connecting and similar interactions happen via digital signals and devices, constituting a *cyber-physical system of systems* ubiquitously available to customers at their locations and embedded in their daily activities. In the context of smart shopping, the analogy of an online product search on the physical web is the specification of a product or set of products on a human intention level, for instance via voice input, and a guided navigation to the most fitting location for the product, based on pre-planned paths but also dynamically adjusted based on the current user location or evolving price as possible optimisation criteria. When searching for multiple products, for instance to buy ingredients mandated by a recipe, this navigation becomes more complex, especially when also involving indoor segments of larger stores. Furthermore, with increasing pedestrian zones in downtowns, the navigation and guidance should also encompass the transportation to and between stores.

Despite heavy investment, the systems offered by global IT players such as Amazon and Google do not yet meet these consumer expectations even at the starting point of the journey. Figure 1 shows an exemplary Google Maps search for butter in the city of Seattle, USA. Despite the maps service being optimised for customers in terms of businesses (hotels, pharmacies, ATMs), it does not drill down into the product level and therefore gives a wrong recommendation to a housewares shop with a brand name containing butter. Hence, a product-level understanding and secondary mapping from products to stores and their locations, as well as product properties such as prices and available quantities, needs to be achieved by a smart shopping guide targeting a physical web search.

The key research question is in the design of an adequate software and hardware system that takes product semantics, customer needs, and product signalling into account so that the physical web search becomes competitive to existing online product search approaches. To address the research question, we propose an end-to-end physical web search process that is people-centric and responsive. To validate the process, we also provide software architecture for such an end-to-end shopping process and explain relevant parts of the architecture at the implementation or experiment levels. Moreover, we discuss latency and cost concerns from a practical adoption perspective, and we outline additional challenges that may emerge from a larger-scale implementation across cities and regions with potentially thousands of concurrent shopping processes.

The work extends our previous work [37] on indoor navigation with the intent capturing and outdoor navigation perspective. The focus in the text is specifically to investigate the feasibility of cost-effective augmented product search in urban shopping areas and within the stores. Customers interested in fully defined products, brands or less

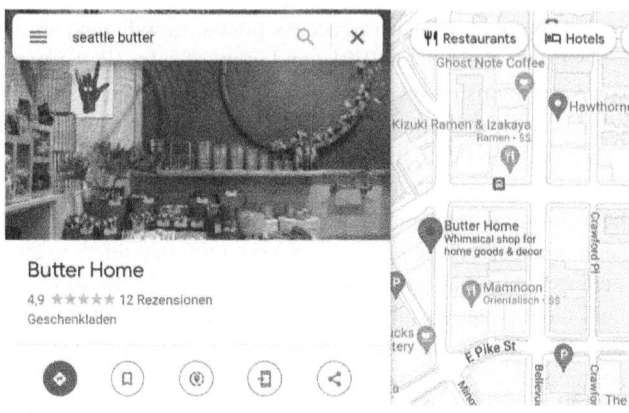

Fig. 1. Incorrect product search in Google Maps.

defined categories need assistance in expressing their interests, getting an overview situation about the availability, and receiving guidance through signalling and navigation to ensure that the chosen products end up in the basket. From a technology perspective, this requires a complex workflow encompassing an interactive device (usually the consumer's mobile phone), beacons for indoor/outdoor positioning, and shelf labels associated to products. Building an unconstrained lab-level technology could address this problem but would not have chances of being adopted on the market. Instead, we opt for a real-tech approach, intending to design and validate a solution that works in the constrained environments found in real stores and matches real cost requirements.

We claim the following contributions: First, an end-to-end workflow for personalised and privacy-preserving physical product search covering outdoor and indoor segments of the customer journey. Second, a realisation of the workflow with mobile application, web application, backend services and shelf labels. Third, a validation in a smart shopping lab environment involving technologies in use in stores today, to emphasise the feasibility of industry adoption.

In the following sections, we first present related works (Sect. 2) to give sufficient background information on our research motivation. Next, we give details on the research objectives and method (Sect 3) and convey information on relevant technologies (Sect 4). Adding our contributions, we present an in-depth application scenario and end-to-end smart shopping workflows (Sect 5), and the resulting system design and implementation (Sect 6 and 7). We evaluate the system according to the scenario workflow (Sect 8) before concluding the paper (Sect 9).

2 Related Work

Shopping is an activity covering multiple channels: Traditional purchases in stores, online purchase with delivery, or online purchase with pickup are among those channels that are well understood according to the literature on multi-channel, cross-channel and omni-channel processes including logistics and marketing [12, 39]. A recent trend, ship-from-store [2], extends the channels by involving stockless merchants who upon the arrival of an order proceed to determine a suitable nearby seller.

Smart shopping concepts align with these trends by supporting the involved stakeholders with adequate technology. The term originated with the rise of e-commerce and the need for brokering in the 1990s [34] and became soon associated with interactive software solutions such as the ontology-based Smart Shop Assistant [29]

About a decade ago, the focus of smart shopping shifted towards the blending of physical technology such as transponders, beacons, sensors and displays. An early example is the SmartCart enhancement to real shopping carts through RFID [20]. The wide-spread possession of smartphones and smart watches further influenced this research direction [22, 30]. More recently, research has been conducted on real-time location services (RTLS) including indoor navigation such as EyeLoc [8] Further research and innovation happened around technology for store owners, such as cleaning and restocking robots. We omit this side due to our work's focus on the customer.

While the potential of revitalisation of downtown stores and tourist shopping areas has been acknowledged by the literature [16], its realisation in particular through COVID-19 pandemic and post-pandemic measures is still ongoing. Holistic system designs starting from the outdoor perspective are needed in order to convey the benefits of smart shopping solutions to stakeholders like city planners and store owners.

Research on digital shopping assistance especially around navigation to products in the physical space has been a niche topic for a long time but has seen progress in the recent years. For visually impaired people, assistance is obligatory and can be addressed with autonomous navigation based on computer vision, text recognition and text synthesis [26] as well as combinations of computer vision and barcode detection [11] and the combined use of accelerometer, gyroscope and magnetometer [32]. The effectiveness of search increases with the data and suitable data structure modelling and visualisation, and therefore research has also been conducted on taxonomies and ontologies such as OntoNavShop [36].

Specifically for indoor environments, researchers have also explored connected devices in shops for other purposes beyond impairment such as smart shopping carts that follows the consumer autonomously [19], technology-enabled personalisation (TEP) [35], and the effects of using mobile devices with augmented reality on consumer behaviour [10]. A previous work studied product-awareness shopping through RFID [9] but required the consumer to be already close to the product to retrieve its information. Many of the studies are conducted with an economics background and do not dive deep into technical matters of feasibility and realisation. In contrast, our work combines physical product finding and hybrid notification about products of interest, an aspect lacking from many of the proposed approaches, and establishes a technological grounding. The hybrid notifications exploit the growing deployment of electronic shelf labels, a technology already investigated from a psychological perspective in terms of revenue effects [5] and customer acceptance [15] but not yet in the context of navigation.

From an innovation perspective beyond the research, indoor navigation and physical product search is increasingly commercialised by startups such as MobiDev and Hyper, and attracting the interest of large mobile platform operators and advertisement brokers such as Apple and Google. However, the combination of indoor and outdoor navigation in an end-to-end process has not been conducted so far.

3 Research Objective and Method

The research objective is the investigation and design of a novel end-to-end phyiscal web search in the domain of shopping that fulfils certain minimum requirements:

1. Domain-specific intent detection. According to the related work analysis, IoT-supported shopping processes exist but only cover a part of the process by not starting with the expression of intent, whereas intent detection in IoT has been explored for a long time [27, 28]. We contribute a domain-specific intent detection for atomic and compound food products based on a taxonomy represented as tag hierarchy.
2. People centrism. The search process can be initialised by text or voice input, including the consideration of local dialects based on a custom-trained text corpus [33]. The mobile device under the control of the customer is the sole information holder at any step of the shopping process and makes the invisible visible. However, the approach also assists people without mobile devices, for instance by initiating a product search in a browser or kiosk system and then relying on environmental signalling through ESLs. This design choice aligns with existing people-centric digitalisation in smart cities and regions [6].
3. Cost effectiveness and technological grounding. In order for the solution to be adopted by businesses, in particular smaller shops, it needs to be affordable and involve equipment already purchased in the industry today. Hence, a solution must be validated to perform in such an environment.

To achieve the goals, we take a design science approach and propose a distributed software architecture, deployable as needed to things, devices and the cloud, that smartly supports the shopping process by considering three distinct aspects to support the intent detection and people centrism: product semantics, product signals, and latency.

The software architecture should support the process along its steps: Multimodal search inquiry specification, including privacy-preserving and localised support for voice recognition; mapping of search terms to locations and product taxonomies, including complex products such as recipes; location refinement with a mapping of products to stores; and end-to-end navigation involving both outdoors (e.g. based on GNSS but also outdoor-placed BLE beacons) and indoors (WiFi, BLE beacons, ESLs).

4 Preliminaries

Localisation of moving entities, such as customers in a store, is possible with multiple techniques. Recent research reports about a precision of around 2 cm that can be achieved with a high number of Ultra-Wide Band (UWB) nodes, for instance [40]. High deployment cost, low mobile device adoption and less stringent application requirement however lead to more balanced decisions on localisation technologies. Moreover, privacy concerns have been raised in the camera-based first smart shopping discussions [3], even leading to broad media coverage[1], leading to further trade-offs. QR codes alleviate these concerns but require active scanning, similar to NFC tags. Bluetooth Low Energy (BLE) beacons are another contender in this space but require dense deployments to achieve tolerable precision and expose a highly device-specific performance [14]. BLE technology is affected by the influence of obstacles [24]. Limitations of precision or acceptance have little effect on the use case analysed in this paper. In our high-level workflow, we do not make any specific assumption and instead merely assume the presence of a suitable localisation subsystem. Table 1 gives a high-level indication of advantages and disadvantages of the main method families.

Table 1. Localisation methods and technologies [37].

Method	Indoor	Cost	Precision
GSM tracking	yes	high	low
Camera tracking	yes	high	med-good
GPS/GNSS	no	low	medium
BLE beacons	yes	medium	med-good
BLE AP	yes	high	medium
UWB	yes	high	good
QR codes, NFC	yes	low	–

Similar to the localisation, there is an open design space concerning the notification channels for searching as well as guiding and navigating users. Technologies should be inclusive, not requiring any particular device (assuming the search could be initiated with a kiosk at the entrance or via a service robot), and be of low cost from the store owner perspective. The corresponding overview is given in Table 2. It is evident that using the personal mobile phone has the advantage of supporting both visual and audible notifications. Electronic shelf labels (ESLs) are less intrusive and, despite having a certain installation and maintenance cost as well as potential security challenges [25], can be a suitable choice if already installed especially due to their proximity to the products. Again, our workflow abstracts from the possible notification options and only assumes the presence of at least one.

---

[1] e.g. Swiss railways shops https://awiebe.org/en/sbb-uses-cameras-for-facial-recognition/.

Table 2. Notification methods and technologies [37].

Method	Inclusive	Cost
Mobile phone	no	low
Mobile scanner	yes	high
Earplugs	no	low
ESL LED	yes	medium (battery)
ESL pageflip	yes	low
Kiosk screen	yes	high

5 Application Scenario and Workflows

For a better understanding of the research challenge, we start by describing a typical customer-facing smart shopping scenario in greater detail. Shopping may in principle refer to food or non-food products, or to services. These shopping targets are subject to diverse relationships such as bundles and compound products (sets) as well as products and services that are often bought together, based on statistical analysis.

5.1 Overall Workflow and Outdoor Perspective

A generic end-to-end customer workflow that can be applied to the procurement of goods in the physical web is shown in Fig. 2. A customer expresses the intent to get products, using multimodal input including voice, plain text, category browsing or a product photo. Compound products, such as recipes, are broken down into individual products as part of this process. Next, the customer receives map navigation to the stores able to fulfil the desired order. Alternatively to proceeding along this navigation, the list of products and services is saved and used as trigger for nearby offerings, based on GNSS and/or beacons. Finally, in each store, navigation and guidance through notifications is offered to the desired products.

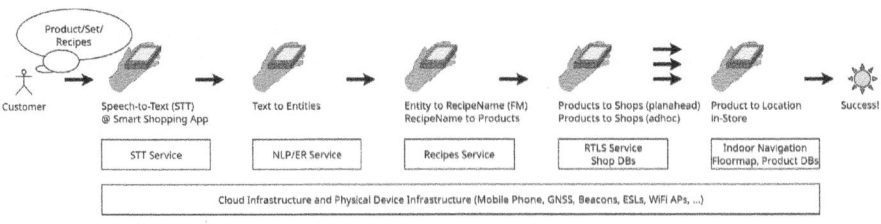

Fig. 2. Customer workflow from intent expression to fulfilment.

The workflow itself, while sophisticated, is composed of existing technologies and engineering methods. However, its cost-effective realisation is challenging, and achieving it helps to find an answer to the research question. To narrow down the focus for our research, we have implemented the proposed workflow specifically for food products in supermarkets, including appropriate data modelling and curation.

5.2 Indoor Subworkflow

The workflow shall be characterised by combining personalisation, i.e. considering the consumer's search preferences, and privacy preservation, i.e. allowing anonymous use. In the last part referring to the indoor navigation, these characteristics furthermore relate to the coupling of search and notification through temporarily assigned unique notification symbols such as numbers or colours, depending on the notification channel, in order to support multiple concurrent physical product search activities within a store.

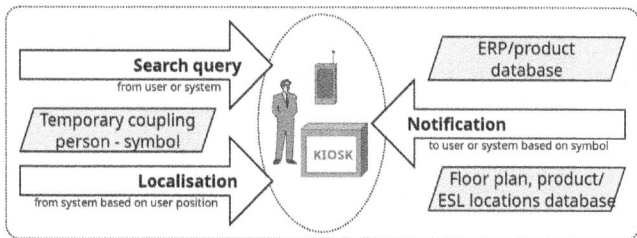

Fig. 3. Scope for the personalised shopping workflow (based on [37]).

In conjunction with the various options for localisation and notification, the scoping of the workflow is determined according to Fig. 3. It connects the three main activities with the necessary data structures, indicating an initial data curation effort by the store owner which can however draw on what stores using shelf labels already have, thus not causing additional cost related to the input data.

Referring to the detailed workflow specification expressed as sequence diagram in Fig. 4, each phase will be described with greater attention to the most innovative technological components. The workflow either starts from the consumer who desires to search for a product in the shop, or by the system upon the consumer entering the shop with previous preferences saved. For simplicity, we focus on the first variant (Step 1 - User search product in the shop). The user types a text reference of the product (possibly using voice recognitition and speech-to-text conversion) and chooses the one that interests him/her from the list of available products, or a set of products matching a desired category. Again, for simplicity, we focus on the single product search case. At this point the application sends the data with the searched product to the Backend server (Step 2 - Receives user request through API). The server checks the availability of the product in the database (Step 3 - Looking for product availability). The database is updated by the shop owner or automatically from the shop management system. The Backend Server responds to the User App with a positive or negative ack of the research (Step 4a - Send Response). If successful, it returns the position of the product and some information. In parallel, the indoor navigation algorithm calculates the initial route to reach the product

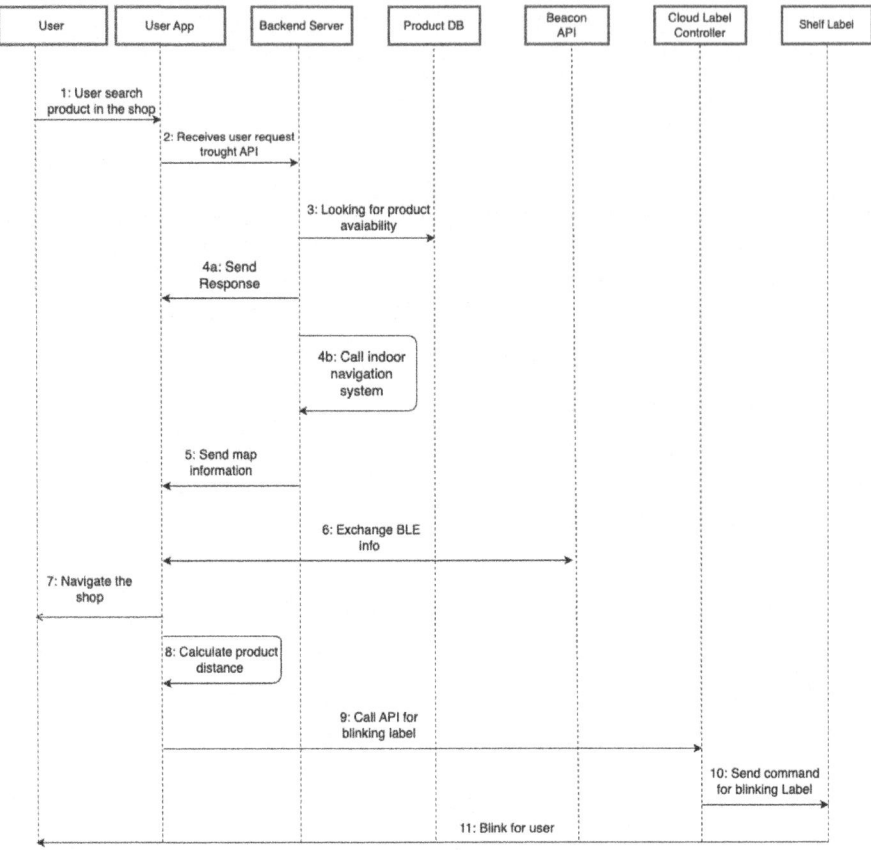

Fig. 4. Sequence diagram of indoor consumer interaction [37].

(Step 4b - Call indoor navigation system). Map and navigation information is then sent to the User App (Step 5 - Send map information).

The User App communicates via API with the positioning devices installed in the store; again for simplification, we refer to one option, BLE beacons (Step 6 - Exchange BLE info). The data exchange allows the indoor navigation algorithm to guide the user towards the shelves with the product (Step 7 - Navigate the shop). The User App is updated indicating the distance from the product which is recalculated during navigation (Step 8 - Calculate product distance). When the user arrives within "visibility" distance of the labels on the shelves, the User App via API passes the information to the Cloud Label Controller (Step 9 - Call API for blinking label). This component knows the position of the labels for each product. Moreover, depending on the chosen notification method, it is aware of the assigned color of the LED or number on the flipped label itself that the user expects to see. If the label exists and is working, the Cloud Label Controller sends a command to the label to make it flash or pageflip (Step 10 - Send command for blinking label). At this point, the label containing the information on the product sought flashes with a specific color or number which will be recognised by the User (Step 11 - Blink for user). The workflow described allows a user who is looking for a specific product in a shop to check its characteristics and availability and search for it on the shelves without wasting time physically searching for it. The flexibility of the workflow opens up the possibility of future developments that can, for example, suggest a product to the user on the basis of a profiling process and allow him/her to reach it, take it and paying the product directly in the app.

5.3 Assumptions

The shortest path for searching for the product depends on its position in the store. The store owner must be able to organise the shelves according to marketing needs. It is essential that an indoor navigation system for personalised shopping allows for easy setup of IoT devices in correspondence with the map and the association between shelf and product. For this purpose, the indoor system needs to provide administration functions that mirror the geolocation functionality available outdoors. This functionality allows the loading of the floor map in image format and the related display of the beacons. The map will be displayed to the user during navigation. The software then allows to associate the products it contains with each shelf. In this way, the store manager will be able to move the products according to business needs and subsequently update the system. The products with related images and information will be imported directly from the company management system such as an ERP. The association with the label can occur subsequently either manually or via automatic systems, for instance, through service robots.

6 Mobile Interaction and Navigation System Architecture

This part of the paper discusses customers' interaction with the mobile application and underlying technologies, following the phases of the workflow. For the purpose of a better understanding of the technologies, the case of the search for a single food product is reported, even though lists of products and compound products are also supported. The mobile application is designed for the user's smartphone. Nowadays many people use smartphones on a daily basis. These devices are designed to work with different technologies including BLE-optimising battery consumption.

There are four subsections through this section: Search Store for Product, typically initiated outdoors before deciding on what store to go to; Locate User, the part where the indoor navigation process takes place; Search Product, where the customers search for a specific product they want to buy; and Navigate to Product, detailed information about the searched product. Each of those refers to a subprocess from the previously explained workflow, providing a concrete realisation for the mobile device side while remaining flexible for the infrastructure side in terms of beacons and ESLs.

6.1 Search Store for Product

The system design follows a distributed approach with functionality decomposed into multiple backend services, combining custom development with existing APIs and services resulting from other research activities.

The services are primarily consumed through two mobile applications. The first, responsible for beacon scanning and signal transmission, runs as native application on the device, for instance a mobile phone or tablet. The second, responsible for the user interaction, is delivered through a dynamic web interface and can also be consumed on other devices. For simplicity, both are collectively referred to as mobile application in the remainder of the text.

The mobile application is implemented with its own API and bindings to the other APIs, a document database containing information on products and locations as well as tags, and dynamic notifications based on web sockets. Figure 5 summarises the implementation architecture in the context of the physical world with beacons associated to the locations and location/product-specific messages.

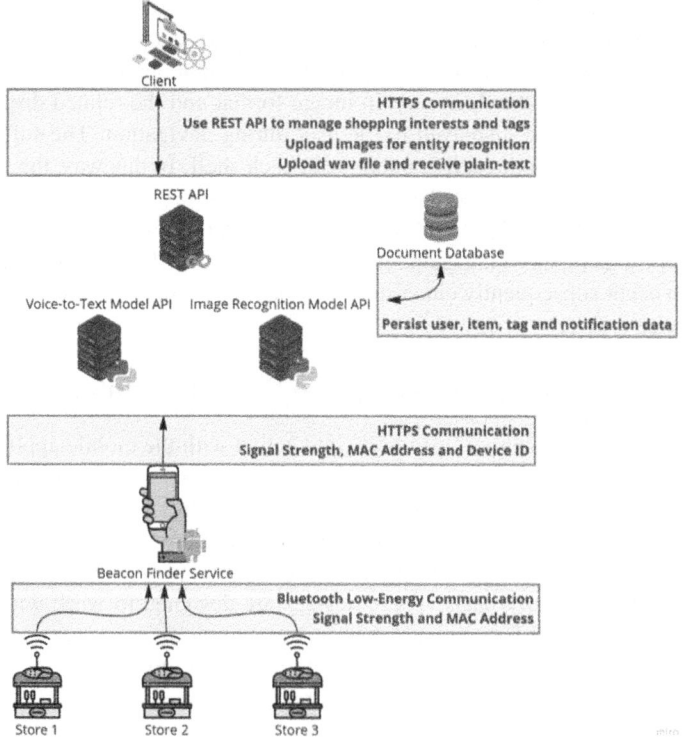

Fig. 5. System architecture encompassing mobile application and backend services.

Products are registered as triplets consisting of a textual and visual information (name, brand, description, image), a price, and a set of associated tags. The tags are organised in a hierarchy and allow for expressing product similarity through narrow or broad categories. For instance, two bags of pepper may be branded and priced differently but would both fit under the narrow tag 'pepper' for most consumers, as well as under the broader tag 'spices'.

Stores are registered as similar triples, consisting of textual and visual identity, geographic location, and references to available products. The expression of dynamic availability or quantity is omitted but could be provided by an inventory system or enterprise resource planning system. Figure 6 exemplifies the outdoor routing result as part of a search process.

An impression of the mobile application to initiate the smart shopping process in urban areas is given in Fig. 7. The example shows a multilingual product search based on multimodal input. The result includes planahead routes but also adhoc notifications that were not part of the initial search while they might be of interest to the customer from nearby places on the shopping path.

6.2 Locate User

The interaction-centric indoor workflow is based on a distributed software architecture connecting the necessary system components for search, localisation and notification as shown in Fig. 8.

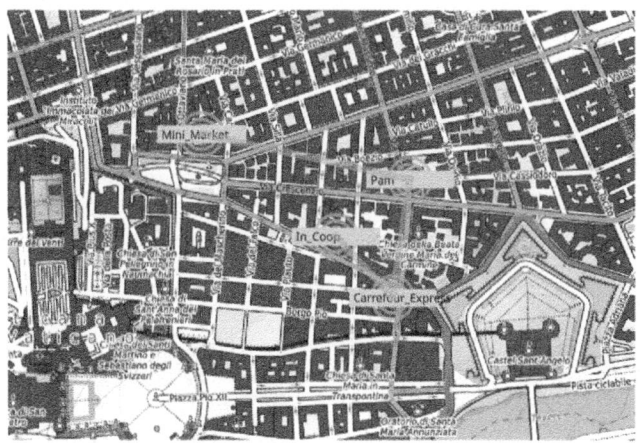

Fig. 6. Map visualisation of suggested shortest outdoor path.

On the mobile application home screen, there are two main paths on with which customers interact: Locate User and Search Product. On the Locate User path, there is a straightforward process: indoor navigation using BLE and locating the customer on the floor map of the shopping store. Depending on the physical deployment, the Bluetooth signals may arrive from a ceiling-mounted access point; in this case, either a single AP provides angle-of-arrival support to determine the direction (and the user's mobile device supports the necessary BLE protocol version), or multiple APs are used for trilateration. Alternatively, if no AP is available or does not provide a suitable API, a mesh of BLE beacons can be deployed, calibrated and used for the same purpose, with configurable density to balance deployment cost and localisation precision.

172   M. C. Sakman et al.

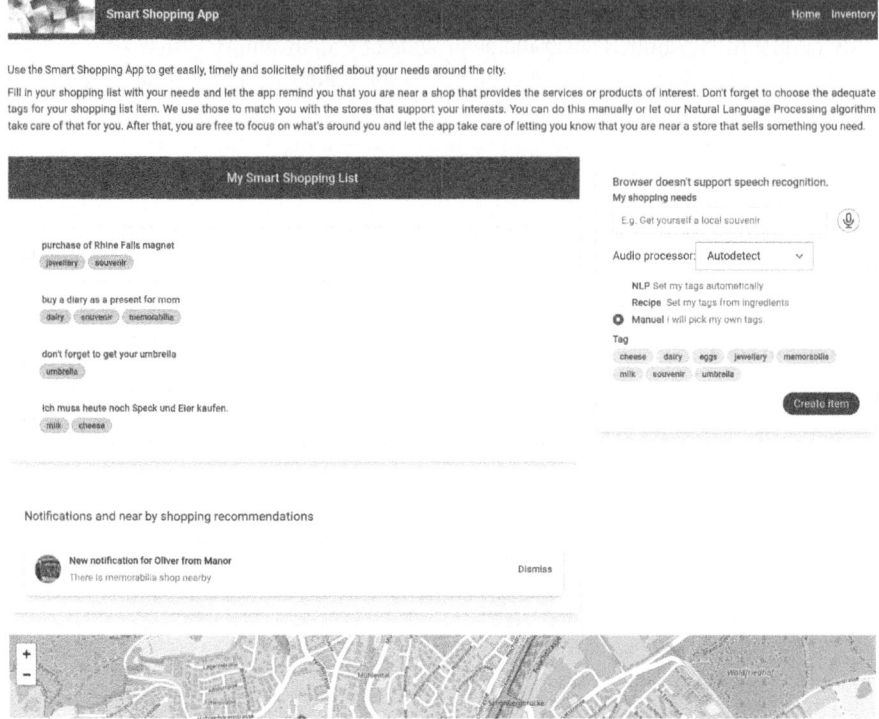

Fig. 7. Mobile application serving as multimodal interface for consumers.

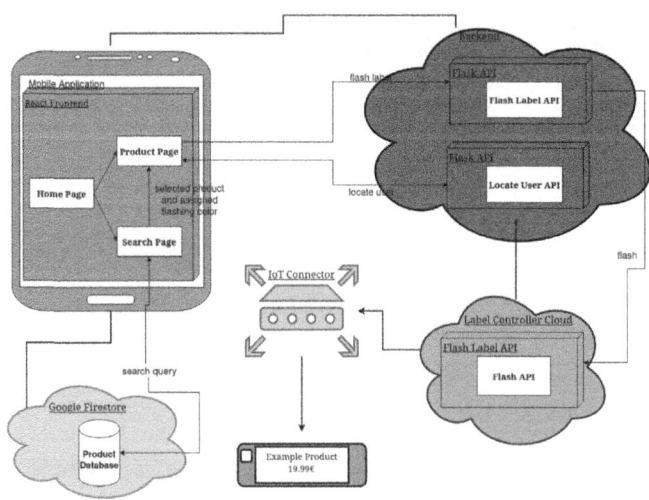

Fig. 8. Indoor mobile application architecture [37].

In our implementation, based on existing research we provide a Neural Network-based navigation algorithm which is competitive in accuracy. Combination of Bluetooth fingerprinting, a Neural Network, and a Kalman filter to predict the position of a user is used for the navigation, as expressed in Fig. 9. The algorithm is separated into two phases, which we refer to as the preparation and localization phases. For the preparation phase, training data is collected by moving a Bluetooth receiver device between as many different points on the shop floor as possible and collection signal strength (RSSI) measurements from the BLE beacons. This data forms our BLE fingerprint database and serves as the training data for a feed-forward neural network. It should be noted that by conventional terms this model is over-fitted, as all the training data is collected from the same location and so it would not work in a different location unless retrained. This is however the state-of-the-art in neural network-based fingerprint localisation, and the traditional alternative of multilateration based on the RSSI measurements [7] also requires manual calibration on location. The model can then predict the location of the receiver (a user's smartphone) and the prediction passes through a Kalman filter for smoothing in between measurements to reduce the jittering of the position the user sees on their screen.

6.3 Search Product

The Search Product path in the application is designed for sending search queries to the database where all the products are stored, typically an ERP, but alternatively a Firestore database with generic schema that works out of the box in our implementation. Customers can easily search for any products they want on this page and then connect to the localisation to correlate both the customer position and the product position. In addition to the search query feature of this page, the other important function is the personalised assignment of an anonymised results indicator, in the form of a colour or number related to the notification channel.

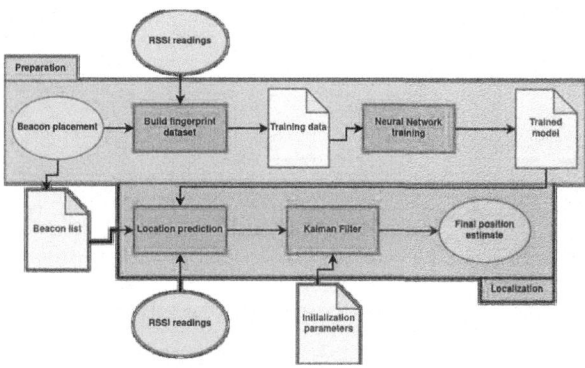

Fig. 9. Beacon-based indoor navigation algorithm [37].

The ESLs available on the market and used in that research have limited flashing colours for flashing commands, and limited preloaded e-ink pages for pageflipping. To avoid customer confusion, each customer should have a unique flashing colour or display number to track the ELSs applying to the appropriate search results. Nevertheless, it is impossible to assign unique colours or numbers to each customer with the current hardware technology. Colours are usually limited to single-digit amounts, and e-ink pages to low double-digit amounts. Therefore, each customer will be assigned different colours or numbers temporarily during the product search, with the mobile application informing about the assignment. If all possible colours or numbers are occupied, customers will be informed and move to the standby list if they wish. Other possible approaches to increase the physical notification options beyond the phone itself are possible, but not currently implemented by us, such as combinations of colours and numbers, or different blinking LED frequencies or patterns.

A sample view of the Search Product entry page for a hypothetic store associated to our physical research lab premises, as outlined in the validation section below, is shown in Fig. 10.

6.4 Navigate to Product

Customers will arrive at the Navigate to Product Page if they search for a product and click that product on the Search Product page. The Navigate to Product step is the final yet potentially longer-run destination of the customer. Here, customers can find information about the product, such as product location on the floor map, distance from

Fig. 10. Search Product sample view [37].

the product, price, and a descriptive image. In case no assignment was performed yet, the assigned colour or number will be first displayed on the Navigate to the Product page. The same assignment is then shown as a reminder on the Navigate to the Product page. In case of all colors are occupied, customers will see that in the pop-up screen, and if they wish, they will move to the standby list until a color becomes available. Even without assigned colour, the map-based navigation on the mobile device itself provides a suitable fallback, although it excludes customers without a phone or without the application installed.

Again, a sample view of this subprocess is provided in Fig. 11. It shows the floor map on the left side, with an overlay for navigation consisting of two to three main items of information: The current location of the customer, the location(s) of the product(s) resulting from the search, and possibly, although not presently implemented by us, a preferred path to collect all products, for instance based on the shortest path navigation. The addition of the path would be more useful in practice in larger stores or malls. On the right side, the page shows the next product in the results list along with navigation information and the assigned personalised indicator.

7 Technology Fitting

7.1 Mobile and Cloud Messaging

To initiate the search of stores for certain products, a low-latency messaging between the customer's VUI interface on the mobile phone and backend cloud services is needed.

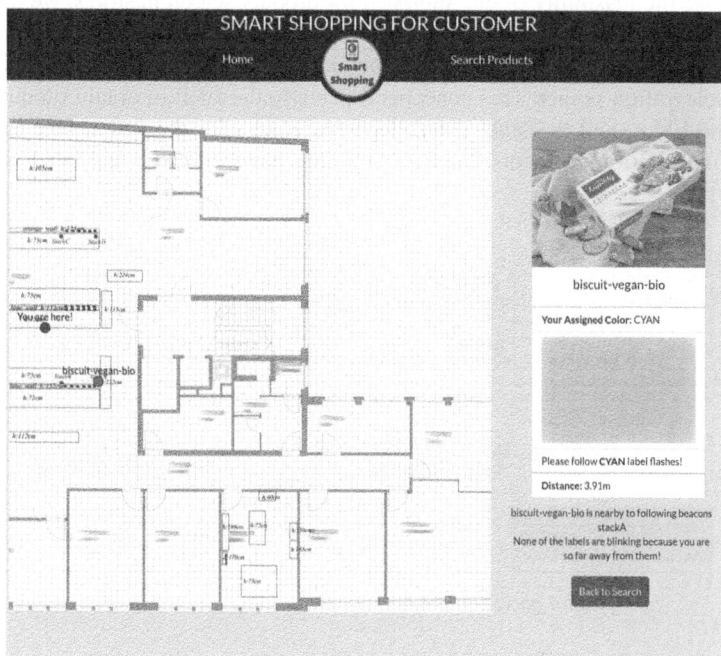

Fig. 11. Navigate to Product sample view [37].

The first stage of the end-to-end workflow consists of the following message transmissions between devices and software components:

1. Voice input from microphone via web browser to STT API, returning a list of recognised entities to the app frontend. Web browser support for microphone input varies, for instance in Chrome with a fixed binding for English language detection. Our app can use both the built-in support or transcode the resulting WebM format to WAV for further handover to a WAV-processing service supporting a second language. Additionally, it can use an autodetection service which will probe both language services and decide on the likely language based on scoring.
2. Entity input from app frontend via backend to a recipes API, with the capabilitiy of returning a list of products including tags, locations and prices. The service performs a fuzzy matching of recipe names to a database of recipes, and normalises product quantities as part of this process.
3. Placement of these products into the virtual basket of the frontend, and interfacing with the maps API to display nearby physical stores that are able to supply the desired products.
4. Further post-processing such as shortest path determination.

The message flow between internal system components implemented by us and external components provided by third parties is summarised in Fig. 12.

7.2 Indoor Navigation Equipment

To determine the feasibility of our approach for product search in stores, we have validated it under realistic conditions, in a research laboratory for smart technologies, following a real-tech approach by using commercial technology widely deployed in stores today as integration points. This concerns especially the ERP to obtain product information, the ESLs, and the label controller to interact with the ESLs. Due to proprietary communication protocols, the tight coupling between ESLs and label controller

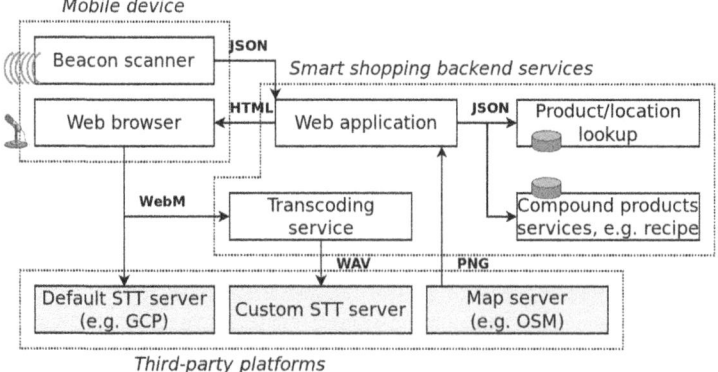

Fig. 12. Message flow between internal and external system components.

is unavoidable, whereas the other technological choices permit a degree of flexibility. Table 3 contains the details on all chosen integration points. The table also informs about an approximate and rounded price point in € in order to facilitate the discussion on how economic the resulting solution can be especially for smaller stores. Of particular research interest in this context is the ability to replace existing functionality with an open source implementation that can be used to foster innovation. This analysis provides our third contribution.

Table 3. Integration points (APIs, portals) for end-to-end validation and comparison [37].

Category	Solution	Cost
ERP	ExtendaGo	100 €/y
Label designer	Vusion Studio	400 €/y
Label controller	Vusion Optipick	350 €/y
Self-localisation	Mist API	300 €/y
Self-localisation	*our approach*	–
Mobile application	*our apporach*	–

7.3 Indoor Navigation Testbed

Our indoor testbed setup resembles a small store with three longer shelves, a total of 30 ESLs in use to mark products, and 12 BLE beacons. The one-time hardware cost is around 200 € for the ESLs, 200 € for the IoT adapter, 700 € for the AP and 120 € for the beacons. In order to have greater flexibility for investigating mobile device behavior, we have used a Linux-based notebook instead of a mobile phone to interact with the system.

By interacting with the ERP and generating label images dynamically on our backend system, both for the product and the numbered pageflip pages, we are in a position to discard the label designer. Moreover, by being able to tap into beacon-based positioning, we are also able to discard the existing localization API. Store owners who prefer to use those online platforms will still be able to do so with our implementation.

We set up the products on the shelves with a 1:1 mapping to ESLs. For labels that emit BLE signals, these could be used as a high-density grid for the navigation. However, most products on the market do not emit signals. Therefore, in our testbed, we assume one beacon per running shelf meter, with the aim to lure customers nearby the target shelf area. Once nearby, the local notifications such as label flashing and pageflipping can occur. An impression of the testbed is given in Fig. 13.

In the experiment environment, 12 BLE beacons were positioned in the research lab space at specific places to create a 4 m x 7.2 m grid spaced by 2 m representing the shopping store along room dividers representing the shelves. The schematic grid is shown in Fig. 13, left side. RSSI measurements were then collected at different positions to collect a fingerprint dataset to train the Neural Network model. The dataset was used

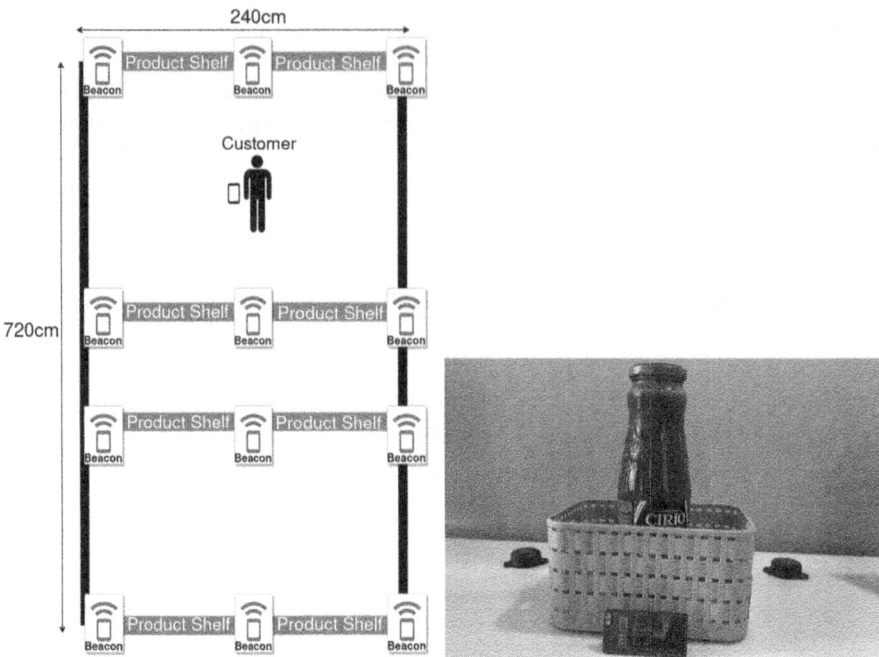

Fig. 13. Schematic view of physical experiment layout, and impression of a product [37].

as training data to generate a Neural Network model that predicts customers' positions based on RSSI readings. The RSSI readings are collected in the background from the 12 beacons in the grid every 4 s. The frequency of 4 s was selected to ensure all beacons are given the chance to advertise and be received by the mobile device. The neural network inference itself is actually much faster. Since that technology will be used in shopping stores, the Neural Network model is purposefully overfitted to get more accurate predictions, meaning the model is only usable in the location it is trained in. Once the model is trained, it is used to predict a position which then passes through a Kalman filter to smoothen the value and rule out spikes. The output of the filter is the final output exposed by the localisation service. The final result represents the location of the customer on the floor map.

7.4 Indoor Navigation Software Implementation

The implementation of the web application used for validation purposes was built using several underlying technologies. For the front end, React JS was used to create the user interface. React JS is a widely used JavaScript library for building user interfaces and allows for the efficient and scalable development of complex web applications. The back-end service was built using Flask API, a microweb framework written in Python. Flask API allowed for the creation of RESTful APIs that could be used to interact with physical devices (label controller for ESLs, beacon/WiFi scanner). Requests sent through the React front-end were able to interact with these APIs to retrieve data from and send data to the IoT devices. Finally, the Google Firebase platform was used as the database for the web application. Firebase is a cloud-based database service that provides real-time updates, secure user authentication, and scalability, making it a reliable and effective choice for the web application's database needs.

The software implementation resulting from our research is available as open source [38]. We expect that it helps accelerating the setup of real-labs for personalised shopping and product search in the future.

8 Evaluation

8.1 Outdoor Navigation Findings

The system's services and backend components were deployed on an 2.5 GHz octocore OpenStack cluster with 16 GB RAM. To validate the system at scale, we re-use the RecipeNLG dataset from University of Poznań [4] containing more than 2.2 million recipes with around 234,000 unique ingredients extracted from plain text with named entity recognition. Our evaluation data set limits this to the first million recipes for a meaningful baseline. Due to a lack of public ERP databases, we then generated a synthetic dataset of 1000 shops, each containing between 1000 and 25000 products.

A 2.6 s audio record representing a single recipe name serves as reference input data to the shopping process. Due to process and network interferences in the shared environment, all measurements were conducted 20 times and the fastest measurements were included, noting that additional delays may be significant but depend on the deployment. The audio record represents a recipe with 13 ingredients which were eventually spread across 11 shops.

Figure 14 summarises the trade-off in time/resource utilisation in looking up the constituent products by compound product name. Accordingly, due to the optimum lookup time being reached with optimisation level 4, this level has been chosen for the implementation and subsequent experiments.

Table 4 contains the full account on roundtrip time for the entire search process, from the submission of the audio record from the web browser to the generation of the trip plan ready for visualisation on a map. With $1/2$ s roundtrip time, the approach is considered attractive to customers and implementable in practice.

8.2 Indoor Navigation Findings

Our findings cover both economic and technological considerations. Concerning the localisation, we can confirm that indoor navigation based on beacons is feasible for a shop environment concerning the navigation precision towards an area close to the target shelf, and that despite additional investment, the overall cost may be lower if such a deployment is planned from the start.

The mean positioning error of the model is typically 50–100cm (the resolution of the grid), although spikes occasionally occur (Step 6 - Exchange BLE info and Step 7 - Navigate the shop). The accuracy is generally higher than RSSI-based multilateration

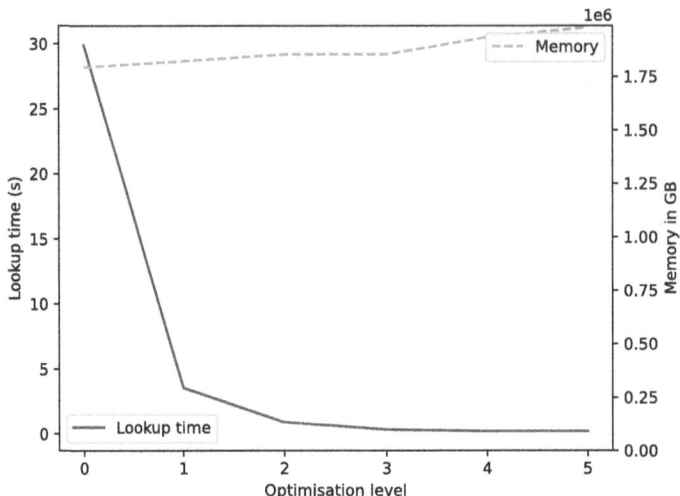

Fig. 14. Trade-off between compute time and memory utilisation for fuzzy compound product lookup.

Table 4. Latency-optimised physical web search delivery.

Message	Fastest roundtrip	Naïve baseline
WebM (2.6 s) to WAV	0.089 s	– /same
WAV to text	0.280 s	– /same
text to recipe (1:1M)	0.002 s	29.902 s
recipe to products	0.001 s	0.168 s
network overhead	0.016 s	– /same
products to locations (13:1000)	0.001 s	2.822 s
locations to trip plan	0.001 s	– /same
network overhead	0.022 s	0.022 s
TOTAL	0.412 s	33.300 s

as used in the state-of-the-art and comparable with more advanced solutions such as angle-of-arrival-based detection [31] or UWB [40] which is more expensive to install and also incompatible with the majority of customer smartphones. With further training rounds, which could be automated by piggy-backing on cleaning or restocking robots in stores, the precision can be expected to increase slightly.

Assuming a write-off period of five years for personalised shopping equipment, store owners today will have to invest 6850 € (including all hardware except for the beacons) to get production-grade support for introducing ESLs and for being able to access a raw positioning API. At this cost, they would still need an on-top solution for personalised navigation and physical product search. In contrast, our solution requires

Fig. 15. Augmented reality integration prototype (based on [37]).

the beacons but is able to discard two existing platforms and the AP as mentioned above. If WiFi is required in the store, a more reasonably priced AP could replace it, with a presumed cost of 200 €. This results in a total cost of 2970 €, equivalent to 43% of the comparative investment, and with the added benefit of obtaining an integrated solution for search and navigation.

9 Conclusions

We confirm the technical and economic feasibility to realise digitally assisted end-to-end shopping processes from any location to the final products in the store. The technical feasibility is backed up by implementations of outdoor and indoor navigation workflows, starting from the specification of the desired product to the final signalling of the shelf location. The economic feasibility is backed up by the validation in an environment consisting of industrially applied technologies which can be re-used, thus not requiring additional investment into equipment, installation, maintenance and operation (including electricity cost). The amount of additionally required data points, such as the mapping of products to shelf locations, can be automated or guided as shown by us, thus remaining tolerable from a business perspective. Stores that have not yet invested into equipment at all also gain an economic value proposation and can realise the indoor navigation part for a four-digit amount.

For the customers outdoors or in the store, a privacy-preserving and inclusive experience is provided. The results can be exploited commercially to drive revenues in physical stores and shopping areas that are under pressure from online shopping. The prototypical software implementation is available under an open source licence [38] so that a commercialisation by digitalisation providers in the retail industry also becomes feasible.

Our research has focused on support for hybrid notifications including navigation on the mobile device. From a human-computer interaction perspective, additional modalities to receive nagitation advice and notifications could be built on top of our work. This includes augmented reality (AR) navigation to maintain the overview in larger shops with multiple separate shelves hosting the desired products. Our implementation is prepared for this modality and we have already coupled it to a first AR-based navigation system as sketched in Fig. 15.

Based on this outlook, we see a number of follow-up research, experimentation and innovation angles in smart shopping interaction beyond AR. One factor is sustainability and autarky on the electricity side, supported by solar-powered ESLs and beacons that work well in stores due to good natural or artificial lighting conditions, along with charging stations for mobile devices and regional production and distribution of electricity through microgrids [13]. Another factor is improved data quality through multi-sensor fusion and multi-perspective consensus voting [17]. Along this path, the application will suggest additional products nearby to the customer as they navigate through the market. If the customer accepts any of the recommended products, the application will automatically generate a new walking path with the same logic. This feature will provide a seamless shopping experience for users, helping them discover new products while efficiently navigating through the store.

Acknowledgements. Research partially supported by Innosuisse - Swiss Innovation Agency in project Indoor Navigation for Personalised Shopping/62895.1 INNO-ICT. This work has been partially supported by the European Union - FSE, PON Research and Innovation 2014–2020 Axis I - Action I.1 "Dottorati innovativi con caratterizzazione industriale" CUP: J75F20000100007.

References

1. Amaxilatis, D., Giannakopoulou, K.: Evaluating retailers in a smart-buying environment using smart city infrastructures. In: 2018 IEEE International Conference on Pervasive Computing and Communications Workshops, PerCom Workshops 2018, Athens, Greece, March 19-23, 2018, pp. 284–288. IEEE Computer Society (2018). https://doi.org/10.1109/PERCOMW.2018.8480304
2. Bayram, A., Cesaret, B.: Order fulfillment policies for ship-from-store implementation in omni-channel retailing. Eur. J. Oper. Res. **294**(3), 987–1002 (2021). https://doi.org/10.1016/j.ejor.2020.01.011, https://www.sciencedirect.com/science/article/pii/S0377221720300321
3. Bermejo, C., Chatzopoulos, D., Hui, P.: Eyeshopper: estimating shoppers' gaze using CCTV cameras. In: Proceedings of the 28th ACM International Conference on Multimedia, pp. 2765–2774 (2020)
4. Bień, M., Gilski, M., Maciejewska, M., Taisner, W., Wisniewski, D., Lawrynowicz, A.: RecipeNLG: a cooking recipes dataset for semi-structured text generation. In: Proceedings of the 13th International Conference on Natural Language Generation, pp. 22–28. Association for Computational Linguistics, Dublin, Ireland (Dec 2020). https://www.aclweb.org/anthology/2020.inlg-1.4

5. Boden, J., Maier, E., Dost, F.: The effect of electronic shelf labels on store revenue. Int. J. Electron. Commer. **24**(4), 527–550 (2020)
6. Brandt, T.: Interview with David Prendergast on "mediating between technology and people in smart city transformations". Bus. Inf. Syst. Eng. **60**(3), 265–267 (2018). https://doi.org/10.1007/s12599-018-0531-7
7. Cantón Paterna, V., Calveras Augé, A., Paradells Aspas, J., Pérez Bullones, M.A.: A bluetooth low energy indoor positioning system with channel diversity, weighted trilateration and kalman filtering. Sensors **17**(12), 2927 (2017). https://doi.org/10.3390/s17122927, https://www.mdpi.com/1424-8220/17/12/2927
8. Cao, Z., Du, J., Liu, M., Zhou, Q.: Eyeloc: Smartphone vision enabled plug-n-play indoor localization in large shopping malls. In: 2019 IEEE International Symposium on Dynamic Spectrum Access Networks (DySPAN), pp. 1–10 (2019). https://doi.org/10.1109/DySPAN.2019.8935776
9. Chen, C., Huang, T., Park, J.J., Tseng, H., Yen, N.Y.: A smart assistant toward product-awareness shopping. Pers. Ubiquitous Comput. **18**(2), 339–349 (2014). https://doi.org/10.1007/s00779-013-0649-z
10. Chen, J.V., Ruangsri, S., Ha, Q., Widjaja, A.E.: An experimental study of consumers' impulse buying behaviour in augmented reality mobile shopping apps. Behav. Inf. Technol. **41**(15), 3360–3381 (2022). https://doi.org/10.1080/0144929x.2021.1987523
11. Deshmukh, S., Fernandes, F., Chavan, A., Ahire, M., Borse, D., Madake, J.: SANIP: shopping assistant and navigation for the visually impaired. CoRR arXiv preprint arXiv: abs/2209.03570 (2022). https://doi.org/10.48550/arXiv.2209.03570
12. Do Vale, G., Collin-Lachaud, I., Lecocq, X.: The new retail model: global reach demands omni-channels. J. Bus. Strategy **43**(6), 339–349 (2021)
13. Ferrari, M., Ollis, B., Starke, M., Massol-Deyá, A.: Why the Next Microgrids Will Be Well Connected. IEEE Spectrum (September 2023)
14. Fürst, J., Chen, K., Kim, H.S., Bonnet, P.: Evaluating bluetooth low energy for iot. In: 2018 IEEE Workshop on Benchmarking Cyber-Physical Networks and Systems (CPSBench), pp. 1–6 (2018). https://doi.org/10.1109/CPSBench.2018.00007
15. Garaus, M., Wolfsteiner, E., Wagner, U.: Shoppers' acceptance and perceptions of electronic shelf labels. J. Bus. Res. **69**(9), 3687–3692 (2016)
16. García-Milon, A., Pelegrín-Borondo, J., Juaneda-Ayensa, E., Olarte-Pascual, C.: The smartphone: the tourist's on-site shopping friend. an extended cognitive, affective, normative model. Telematics Inform. **61**, 101618 (2021). https://doi.org/10.1016/j.tele.2021.101618
17. Gkikopoulos, P., Kropf, P.G., Schiavoni, V., Spillner, J.: AVOC: history-aware data fusion for reliable IoT analytics. In: Zhang, K., Gherbi, A., Bellavista, P. (eds.) Proceedings of the 23rd International Middleware Conference: Industrial Track, Middleware 2022, Quebec, Quebec City, Canada, November 7-11, 2022. pp. 1–7. ACM (2022). https://doi.org/10.1145/3564695.3564772
18. Gong, T., Wang, C.Y., Lee, K.: Effects of characteristics of in-store retail technology on customer citizenship behavior. J. Retail. Consum. Serv. **65**, 102488 (2022) https://doi.org/10.1016/j.jretconser.2021.102488, https://www.sciencedirect.com/science/article/pii/S0969698921000540
19. Heyns, R., Ndiaye, M., Abu-Mahfouz, A.M.: Enabling user-oriented features at the edge: a case of an IoT-based smart shopping cart. In: 30th IEEE International Symposium on Industrial Electronics, ISIE 2021, Kyoto, Japan, June 20-23, 2021, pp. 1–6. IEEE (2021). https://doi.org/10.1109/ISIE45552.2021.9576473
20. Kahl, G., Spassova, L., Schöning, J., Gehring, S., Krüger, A.: IRL smartcart - a user-adaptive context-aware interface for shopping assistance. In: Proceedings of the 16th International Conference on Intelligent User Interfaces, pp. 359-362. IUI '11, Association for Computing Machinery, New York, NY, USA (2011). https://doi.org/10.1145/1943403.1943465

21. Kellermayr-Scheucher, M., Hörandner, L., Brandtner, P.: Digitalization at the point-of-sale in grocery retail - state of the art of smart shelf technology and application scenarios. Procedia Comput. Sci. **196**, 77–84 (2022). https://doi.org/10.1016/j.procs.2021.11.075, https://www.sciencedirect.com/science/article/pii/S1877050921022146, international Conference on ENTERprise Information Systems / ProjMAN - International Conference on Project MANagement / HCist - International Conference on Health and Social Care Information Systems and Technologies 2021
22. Lee, S., Min, C., Yoo, C., Song, J.: Understanding customer malling behavior in an urban shopping mall using smartphones. In: Proceedings of the 2013 ACM Conference on Pervasive and Ubiquitous Computing Adjunct Publication, pp. 901-910. UbiComp '13 Adjunct, Association for Computing Machinery, New York, NY, USA (2013). https://doi.org/10.1145/2494091.2497344
23. Linzbach, P., Inman, J.J., Nikolova, H.: E-commerce in a physical store: which retailing technologies add real value? NIM Mark. Intell. Rev. **11**(1), 42–47 (2019). https://doi.org/10.2478/nimmir-2019-0007
24. Ližbetin, J., Pečman, J.: Possibilities of using bluetooth low energy beacon technology to locate objects internally: a case study. Technologies **11**(2), 57 (2023). https://doi.org/10.3390/technologies11020057, https://www.mdpi.com/2227-7080/11/2/57
25. Mandyam, G.D., Scagnol, M., Graube, N.: Secure onboarding and management of electronic shelf labels in retail. In: 2023 15th International Conference on Communication Systems & NETworkS (COMSNETS), pp. 96–101 (2023). https://doi.org/10.1109/COMSNETS56262.2023.10041323
26. Miralles, P.S., Gonzalez, L.F., Yu, X., Saniie, J.: Assisting visually impaired people using autonomous navigation system and computer vision for grocery shopping. In: 2022 IEEE International Conference on Electro Information Technology, EIT 2022, Mankato, MN, USA, May 19-21, 2022, pp. 203–208. IEEE (2022). https://doi.org/10.1109/eIT53891.2022.9813952
27. Mukherjee, S., Verma, A., Church, K.W.: Intent classification of voice queries on mobile devices. In: Carr, L., et al. (eds.) 22nd International World Wide Web Conference, WWW '13, Rio de Janeiro, Brazil, May 13-17, 2013, Companion Volume, pp. 149–150. International World Wide Web Conferences Steering Committee / ACM (2013). https://doi.org/10.1145/2487788.2487860
28. Ni, P., Li, Y., Li, G., Chang, V.: Natural language understanding approaches based on joint task of intent detection and slot filling for IoT voice interaction. Neural Comput. Appl. **32**(20), 16149–16166 (2020). https://doi.org/10.1007/s00521-020-04805-x
29. Niemann, M., Mochol, M., Tolksdorf, R.: Smart shop assistant - using semantic technologies to improve online shopping. In: Zseby, T., Savola, R., Pistore, M. (eds.) Future Internet - FIS 2009, pp. 106–115. Springer, Berlin Heidelberg, Berlin, Heidelberg (2010)
30. Ohta, M., Nagano, S., Takahashi, S., Abe, H., Yamashita, K.: Mixed-reality shopping system using HMD and smartwatch. In: Adjunct Proceedings of the 2015 ACM International Joint Conference on Pervasive and Ubiquitous Computing and Proceedings of the 2015 ACM International Symposium on Wearable Computers, pp. 125-128. UbiComp/ISWC'15 Adjunct, Association for Computing Machinery, New York, NY, USA (2015). https://doi.org/10.1145/2800835.2800888
31. Paulino, N., Pessoa, L.M., Branquinho, A., Gonçalves, E.: Design and experimental evaluation of a bluetooth 5.1 antenna array for angle-of-arrival estimation. In: 2022 13th International Symposium on Communication Systems, Networks and Digital Signal Processing (CSNDSP), pp. 625–630 (2022). https://doi.org/10.1109/CSNDSP54353.2022.9907908

32. Perera, G.S.T., Madhubhashini, K.W.R., Lunugalage, D., Piyathilaka, D.V.S., Lakshani, W.H.U., Kasthurirathna, D.: Computer vision based indoor navigation for shopping complexes. In: ICVISP 2020: 4th International Conference on Vision, Image and Signal Processing, Bangkok, Thailand, December, 2020, pp. 1–6. ACM (2020). https://doi.org/10.1145/3448823.3448828
33. Plüss, M., et al.: SDS-200: a swiss German speech to standard German text corpus. CoRR arXiv preprint arXiv: abs/2205.09501 (2022). https://doi.org/10.48550/arXiv.2205.09501
34. Ravindran, S., Barua, A., Lee, B., Whinston, A.B.: Strategies for smart shopping in cyberspace. J. Organ. Comput. Electron. Commer. **6**(1), 33–49 (1996). https://doi.org/10.1080/10919399609540266
35. Riegger, A.S., Klein, J.F., Merfeld, K., Henkel, S.: Technology-enabled personalization in retail stores: understanding drivers and barriers. J. Bus. Res. **123**, 140–155 (2021) https://doi.org/10.1016/j.jbusres.2020.09.039, https://www.sciencedirect.com/science/article/pii/S0148296320306214
36. Ruijgrok, P., Frasincar, F., Vandic, D., Hogenboom, F.: OntoNavShop: an ontology-based approach for web-shop navigation. J. Web Eng. 241–269 (2018)
37. Sakman., M., Gkikopoulos., P., Martella., F., Villari., M., Spillner., J.: Indoor navigation for personalised shopping: a real-tech feasibility study. In: Proceedings of the 20th International Conference on Smart Business Technologies - ICSBT, pp. 43–53. INSTICC, SciTePress (2023). https://doi.org/10.5220/0012085100003552
38. Sakman, M.C., Gkikopoulos, P., Martella, F., Villari, M., Spillner, J.: Smart personalised shopping web prototype (Apr 2023). https://doi.org/10.5281/zenodo.7859411
39. Verhoef, P.C.: Omni-channel retailing: some reflections. J. Strateg. Mark. **29**(7), 608–616 (2021). https://doi.org/10.1080/0965254X.2021.1892163
40. Vey, Q., Dalcé, R., van den Bossche, A., Val, T.: Indoor UWB localisation: LocURa4iot testbed and dataset presentation. In: Oteafy, S., Bulut, E., Tschorsch, F. (eds.) 47th IEEE Conference on Local Computer Networks, LCN 2022, Edmonton, AB, Canada, September 26-29, 2022, pp. 258–260. IEEE (2022). https://doi.org/10.1109/LCN53696.2022.9843513

Author Index

A
Addo-Tenkorang, Richard 41
Alves, Paulo 61
Andonoff, Eric 132

B
Ben Said, Imen 132
Bouaziz, Rafik 132
Branco, Frederico 61
Broneske, David 76

C
Chaâbane, Mohamed Amine 132
Chen, Kuan-Lin 41
Cvetkovski, Oliver 160

G
Ghezzi, Antonio 24
Gkikopoulos, Panagiotis 160
Gry, Soeren 1

H
Hasan, Mahady 99
Heras, Federico 113

I
Ilapavuluri, Devi Prasad 76

L
Lodi, Aena Nuzhat 1

M
Manotti, Jacopo 24
Martella, Francesco 160
Mohammad Abu Bakar, Nabil 99
Moiana, Davide 24
Møller, Charles 41
Mutz, Marcel 1

N
Niederlaender, Marie 1

O
Obionwu, Chukwuka Victor 76
Oukharijane, Jamila 132

R
Rangone, Andrea 24
Reis, Arsénio 61

S
Saake, Gunter 76
Sakman, Mehmed Cihan 160
Sequeira, Nuno 61
Spillner, Josef 160

V
Villari, Massimo 160

W
Werth, Dirk 1

SPRINGER NATURE

GPSR Compliance

The European Union's (EU) General Product Safety Regulation (GPSR) is a set of rules that requires consumer products to be safe and our obligations to ensure this.

If you have any concerns about our products, you can contact us on ProductSafety@springernature.com

In case Publisher is established outside the EU, the EU authorized representative is:

Springer Nature Customer Service Center GmbH
Europaplatz 3
69115 Heidelberg, Germany

The manufacturer's authorised representative in the EU is Springer Nature Customer Service Centre GmbH, Europaplatz 3, 69115 Heidelberg, Germany. If you have any concerns regarding our products, please contact ProductSafety@springernature.com

Printed and bound by CPI Group (UK) Ltd, Croydon, CR0 4YY
25/03/2026
02078187-0006